T0323406

Doing Process Research in Organizations
Noticing Differently

Doing Process Research in Organizations

Noticing Differently

Edited by

Barbara Simpson
Line Revsbæk

OXFORD
UNIVERSITY PRESS

Great Clarendon Street, Oxford, OX2 6DP,
United Kingdom

Oxford University Press is a department of the University of Oxford.
It furthers the University's objective of excellence in research, scholarship,
and education by publishing worldwide. Oxford is a registered trade mark of
Oxford University Press in the UK and in certain other countries

© Oxford University Press 2022

The moral rights of the authors have been asserted

Impression: 1

Published in the United States of America by Oxford University Press
198 Madison Avenue, New York, NY 10016, United States of America

British Library Cataloguing in Publication Data
Data available

Library of Congress Control Number: 2022934633

ISBN 978–0–19–284963–2

DOI: 10.1093/oso/9780192849632.001.0001

Printed and bound by
CPI Group (UK) Ltd, Croydon, CR0 4YY

Preface

It is fifty years since John Berger's ground-breaking 'Ways of seeing' was first broadcast on British television. In this series, and its subsequent book adaptation, Berger (1972) develops the then-radical proposition that what we 'see' when we look at a work of art is profoundly and often unconsciously influenced by the political and social systems within which we, as viewers, are entangled. He invites a critical attitude that acknowledges the diversity of possible responses to any creative work as a valuable source of new insight. This argument is now widely accepted, informing a whole culture of critique that applies not only to the visual and performing arts, but also to literature and the activities of reading and writing more generally.

In this book, chapter authors are particularly concerned with the reading and writing (i.e. the doing) of organizational research, where understanding that what we 'see' in any particular situation may not necessarily accord with what others 'see'. Different noticings, as they arise in various circumstances, guide us in responding differently, engaging differently, and thus creating our world(s) differently. Following Berger, when we allow ourselves to be struck by these differences, we produce fertile ground upon which to create new ways of appreciating organization and the dynamics of organizing. By noticing something that has previously gone unnoticed, that is by 'noticing differently', we can better direct our attention away from well-known and predictable 'facts', towards the emergence of genuinely novel knowings and the worldmaking this implies. Whilst this may seem an appealing, even obvious idea, the skills and capacities for 'noticing differently' remain under-developed in the organization studies research community. Indeed, understanding of process ontology in the doing of organization research is still nascent. In recognition of this deficit, this book seeks to contribute specifically to the practising of organizational researching, and also to adjacent areas of inquiry such as posthuman and post qualitative studies, social anthropology, human geography, and education.

It is not our intention though, to suggest that this book somehow provides all, or even limited answers. There is no formula or failsafe recipe for doing process ontological research. Rather, we hope readers will find inspirations here—different noticings of their own—that develop process ontological sensibilities in their own journeys of inquiry. Committing, in this way, to the continuous evolution of knowing, is consistent with the ontological orientation that runs as a linking thread throughout the chapters of this book, and which obliges us always to notice differently in the continuous unfoldings of experience. It is also consistent with the intellectual trajectories that we (Barbara and Line) have travelled, and continue to travel, in our own questing for previously unnoticed and potentially transformative differences. We have both benefitted immeasurably from the process thinking of the American Pragmatists, who challenge us to consider actions not in terms of their antecedents, but their practical consequences. This performative and future orientation reminds us that we are already entangled with the becomingness of the world and the people to come, which in turn implies certain responsibilities to engage (and engage differently) in transformational change. Pragmatism also provides a natural segue to more contemporary philosophical thinkers such as Gilles Deleuze, Rosi Braidotti, Karen Barad, and Donna Haraway, each of whom has offered us, and many of the chapter authors in this book, new opportunities to notice differently.

Our journeying has been further enriched by a number of communities of inquiry including the annual Process Organization Studies (PROS) symposia, the Complexity and Management Centre at the University of Hertfordshire, the EGOS Standing Working Group on 'Doing Process Research' (2017–2020), the ResearchGate online community for Pragmatism and Organization Studies, and the supportive collegial atmospheres that we have enjoyed at Aalborg University (DK) and Strathclyde Business School (UK). All of these have offered an abundance of opportunity to notice differently and create afresh. Words cannot adequately express our gratitude for these opportunities to discuss, chew over, debate and generate together. And finally, where would we be without the sustained relationships we enjoy with our doctoral supervisees, research collaborators, and students? Their willingness to step off well-trodden paths has created the conditions for both them, and us, to continue to invent and grow. What joy!

BS & LR

Berger, John (1972). *Ways of Seeing*. London: British Broadcasting Corporation / Penguin Books.

Contents

List of Illustrations

List of Contributors

Ariana Amacker is currently studying somatic pedagogy at ISLO in eastern Finland and was previously a Senior Lecturer in Design at the University of Lincoln. Her experiential inquiry, based in Classical Pragmatist philosophy, explores intersections between design, performance, movement, and imagination.

Anne Augustine is a senior teaching fellow in leadership and organisational dynamics at Strathclyde Business School, and an independent organisational consultant. She is writing up her doctoral thesis on practising caring in organisations and organising. As a transdisciplinary researcher, Anne enjoys collaborative explorations into the practical applications of social ethics, classical pragmatism, feminist technoscience, and post qualitative inquiring. As an organisational consultant and teaching fellow, she facilitates experiential learning and purposeful action on leadership, strategy, and social impact. Anne has an MBA from the University of Oxford, and a Masters in Organisational Consultancy from the Tavistock and Portman NHS Foundation Trust. She is a Fellow of the Royal Society for the Encouragement of Arts, Manufactures and Commerce.

Katie Beavan is a practitioner–researcher and an adjunct professor in the School of Professional Studies, New York University. She has had a long career in business working in many parts of the world. Her undergraduate degree is from Cambridge University. As a mature part-time student, she obtained a Master's from INSEAD, a PhD from the University of the West of England and a Master's in Fine Arts (MFA) (Creative Writing and Poetics) from the Jack Kerouac School of Disembodied Poetics, Naropa University. A transdisciplinary, feminist practitioner–scholar she enjoys blurring boundaries, engaging with multiplicity, and a focus on collaborative doing–of–knowing. She is interested in practice-based research and praxis, pragmatism and posthuman and creating critically aesthetic, affective performative texts as poetics of disquiet. In 2021 she became an entrepreneur co-founding a business aimed at helping Generation Z and Millennials anywhere in the world looking for career advice and personal development in key life and work skills.

Timon Beyes is Professor of Sociology of Organization and Culture at the Institute for Sociology and Cultural Organisation, Leuphana University Lüneburg (Germany), and at Copenhagen Business School's Department of Management, Politics and Philosophy (Denmark). He is trying to write a book on the chromatics of organization. This is part of a more general effort to reconsider organization as a primary concern of cultural theory, and cultural theory as a primary concern for the study of organization.

Boris H. J. M. Brummans (PhD, Texas A&M University, 2004) is a professor in the Département de Communication at the Université de Montréal in Canada. His research interests include agency, conflict management, mindful organizing, organizational communication, organizational ethnography, and process philosophy. He has contributed chapters to several edited books and his articles appear in international peer-reviewed journals such as *Communication Monographs, Human Relations, Information, Communication & Society, Journal of Communication, Management Communication Quarterly, Organization Studies,* and *Qualitative Inquiry.* His edited volume, *The Agency of Organizing: Perspectives and Case Studies* (published by Routledge), received the 2018 Outstanding Edited Book Award from the Organizational Communication Division of the National Communication Association, and he served as an Associate Editor of *Management Communication Quarterly* from 2015 to 2019.

Michela Cozza is Associate Professor and member of the New Organization and Management Practices (NOMP) group at the School of Business, Society and Engineering (EST) at Mälardalen University (Sweden). In her work, she has developed an interdisciplinary research agenda on the use and design of technologies for older people that combines concepts and theories from STS (in particular Feminist technoscience and Post-humanism), Organization studies (with regards to

Practice-based studies) and Age Studies (especially, Critical gerontology).

Silvia Gherardi is senior professor of sociology of organization at the Department of Sociology and Social Research (University of Trento, Italy), where she founded the Research Unit on Communication, Organizational Learning, and Aesthetics (www.unitn.it/rucola). She is also professor II at the School of Business, Society and Engineering, Mälardalen University (Sweden). She received the degree of 'Doctor Honoris Causa' from Roskilde University (2005), East Finland University (2010), and St Andrews University (2014). Her research interests include: feminist new materialism, entrepreneurship, epistemology of practice, and post-qualitative methodologies in organization studies. She published two books on practice-based studies with Edward Elgar: *How to Conduct a Practice-based Study* (2019) and *Learning and Knowing in Practice-Based Studies* (2012), co-authored with Antonio Strati. Several articles have been published in journals like *Organization, Management Learning, Gender, Work and Organization, Qualitative Research in Organizations and Management, International Journal of Gender and Entrepreneurship, Academy of Management Review.*

Alecia Y. Jackson is Professor of Educational Research at Appalachian State University in Boone, NC—where she is also affiliated faculty in the Gender, Women's, and Sexuality Studies programme. Dr Jackson's research interests bring feminist, poststructural, and posthuman theories of power/knowledge, language, materiality, and subjectivity to bear on a range of overlapping topics: deconstructions of voice and method; conceptual analyses of resistance, freedom, and agency in girls' and women's lives; and qualitative analysis in the 'posts'. Her work seeks to animate philosophical frameworks in the production of the new, and her current projects are focused on the ontological turn, qualitative inquiry, and thought.

Stephen Linstead is Professor of Management Humanities and Co-Director of the Management and Humanities Research Theme at the University of York Management School. His transdisciplinary research began with shopfloor anthropology and has since extended to varieties of organizational aesthetics and philosophy, including televised documentary film, recorded musical performance and published poetry.

Lisa A. Mazzei is Alumni Faculty Professor of Education at the University of Oregon, USA where she also holds a courtesy appointment in the Department of Philosophy. She is a feminist qualitative methodologist and is interested in philosophically informed inquiry. Professor Mazzei has produced a body of work that considers silence in qualitative research and a mapping of inquiry as a process methodology. She is a methodological innovator and her work is widely read and cited across disciplines such as education, psychology, sociology, political science, anthropology, business, and medicine. She is co-author, with Alecia Jackson, of *Thinking with Theory in Qualitative Research*.

Sideeq Mohammed is a Lecturer in Organizational Behaviour/HRM at the University of Kent. Sideeq's work is interested in engaging with philosophy in order to critically reflect on the problems posed by and to 'organization' in the contemporary milieu. He has a particular fondness for the works of Gilles Deleuze and Felix Guattari and has published work that draws heavily on their mode of experimenting with 'concepts' in order to think about organization in more robust ways including the monograph: *Stories and Organization in the Anthropocene: A Critical Look at the Impossibility of Sustainability* published by Palgrave Macmillan. Sideeq lives in Canterbury, UK.

Line Revsbæk is Associate Professor of Organizational Processes in the Department of Culture and Learning at Aalborg University, Denmark. Building on her background as an organizational psychologist, Line's research interests are innovation and learning dynamics, and participatory and change-oriented processes in organizations. She works from process philosophy, particularly Pragmatism and the philosophy of George Herbert Mead, to innovate methodologically and her work is published in *Qualitative Inquiry* and *Qualitative Studies*. Line has co-convened an EGOS PDW on *The Challenge of Writing about Emergence and Temporality in Empirical Studies of Time and Process*, and an EGOS Subtheme on *Pragmatism and Organizing for Change*. She has also been a co-convener of the EERA Network 32 *Organizational Education* since 2015.

Anna Rylander Eklund is a senior researcher at Chalmers University of Technology, Division of Innovation and R&D Management, Gothenburg, Sweden, where she conducts research on self-managed forms of organizing and artistic practices in design work. Her research is guided by the classical American Pragmatists, especially John Dewey, William James and Mary Parker Follett.

Barbara Simpson is Professor of Leadership and Organisational Dynamics at Strathclyde Business School, Adjunct Professor of Learning and Philosophy at Aalborg University, and a Visiting Professor in the Faculty of Industrial Design Engineering at TUDelft. Her research and teaching interests are shaped by the writings of process philosophers, especially the American Pragmatists, and the challenges of practising in ways that are ontologically processual, both of which she diffracts through her earlier career experience in physics as well as her active interests in musical performance, theatre, the arts, and literature. She takes particular delight in collaborating across disciplinary boundaries, most recently working with an arts organization, engineers and designers, and health and social care professionals.

Charlotte Wegener is Associate Professor in the Department of Communication and Psychology, Aalborg University, Denmark, where she researches and teaches social innovation from a learning perspective. She is also passionate about writing and runs doctoral courses and writing workshops for students and faculty. Drawing on her background in music science and literature, she seeks to expand academic writing by involving fiction, music, dreams, and everyday life experiences. Her latest publications about writing include 'Co-Production as a Research Method: Reflections From a Collaborative Writing Workshop'. In: Thomassen, A. O. & Jensen, J. B. (eds), *Processual Perspectives on the Co-Production Turn in Public Sector Organizations*. IGI Global, pp. 255–269 (2020), and the editorial 'Rhythms' for a special issue of the journal *Qualitative Studies* (2021).

1

Why Does Process Research Require Us to Notice Differently?

Line Revsbæk and Barbara Simpson

> Process is process because it is forever deferring its own comple-
> tion in the dynamic form of more becoming. Process is always in the
> process of exceeding itself in its own carrying forward. This makes it
> transcendental not only in relation to its determinate products, but
> in relation to itself. It is always moving into its own beyond. Process
> is the transcendental in person. Or, more precisely, in *movement*.
>
> **Massumi (2013, xii)**

Process philosophy sets out to trouble familiar ontological concerns about the stable entities or 'things' that are normally taken to be constitutive of our world(s). A process ontology instead treats entities as secondary manifestations of the continuous movements of lived experience, which, like a picture that paints a thousand words, is always a multiplicity, always *more-than* any entities that might be abstracted from it. They rise as ephemeral emergents from the tide of experience, and once they have served their immediate purpose in the processes of living, they subside back into the undifferentiated swell to be reformed (differently) as and when required. As Brian Massumi argues, there is neither a beginning nor an end to process; rather it is conceived as a perpetual becoming that makes and re-makes knowings as we continuously re-compose our world(s). Process is, therefore, profoundly generative as it invites researchers to continuously engage with the movements and moments, the sudden mutations and gradual accretions that emerge from differences experienced in our relatings; relatings that are by no means limited to the human–human interface, as they also incorporate the non-human and material dimensions of experience. Process philosophy invites us as researchers to create worldings, ever

Line Revsbæk and Barbara Simpson, *Why Does Process Research Require Us to Notice Differently?*
In: *Doing Process Research in Organizations, Noticing Differently.* Edited by Barbara Simpson and Line Revsbæk,
Oxford University Press. © Oxford University Press (2022). DOI: 10.1093/oso/9780192849632.003.0001

differentiating and shimmering worldings that call us out from the safe havens of epistemology. Indeed, it is 'the way in which the ongoing and the surprise come punctually together to determine a burst of life' (Massumi, 2013, xvii).

The contention of this edited collection is that process ontology demands a re-imagining and ongoing re-invention of how we inquire as researchers, especially in our engagements with the processes of worlding. As a scholarly community, we are all already well schooled in the methods and methodologies of entity-based research, and indeed, future generations of social science researchers continue to be inducted into these approaches to theory development and application. It is here we learn that the 'gold standard' for research requires accurate representations of the objective entities that are given, already formed in 'reality', so that we may make generalized assertions about how our world works. In circumscribing these entities, we are imposing dualistic, or divisionary thinking that simplifies and reduces our world(s) to contrasting categories—by defining 'this' we simultaneously define 'that' as its alterity. However, this obtrusion of dualistic categories is less a representation of something 'real', than an agential cut that is far from innocent. Arguably, it is an act of violence, a power move by those who claim a privileged access to objectivity, creating a black-and-white world from which nuance and difference have been erased in the pursuit of a narcissistic and self-serving universalism. These bounded dualistic entities thus become an 'iron cage' that conditions the ways in which we notice what is happening around us and through us.

Entity-based approaches to researching have, of course, produced many valuable insights—we do not seek to deny this—but because they are founded on normalized entities presumed to be pervasive and immutable, they are not well suited to inquiries that seek to engage with the fluid and ever-changing dynamics of living experience. The problem is that although this devotion to categories and 'things' has undoubtedly enabled us to grasp some aspects of experience, it fails to notice nuances and differences, which tend to be relegated as externalities and outliers in relation to the field of research. Cooper (2005, 1701) describes these unacknowledged, or ghostly aspects of lived experience in terms of latency, which he takes to be 'always present as a motivating absence of human agency' but at the same time it 'withdraws from all attempts to make it visible'. Latency hints at the *more-than* that can never be captured by static representations, and yet as a matter of necessity, we must always strive to engage with its dynamic expressions as ephemeral forms of life.

Similar arguments have been made by Vattimo (1996, cited by Deslandes, 2020), who developed the idea of 'weak thought' as knowledge that is fragile, vulnerable, plural, and always attentive to the subtleties of experience. By contrast, 'strong thought' is concerned with those singular objective truths that are the familiar products of objective science[1]. These ideas of latency and weak thought resonate with the concept of vitalism, which was overwhelmingly rejected in the philosophical debates of the nineteenth century as positivist science rose to ascendancy in Western epistemology. With the passage of time, however, scientific inquiry is increasingly challenged to reach beyond reductionist thinking to find ways of working with ever-more complex and dynamic problems. 'A new ontological realm of inquiry would seem to be required, concerned not with acquiring new *knowledge* as such, but with developing our *embodied sensitivities* to previously unnoticed aspects of circumstances troubling us' (Shotter, 2015, 56, emphases in original). What we need is a new science of indeterminacy (Lather, 2016), one that invites attention to previously unacknowledged goings-on by focussing on novelty, invention, and creativity, drawing the dynamics of emergence into the centre of research rather than merely describing them from a (safe) distance.

We propose that a process ontology offers just such possibilities for a different approach to research, one that is more about the becoming-ness of the worlds we are opening up and making than describing those we have historically or currently inhabited. This alternative approach already has deep roots in both Western and Eastern thinking, providing rich intellectual resources to draw upon. For instance, Buddhist practice offers two and a half millennia of experience in the practicalities of becoming, while in the West, philosophers such as Georg Simmel, Henri Bergson, A. N. Whitehead, and the Pragmatists, especially G. H. Mead and John Dewey,[2] take inspiration from relativistic and quantum physics, which profoundly unsettles assumptions about Euclidean space and time as a universal and objective frame within which all experience may be explained. Their ideas have been carried forward by contemporary philosophers such as Gilles Deleuze and Félix Guattari, Nicholas Rescher, and Martin Heidegger, all of whom seek a more fluid and precarious involvement in their worldings. In

---

[1] We note that Vattimo's distinction between weak and strong thought is, somewhat confusingly, opposite to the strong and weak process theories proposed by Chia & Langley (2005; see also Langley & Tsoukas, 2010, 2017a), where strong process affords ontological priority to movement and flow, while weak process privileges entities that move.

[2] The lists of scholars provided in this paragraph are intended to be indicative rather than exhaustive.

the humanities, process ontology is being rapidly elaborated by disciplines such as anthropology (e.g. Tim Ingold, Erin Manning, Brian Massumi, Kathleen Stewart, and Eduardo Viveiros de Castro), feminist studies (e.g. Karen Barad, Rosi Braidotti, Donna Haraway, and Patti Lather), Science and Technology Studies (e.g. Bruno Latour, John Law, and Annemarie Mol), and education (e.g. Alecia Jackson, Lisa Mazzei, and Elizabeth St Pierre). In organization studies also, there has been growing interest in process philosophy, as evidenced by two comprehensive Handbooks (Helin, Hernes, Hjorth, & Holt, 2014; Langley & Tsoukas, 2017b) as well as an ongoing book series published by OUP (Perspectives on Process Organization Studies, Volume 10 published in 2020) and a recent special issue in *Organization Studies* (Simpson, Harding, Fleming, Sergi, & Hussenot, 2021). All of this activity has massively increased awareness of the philosophical conundrums that come with process ontology, but as yet, their implications for the actual doing of process research remain hauntingly at, or beyond, the margins of scholarly awareness.

Doing, Reading, and Writing in Process Ontological Inquiry

We argue that the practice of doing empirical process research is inseparable from the scholarly processes of reading and writing. Indeed, it is in the confluence of doing, reading, and writing that this edited volume seeks to contribute to ongoing conversations about process research. The key issue, it seems to us, is how process ontology re-conditions the ways in which we notice what is happening around us, shifting our attention away from the abstracted constraints of centralized and dualistic frameworks, and towards the situated invention of engaged practices that move flexibly with and within purposive action, generatively entangling the converging and diverging dynamics of relating-together and living-with. A fundamental question then, is 'who/what is doing the noticing?' The modern Humanist notion of an autonomous and authoritative researcher as the knowing 'I' has been thoroughly problematized by critical scholars who, from an explicitly anti-humanist view, argue instead for a decentring that absents the subjective 'I' of the researcher in favour of a similarly privileged 'other' (see also Simpson et al., 2021). Jackson & Mazzei (2008, 300) observe 'more and more reflexivity that would reveal more and more about the researcher's ways of knowing' is not the answer to the limitations of a knowing subject.

The reflexive centring of a subject, whether it is the researcher or an 'other', does not address the subject's 'privilege and authority in listening and telling', and neither does it illuminate 'why one story is told and not another'. As a potentially productive alternative, they suggest a re-imagining of the subjective 'I' as performative; that is, as not only constructing the situation anew, but also changing in itself. Thus the 'I' of the researcher and the situation researched are in continuous and mutual co-production, so the researcher's noticings are part of an *agencement* (Gherardi, 2016) that constitutes and encompasses everything, both co-producing and produced by what is happening.

This idea of a performative 'I' resonates with Rosi Braidotti's (2019) articulation of posthuman subjectivities that somehow negotiate a middle ground between simply tinkering around the edges of the Humanist subject on one hand, and complete rejection of subjectivities in any form on the other. Drawing inspiration from Deleuze and Spivak, amongst others, Braidotti (2019, 41) argues for 'a subject position worthy of our times', which are undeniably times of global upheaval. This subject position is necessarily 'a work-in-progress . . . as both a critical and creative project'. In her view, a posthuman framing of subjectivity must begin from the social and relational capacities through which we become together with the human and non-human materialities of our *agencements*. Subjectivity then, is inherently social, preceding the individual while at the same time emerging from socially engaged experience, 'in constant negotiation with multiple others and immersed in the conditions that it is trying to understand and modify, if not overturn' (2019, 42). This posthuman subjectivity, in its questing for 'a new alliance, a new people' (Braidotti, 2019, 164), is necessarily concerned with the social dimensions of compassion, justice, geopolitics, kinship, sustainable existence, multi- and trans-species studies, and ethical practice (see also Haraway, 2016). It is incumbent upon us as researchers then, to become alive and response-able to our entanglements in the becomingness of these new worldings, and to the performativity of our noticings as they cut across the dappled and shimmering movements of living experience.

How then can we, as posthuman subjectivities and performative 'I's, learn to engage more with the subtle differences that arise in relating, with their continuously shifting nuances and multiplicities of becoming? What is 'real' cannot be reduced to objective truths from which the researcher stands apart. Neither can we access what is 'real' by capturing events in flight, freeze-framing them, indexing them, and arranging them into abstract sequences. Instead the 'real' must be appreciated as an entanglement of material elements (human and non-human) that in their (albeit temporary) togetherness, create something new within the continuities of becoming. The 'real' must, therefore, be appreciated not only by noticing differently, but also by attuning to the different noticings that may contribute to 'an otherness of worlding' (Manning, 2013, 169). Kathleen Stewart (2013, 1) proposes that such 'reals' are 'compositional nodes' that take the form of 'lines of action and mood etched across the sensations, vibrations, movements, and intensities that comprise both experience and states of matter'. Process ontology means considering and engaging with worlds in their multiplicitous becomings, acknowledging that the 'doing' of research is not only *of* the world, but also *in* the world, a worlding practice in itself. The researcher's task then, is to trouble 'reals', admitting doubt and uncertainty as indispensable for the wayfinding that transforms and produces new possibilities, while also acknowledging that we too are becoming-with the entangled elements of our current situation.

The importance of reading—of how and what we read as we shape the 'reals' that guide process inquiry—cannot be over-estimated. Elizabeth St Pierre (2011, 621), inviting 'a simultaneity of living, reading, and writing' in post-qualitative inquiry, argues for a breadth of reading that enables researchers to break free of their normalized discourses in order to think anew. In their 'new analytic' of 'thinking with theory' Alecia Jackson and Lisa Mazzei (2012, 7) illustrate how they 'keep meaning on the move' by co-reading texts with and through other texts, plugging in, diffracting, deconstructing and 'think[ing] *with* whatever we are reading at the moment' (Jackson & Mazzei, 2017, 725). For them, reading theory 'relies on a willingness to borrow and reconfigure concepts, invent approaches, and create new assemblages' (p. 717). As an obvious corollary, we do not need to limit our reading within narrow disciplinary constraints; why not also draw inspirations from the arts, the sciences, philosophy, history, and so on (St. Pierre, 2021)? Attentive reading, especially of differently written empirical studies intended to create (transformative) reading experiences (e.g. Pullen, Helin, & Harding, 2020), admits the reader as a participant in a research *agencement* that requires 'an openness toward literature . . . that allows the [text] to read you, at the same time as you read the [text]' (Helin, 2020, 4).

Gayatri Chakravorty Spivak, reader and translator of Derrida, writes about 'the difficult work of reading theory well'. Reading theory transforms you, she explains, 'you enter the protocol of the other person's theory'

(2014, 77) in ways that may amplify or diminish in future encounters and in the continued doings of related and resonant matters. Sensitivities are transformed, conditioning the environment, relationalities, and circumstances we are able to inhabit, perceive, and respond to, and thus conditioning the worldings we are able to engage in co-creating. Theory 'comes in as a reflex' (Spivak, 2014, 77), not as something to be intentionally or externally applied. In our experience from participatory research engagements, theory-as-reflex comes in as an involuntary noticing differently of phenomena in specific situations and dynamically emergent presents, demanding that we notice differently—sometimes much to our own inconvenience in research endeavours framed by pre-established project goals and strict resource constraints. Re-gaining response-ability on altered grounds, analysing in and with the present (Revsbæk & Tanggaard, 2015), implicates our ability to further our processual development of thought, our *thinking with* (Mazzei, 2021), as well as advancing our sense of what it could mean to do and become-with process research. By not responding to the potentiality of paradigmatic re-arrangement in living research situations, we risk closing down the development of new processual thought (and indeed killing it off entirely) as we socialize ourselves into doings unaffected by those very considerations and sensitivities that have been enabled by our reading and entering into the language and grammar of process philosophy.

The 'difficult work of reading theory well' is reading it 'as if we were writing it' (Spivak, 2014, 77). '[R]eading is writing is reading', Pullen et al. (2020, 2) remind us, encouraging the sort of 'slow inquiry' that heightens awareness (Ulmer, 2017). Reading is a matter of attunement. If you read theory and philosophy, St Pierre (2011) argues, deconstruction happens, not planned or designed, yet thoroughly and intensely worked towards. The process researcher's response-ability is the continual development of writing that is not only *of* but also *with* empirical matters. 'We might cease our endless writing about performances, and become performers ourselves' (Ingold, 2021, 201). Producing stories that perform a grammar of their own, laying out worldings, suggesting and constituting new or unknown dynamics and relationalities, and engaging readers differently, are key activities in process ontological inquiry. Such differently written texts are 'micro-revolutions' (Pullen et al., 2020, 2). Process ontological writings are often characterized by playfulness as they seek to further complex ideas about relationality and temporality by drawing inspirations from a wide range of sources. We find that empirical texts with explicit or implicit ideas of temporality and dynamic relationality encourage us to go on noticing more of what and how our own research practice might be developed as an ontological endeavour, always in new and unforeseen ways, as we seek to develop micro-strategies for engaging differently, and generatively, with whatever is happening in the present moment and circumstances.

As an example, Jenny Helin (2020, 8) introduces the concept of vertical writing as 'writing from within the forces of the instant' (2020, 6). Reminding us that the temporalities at play produce the writing, while writing troubles and creates (other) temporalities, she draws on Bachelard to suggest verticality expresses a concern for depth and height in instances of disruption and discontinuity, as opposed to horizontal writing that is 'organised by the logic of the clock' (2020, 3). Related to affect theory, Kathleen Stewart seeks to write in ways that provoke 'attention to the forces that come into view as habit or shock, resonance or impact' (2007, 1). 'Terms that index', such as factors, dimensions and categories, are 'not helpful (to say the least) in the effort to approach a weighted and reeling present'. Instead, we need concepts that continuously evolve as they travel (Simpson, Tracey, & Weston, 2018), and a working of concepts and problems together 'enabling new thought and connections' (Mazzei, 2021, 676, see also Stengers, 2011). Unacknowledged experiences may invoke a style of writing known as écriture féminine (Cixous, 1976), which is characterized by plurality and multiplicity of meanings, diffuseness, and a resistance to unity, fixation, instrumentality, and closure (Cixous, 1981, cited by Vachhani, 2019). '[I]nterrogating the dualisms that structure thought' (p. 15), writing from the body becomes writing as a form of resistance and a freeing of self. Beyond writing, other performative technologies for inscribing and learning to think, technologies that can engage with a continuously morphing world (e.g. visual imaging, video and audio) must also be included in the inventive experimentation of process ontological inquiries.

Threading Connections across the Chapters of This Book

In preparation for writing the chapters of this book, we invited the authors to join us in a workshop to explore how we each, together and apart, understand and engage process ontology in research, and to identify vibrancies and lines of intersection across the proposed contributions. We set the stage by circulating draft abstracts, and then met one afternoon (European time) in March 2021, to explore. The meeting was conducted on the now ubiquitous Zoom platform, which offered an expedient solution to the constraints imposed on our movements by the global coronavirus pandemic and our considerable geographic spread. The conversation was rich and productive, and as we engaged with each other's ideas, elaborating them and drawing out new inspirations, the *doing, reading,* and *writing* dynamics, as well as the *connecting, responding,* and *cutting* of process ontology appeared as generative movements, flowing within and across chapters, and revealing a shared commitment to research that is generative, on-the-move, and more-than-representational (Ingold, 2011, Lorimer, 2005). Authors took ideas and orientations from this workshop and subsequently wove these into their own chapters. So now, as we (Line & Barbara) read and re-read the final chapters, we find many transversal threads that form a mycelial web of resonances. To induct you into this experience of entanglement, dear reader, we will now trace/weave three of the threads that we found travelling across the chapters, but we hasten to add that these threads should not be taken as discrete themes; rather they are simply aspects that cut across the ongoing entanglements of every chapter. Further, they are by no means the only threads that might be drawn from reading these chapters, so we encourage you to also follow your own tracings. The particular threads that we now develop are *training attention and attuning*; *rhythming and exploring poetics, art, and aesthetics*; and *engaging multiplicity, difference, and diffraction in agencement*.

Training attention and attuning is a recurring activity in a number of the chapters. Ariana Amacker and Anna Rylander Eklund (Chapter 3) explore the use of body-mind techniques and whole-body openness for building a communing connection with a forest as a living organism. They train their attention physically through movement and bodily orientation, sometimes in silence and sometimes in dialogue, working to stretch their imaginative capacities while actively staying receptive and alert to all senses in order to achieve an integrated awareness of a sense of 'forestness'. In Chapter 9, the cultivation of awareness is similarly elaborated by Boris Brummans in his artful combining of texts and images to notice mindfully in accord with Buddhist 'pith instructions'. Here the forms of everyday life are contemplated as emptiness, while this emptiness is also form, suggesting a manner of attuning that halts, albeit temporarily, the incessant clamour of sense-making and the tendency to cling to the certainties of what we 'know'. Silvia Gherardi and Michela Cozza (Chapter 2) take a different approach, practising 'slow seeing' as a way of attuning to atmospheres and affect in their research encounters with a video that promotes the use of welfare technologies in eldercare. They describe 'slow seeing' as a bodily labour of relating that arises in the process of attuning, and which opens a space in experience where abstract oppositions between representation and reality dissolve. At the level of technique, Stephen Linstead (Chapter 6) suggests ways of developing a poetic sensibility that frees the imagination to notice differently, while Charlotte Wegener's (Chapter 4) performative writing illustrates how attention continues listening to life just as it comes, unvarnished and without headings. Anne Augustine (Chapter 5) demonstrates how memories and personal experiences may be engaged diffractively to notice differently, and Sideeq Mohammed (Chapter 8) explores the different noticings afforded when the researcher adopts alternative conceptual personae.

Rhythming formats and exploring poetics, art and aesthetics in the doing of process ontological research is a second thread that we see running across the chapters. Spaceships, nineteenth-century German Romantic paintings, music by Jeff Buckley and 'Machanic Manyeruke and the Puritans', a video art exhibition at the Grand Palais, documentary cinematics of coal and community, a ramshackle summerhouse with stained-glass windows, a rubato waltz, digital excess and decolourization in visual fabulation, a raven dreamed (or maybe not), the noise of a Women's Strike, music streaming while riding on a train, writing in and with the rhythmic stops and starts of a metro train, and Zoom zooming across continents and time zones. These are some of the flickers of poetics, art, and aesthetics that travel across the chapters. They invite us to read and write playfully rather than merely for consumption or the mastery of content (see also Chapter 11). The rhythming formats of noticing differently are exemplified in Chapter 6, where Stephen Linstead demonstrates how poetics are disciplined by the rhythms, sounds, and spaces of activity, as well as by the bringing together of poetic, aesthetic, ethical, and political moments that permit alternative worldings to produce new directions for new futures. Using cinematics to supplement poetics, he argues that using unfamiliar non-textual and non-prosaic media helps researchers to become more attuned to elusive processes. Charlotte Wegener (Chapter 4) presents a rhythmanalysis that sets rhythms of writing in motion by fusing, even confusing, concepts and everyday experience. The question of how to swim in colour opens Timon Beyes' (Chapter 7) exploration of a tender chromatic empiricism that conceives colour as processual force with endless capacity for differentiating form and fleeting order. A 'gut feeling' evoked in the experiencing of video art offers an aesthetic way in to knowing through the body's capacity for affect and to be affected (Chapter 2), while Katie Beavan (Chapter 10) makes the artist present through freewheeling writing that emerges from a whirlpool of correspondences in a Zoom meeting, where conversants engage 'from the waist up' in a meshwork of pandemic-induced non-smellosophic isolation, rhythming zooming as almost, but not quite, living organisms.

Engaging multiplicity, difference, and diffraction in agencement is the third thread that we noticed crossing many of the chapters. In an exercise of depersonalization and proliferating subjectivities, Sideeq Mohammed (Chapter 8) challenges the conventional inference that 'the ethnographer' is an island of stability in a sea of change, developing instead multiple conceptual personae in his study of the multiple reals of shopping centres. Similarly in Chapter 9, Boris Brummans views the researcher as a vector in an unfolding organizational field of relations, co-composing by feeling-with, thereby manifesting not only as a way of noticing mindfully, but also as continuous becoming. Making yourself available for resonances as a plural 'I' in compositional work is illustrated by writing engagements with emergent and morphing multiplicities (Chapters 4 and 10). It is in entangled performativity, which admits affect as an atmospheric force, that *agencement* is produced (Chapters 2, 5, 7, 8, and 9). By allowing unnoticed dynamics, unaccepted feelings, and forces in the body to disrupt indifference, Anne Augustine (Chapter 5) comes to understand caring diffractively as a collective and ongoing reconfiguring of mutual entanglements. And from the blooming and buzzing confusion of re-searching within the labyrinth of an ever-unfolding lifeworld, Katie Beavan (Chapter 10) explores agencing and demonstrates a contemplative poetic attentionality guided by a soft rigour that stays close to the goings-on in the corresponding flow of togethering between human and non-human in an online meeting.

All the chapters vibrate with a latency that hints at the between and the beyond; the chapters are a force field both in themselves and together. Any reading across the chapters is bound to pick up on this latency, as the reader continuously creates new worldings made possible in and through this book. The chapters in this collection, by responding to the intensity that an ontological stance in process research evokes, offer a timely answer to the burning question, 'why is doing process ontological research important?' The answer, we suggest, is because the world is in the here-and-now. There is no 'elsewhere' to be, or that we might more productively occupy in order to create the future to come. If we are not content with the impacts that our current commitments to circumstances, activities, or locations are producing, then we should leap to our feet and move to a setting that is more likely to produce the kind of impact that we are aiming for with our work. Should you choose to do so, we would just point out that you are now working processually, creating change by doing differently. Your efforts to produce process ontological research are much needed. Good luck.

Organization of This Book

The usual, in fact expected way to assemble the chapters of an edited book such as this is to cluster them into groups based on some sort of thematic logic. We, as editors, embarked on this sorting process in good faith, but we very quickly discovered the task we had set ourselves was impossible. As we have just demonstrated, all of the chapters included in this collection are embedded in an intricate web of vibrant interconnections. Like barely visible mycelial threads (Sheldrake, 2020), these connections grow, branching and morphing to produce a dynamic network that not only gives the appearance of (provisional) form, but is also constantly changing. We realized that any cuts we might make across this emerging web would be acts of intellectual violence that would disrupt the continuities within and amongst these chapters. Although the authors are all addressing quite different empirical experiences, like Deleuze and Guattari's (2004) 'Thousand plateaus' each chapter offers a unique entry point into process ontology, so in fact they may be read in any order. We encourage readers, therefore, to dive in wherever their interests take them, following the threads that seem most immediately relevant.

In addition to this introductory chapter in which we have set out our ambitions for this book, there are nine invited chapters each of which exemplifies the doing, reading, and writing of process ontological research, but in very different ways. Then, moving towards (temporary) closure, although with the clear intention of also opening up new directions, we include the transcript of a conversation we had with Alecia Jackson and Lisa Mazzei (Chapter 11), scholars who work in the field of education and who also struggle with questions similar to ours about researching in accord with process ontology and the posthuman condition. But we are still left with the question of how to order our nine contributed chapters: randomly, whatever that means; alphabetically by last name, or even first name; by date of receipt? None of these options makes any sense. We then started to think about how these chapters nudge each other, colliding, opening up rifts of possibility, slipping under and over, together re-worlding, making anew through their multiple interactions.

This brought to mind the dynamic metaphor of plate tectonics, which envisages the continents and oceans of our world as deformable plates that constantly shift in relation to each other along fault lines, subduction zones, and spreading boundaries, generating earthquakes, volcanic eruptions, tsunamis, and building mountains. Extending this geographic metaphor, we decided to order the chapters, because order we must in the linear domain of printed work, according to the geographic location of each chapter and its authors, but also recognizing that these locations are not permanent, and will change in time, perpetually extending the mycelial reach of these ideas. Specifically, the chapters are ordered by latitude, from the most northerly contribution in Mälardalen, to the most southerly in Boston. We hope that readers will enjoy this expression of dynamic engagement as it emerges in their own processes of doing, reading, and writing.

References

Braidotti, Rosi (2019). *Posthuman Knowledge*. Cambridge: John Wiley & Sons.

Chia, Robert & Langley, Ann (2005). Call for Papers: Theorizing Process in Organizational Research. At *First Organization Studies Summer Workshop*. Santorini, Greece, 12–13 June 2005.

Cixous, Hélène (1976). The Laugh of the Medusa. *Signs: Journal of Women in Culture and Society*, 1, 875–893.

Cooper, Robert (2005). Peripheral Vision: Relationality. *Organization Studies*, 26, 1689–1710.

Deleuze, Gilles & Guattari, Felix (2004). *A Thousand Plateaus* (Massumi, Trans.). London: Bloomsbury Academic.

Deslandes, Ghislain (2020). Weak Theology and Organization Studies. *Organization Studies*, 41, 127–139.

Gherardi, Silvia (2016). To Start Practice Theorizing Anew: The Contribution of the Concepts of Agencement and Formativeness. *Organization*, 23, 680–698.

Haraway, Donna J. (2016). *Staying with the Trouble: Making Kin in the Chthulucene*. Durham, USA and London, UK: Duke University Press.

Helin, Jenny (2020). Temporality Lost: A Feminist Invitation to Vertical Writing that Shakes the Ground. *Organization*, 1350508420956322.

Helin, Jenny, Hernes, Tor, Hjorth, Daniel & Holt, Robin (2014). *The Oxford Handbook of Process Philosophy and Organization Studies*. Oxford: Oxford University Press.

Ingold, Tim (ed.) (2011). *Redrawing Anthropology: Materials, Movements, Lines*. Surrey, UK: Ashgate Publishing.

Ingold, Tim (2021). *Correspondences*. Cambridge, UK: Polity Press.

Jackson, Alecia Y. & Mazzei, Lisa A. (2008). Experience and 'I' in Autoethnography: A Deconstruction. *International Review of Qualitative Research, 1*, 299–318.

Jackson, Alecia Y. & Mazzei, Lisa A. (2012). *Thinking with Theory in Qualitative Research: Viewing Data across Multiple Perspectives*. London and New York: Routledge.

Jackson, Alecia Y. & Mazzei, Lisa A. (2017). Thinking with Theory: A New Analytic for Qualitative Inquiry. In Denzin & Lincoln (eds), *SAGE Handbook of Qualitative Research* (5th Edition ed.) (pp. 717–737). Thousand Oaks, CA: SAGE.

Langley, Ann & Tsoukas, Haridimos (2010). Introducing Perspectives on Process Organization Studies. In Hernes & Maitlis (eds), *Process, Sensemaking, and Organizing* (1, pp. 1–27). Oxford: Oxford University Press.

Langley, Ann & Tsoukas, Haridimos (2017a). Introduction: Process Thinking, Process Theorizing and Process Researching. In Langley & Tsoukas (eds), *The SAGE Handbook of Process Organizational Studies* (pp. 1–26). London: SAGE.

Langley, Ann & Tsoukas, Haridimos (eds) (2017b). *The SAGE Handbook of Process Organization Studies*. London: Sage.

Lather, Patti (2016). Top Ten+ List: (Re) Thinking Ontology in (Post) Qualitative Research. *Cultural Studies - Critical Methodologies, 16*, 125–131.

Lorimer, Hayden (2005). Cultural Geography: The Busyness of Being 'More-Than-Representational'. *Progress in Human Geography, 29*, 83–94.

Manning, Erin (2013). *Always More than One - Individuation's Dance*. Durham, NC and London, UK: Duke University Press.

Massumi, Brian (2013). Prelude. In Manning (ed.), *Always More than One* (pp. ix–xxiii). Durham and London: Duke University Press.

Mazzei, Lisa A. (2021). Postqualitative Inquiry: Or the Necessity of Theory. *Qualitative inquiry, 27*, 198–200.

Pullen, Alison, Helin, Jenny & Harding, Nancy (eds) (2020). *Writing Differently*. Bingley, UK: Emerald Publishing.

Revsbæk, Line & Tanggaard, Lene (2015). Analyzing in the Present. *Qualitative Inquiry, 21*, 376–387.

Sheldrake, Merlin (2020). *Entangled Life: How Fungi Make Our Worlds, Change Our Minds, and Shape Our Futures.* London, UK: The Bodley Head.

Shotter, John (2015). On Relational Things A New Realm of Inquiry. In Garud, Simpson, Langley, & Tsoukas (eds), *The Emergence of Novelty in Organizations* (3, pp. 56–79). Oxford: Oxford University Press.

Simpson, Barbara, Harding, Nancy, Fleming, Peter, Sergi, Viviane & Hussenot, Anthony (2021). The Integrative Potential of Process in a Changing World: Introduction to a Special Issue on Power, Performativity and Process. *Organization Studies, 42*, 1775–1794.

Simpson, Barbara, Tracey, Rory & Weston, Alia (2018). Traveling Concepts: Performative Movements in Learning/Playing. *Management Learning, 49*, 295–310.

Spivak, Gayatri Chakravorty (2014). *Readings.* New York: Seagull Books.

St Pierre, Elizabeth Adams (2011). Post Qualitative Research: The Critique and the Coming After. In Denzin & Lincoln (eds), *The SAGE Handbook of Qualitative Research* (4th ed., 37). Thousand Oaks, CA: SAGE.

St Pierre, Elizabeth Adams (2021). Post Qualitative Inquiry, the Refusal of Method, and the Risk of the New. *Qualitative Inquiry, 27*, 3–9.

Stengers, Isabelle (2011). *Thinking with Whitehead: A free and wild creation of concepts.* Cambridge, MA: Harvard University Press.

Stewart, Kathleen (2007). *Ordinary affects.* Durham, USA and London, UK: Duke University Press.

Stewart, Kathleen (2013). Studying Unformed Objects: The Provocation of a Compositional Mode. *Fieldsights.* Retrieved from https://culanth.org/fieldsights/studying-unformed-objects-the-provocation-of-a-compositional-mode

Ulmer, Jasmine B. (2017). Writing Slow Ontology. *Qualitative Inquiry, 23*, 201–211.

Vachhani, Sheena J. (2019). Rethinking the Politics of Writing Differently through Écriture Féminine. *Management Learning, 50*, 11–23.

2

Atmospheric Attunement in the Becoming of a Happy Object

'That Special Gut Feeling'

Silvia Gherardi and Michela Cozza

Introduction

In this chapter, we wish to point to that special 'gut feeling' sometimes experienced during fieldwork, or elsewhere, which brings not only a special mode of deep understanding, but also comes from the body and is deeply embodied. This verbal expression is our key for entering into the realm of 'noticing differently', for introducing the theme of affect into posthumanist practice theory, and for reflecting on research practices intending to appreciate both elusive knowledges (Toraldo et al., 2018) and sensible knowing (Strati, 2009).

To offer an example of what we mean by 'gut feeling', we mention a vivid experience of one of the authors, Silvia:

> In Paris, in 2014, there was a great exhibition of work by Bill Viola, the leading representative of video art, at the Grand Palais. I was familiar with the artist's work and aware that he explores life, death, and transfiguration. The artist and the curators wanted to offer time to the visitors; time to look at the works and think about the concepts. They explained in a presentation of the exhibition that, since video captures image and sound simultaneously, it is very close to real life and makes it possible to experience time as a living moment happening now. After some time immersed in Bill Viola's artistic journey, I felt sick. All my emotions were centred in the pit of my stomach, and I was having a hard time breathing. I thought I couldn't get any more inside, that I would burst. In that moment, I remember that I thought: 'this is affect'. It was the most intense

Silvia Gherardi and Michela Cozza, *Atmospheric Attunement in the Becoming of a Happy Object.*
In: *Doing Process Research in Organizations, Noticing Differently.* Edited by Barbara Simpson and Line Revsbæk,
Oxford University Press. © Oxford University Press (2022). DOI: 10.1093/oso/9780192849632.003.0002

aesthetic experience I can ever remember, and even if this sounds weird, I can say that Bill Viola's art made me appropriate the power of the concept of affect as being affected.

Reflecting in retrospect on this experience, I (Silvia) believe that my stomach attuned itself on the intensity of the works, the lights, the sounds, the moods of other spectators next to me. I sensed the atmospheric context that materialized as bodily nausea; my body could no longer contain my sensations. When the word 'affect' rose to the surface of my consciousness, I 'carnally' knew that affect is pre-conscious, pre-individual, atmospheric, and deeply material. Only later, speaking with Michela, did we think that affect could become a research tool, and that atmospheric attunement, spontaneously experienced, could be cultivated and put into practice through research in the form of affective attuning.

Often the expression 'gut feeling' is used only metaphorically to describe intuition, hunches, premonitions, forms of non-rational knowledge or unexpected insights that may change research design. On the contrary, we point to its materiality highlighting how we know through the body, how the knowledge we produce is embodied, how we are inside research practices as embodied beings which may deploy an affective attuning with what and how we study.

We point this out to critique how our attention, as social science researchers, has been trained in rational and analytic terms. Our professional bodies have been disciplined through a technology of observing, listening, and seeing that prevents us from noticing differently. Even most qualitative methodologies rely on language, sight, and 'authorial voice' (Mazzei, 2016; St Pierre, 2011). In this context, affect theories head towards something that perhaps escapes or remains in excess of the practices of the 'speaking subject' (Gherardi & Strati, 2017; Mazzei, 2013).

Other forms of 'noticing differently' while doing empirical research may be experimented with, learned, or taught, and doing so requires acknowledging embodied knowledge and a conception of the body as process (Latour, 2004). For example, Blackman & Venn (2010), upon introducing a special affect-themed issue of *Body & Society*, mention noticing as a different way to train attention, and illustrate their point with reference to two articles, Game (2001) and Despret (2004), which both use horse–human relationships as a case study. To give just one illustration, Game (2001) recounts the experience of helping her injured horse to regain the ability to trot. She describes how her successful attempt came about through forgetting her separateness from the animal, and equates this forgetting to a release of self-consciousness. In this state, she was able to mount her horse and connect with the subtle movements that the horse was making, in order to help her (the horse) to remember what it felt like to trot with a rider. By attuning to subtle movements, Game and the horse developed a shared kinaesthetic modality of attention. We mention this case study to highlight how noticing may be conceived as a contingent process, through which attention takes place and shapes the sensibility for thinking.

While Bill Viola uses slow motion to perform the transmission of intensity from one body to another, we experiment with 'slow seeing'[1] to illustrate the intensity of the process of atmospheric attunement (Stewart, 2011) while watching a video and discussing our own research practices. Slow seeing can be theorized as a research practice inspired by affective methodologies (Knudsen & Stage, 2015) bringing forward a style of research informed by sensory ethnography (Pink, 2015) and affective ethnography (Gherardi, 2019c). This latter refers to a mode of writing and being in the field that involves the researcher's power to act, and may be described as a style of being in the field, being with, and 'becoming-with' others.

In the following section, we introduce the concept of a research practice *agencement* of material-discursive elements to describe the place of affect within slow seeing.

What Is the Place of Affect in Research Practices?

A posthumanist practice theory (Gherardi, 2019a) positions social practices as the unit of analysis (instead of structures or agencies), conceiving, for example, a research practice as an *agencement* of heterogeneous elements (human bodies, more-than-humans, discourses, knowledges) that achieve collective agency through entanglement, in their capacity to affect and be affected. The reason for preferring to keep Deleuze and Guattari's (1987) French term *agencement*, poorly translated into English as assemblage, is that the French term retains its root in agency and has a processual connotation—the idea of establishing or forming an assemblage—not a fixed state of assembled things. The difference aims to shift attention from what is interconnected towards how the entangled elements achieve agency by being interconnected. Moreover, the power of affect within an *agencement* is formed as the elements' capacity to affect and be affected.

---

[1] We are thankful to Katie Beavan and Tom Kennon who, in a personal mutual communication (7 April 2021), pointed out the importance of 'slow sight'.

Thus the circulation of affect within a research practice can be seen as the agentic capacity of linking or dissolving entangled relationships.

The conception of research practice as an *agencement* better agrees with the posthumanist theory of the de-centring human subject, concerns about the materiality of the world, the social production of the world (not its social construction), and how epistemic practices (the apparatus for knowledge production) shape our empirical ontologies (Law & Mol, 1995). The flow of agency (Hultin & Mähring, 2017) is the key to understanding *agencement* as an active process of agency realization, rather than an assemblage, understood as the static and final product of such a process. For this reason, rather than the more common term of research assemblage, we prefer to retain the term of research *agencement*, which, in accordance with Coleman and Ringrose (2013) and Fox and Alldred (2015), comprises researcher, data, methods, and contexts. When we consider the practice of slow seeing as an *agencement,* we focus on how affect circulates as a force realizing 'agencing'.

Our conception of affect is inspired by Stewart's (2007, 4) definition of ordinary affects as 'moving things—things that are in motion and that are defined by their capacity to affect and to be affected—they have to be mapped through different, coexisting forms of composition, habituation, and event. They can be "seen", obtusely, in circuits and failed relays, in jumpy moves and the layered textures of a scene.' However, we stress that affect is not defined by a difference from emotion. For Massumi (2002, 35), affect 'escapes confinement' in the body, while emotion is the capture of affect, i.e., a sociolinguistic fixing of the quality of an experience. Since emotion is the expression of that capture, this implies that something always escapes. For this reason, Massumi views affect as eluding form, cognition, and meaning. When he asks what a body does 'to earn that name, two things stand out. It moves. It feels. In fact, it does both at the same time. It moves as it feels and it feels itself moving' (Massumi, 2002, 1). He relies on Spinoza's definition of the body in terms of relations between movement and rest, the body's capacity (or power or *potentia*) to affect or be affected, and the variation in intensity as felt bodily. Therefore, this conceptualization of affect offers a way to think about feelings, emotion, and other interior and subjective phenomena, in terms of activity and movement in situated practices in the world and in connection to temporality. Deleuze and Guattari write that 'affects are becomings' (1987, 256).

In characterizing affect, Blackman and Venn (2010, 8) state that a turn to affect 'entails a rethinking of the concept of embodiment, and places work within body-studies in an important position in enfleshing and embodying affect as a particular kind of process-in-practice'. In other words, with affect we leave behind the person as the unit of analysis in favour of pre-personal, and trans-corporeal contact among permeable bodies (human and more-than-human) that encounter each other, affect one another, and jointly become within a research practice *agencement*.

In this framing, attunement as a noun and attuning as a verb (a process) are key concepts. The attunement, as a fundamentally social or practical human phenomenon, has been widely discussed in the writings of both Heidegger and Wittgenstein, as well as Stern (1985), who relates affective attunement to the mother–child relation. However, Manning (2013) suggests that it can also be thought of as a relationship between non-human things: 'Affective attunement need not be solely located on a human scale. If conceived beyond human interaction, affective attunement might well describe the relational environment co-created by movement and sound' (Manning, 2013, 11). She emphasizes sounds and tones, in analogy with tuning a musical instrument, and the materiality of the environment, as an ambient attunement, describing attunement in a broader sense as cultivating an 'affective tonality'. Cultivating new units of sense between the human and the nonhuman (in the form of vibration or tone) encourages researchers to focus on the points of intersection where bodies and objects meet (Ash & Gallacher, 2015).

We want to underline a posthumanist, materialist, and processual conception of attunement, both as a matter of feeling a 'vibe' and of tuning our sensibilities and bodies to appreciate the material forces that structure situations. For this reason, we emphasize atmosphere within a wider affective attunement: 'An atmosphere is not an inert context but a force field in which people find themselves. It is not an effect of other forces but a lived affect—a capacity to affect and to be affected that pushes a present into a composition, an expressivity, the sense of potentiality and event' (Stewart, 2011, 452).

It is here that Stewart's concept of atmospheric attunement helps us to conceive of 'slow seeing' as a situated practice. Stewart describes it as a form of writing and theorizing that sticks with something, becoming atmospheric and resonating with the force of material-sensory something accumulating: 'The effort requires a clearing—a space in which to clear the opposition between representation and reality, or the mind-numbing summary evaluations of objects as essentially good or bad, or the effort to pin something to a social construction as if this were an end in itself.

Attending to atmospheric attunements means, instead, chronicling how in-commensurate elements hang together in a scene that bodies labour to be in or to get through' (Stewart, 2011, 452).

We argue that we can learn how to create this space intentionally, as an inner clearing where we suspend judgment, slow looking and feeling down, and actively try to enter another 'wor(l)ding'. Slow seeing is the bodily dis-cipline that opens the door to atmospheric attuning, to a bodily labouring for relating. In other words, we do not reflect on the world but attempt to sense and understand it 'from within and as part of it' (Barad, 2007, 5). The knower's embodiment is not only about their individual body in a bounded sense, but also about an unbounded bodily embeddedness in the material, earthly world (Lykke, 2009).

Empirically, affect can be traced as a generative force that operates non-representationally even when working through language (Beyes & Steyaert, 2012; MacLure, 2013; McCormack, 2015; Thrift, 2007; Vannini, 2015). An empirical solution for avoiding the *thingification* of affect is to look for the material traces that affect leaves in the becoming of research practices (Gherardi et al., 2018) and in researchers' bodies (Gherardi, 2019c). A trace is a sign of passage, recorded evidence that something occurred in the course of the world's coming into being, contributing to its ongoing renewal (Ingold, 2011). These traces are the materializa-tion of sensed energies reverberating through all kinds of bodies that are not in a steady state of being, but in a continuous relational state of becoming.

Empirically, enquiring into affect's work requires our presence 'there' with our bodies, exercising their capacity to affect and be affected. 'There' is an affective space, in which our bodily presence is performed and acted upon by other material-discursive presences, contravening the pretence of being present only as minds. Within a research practice *agencement*, everything is in a state of becoming together, and we shall illustrate the process of 'becoming-with' (Shotter, 2006), in its flow of agency. Instead of considering a process from the outside, as external observers, we shall follow Shotter's 'withness-thinking', defined as a form of engaged, respon-sive thinking, acting, and talking, which allows us to affect the flow of processes from within our living involvement with them. Among the modes of process research (Abdallah et al., 2019), we position our con-tribution with the so-called performative process stories, which enact a 'becoming-with' process to reveal the co-emergence of materiality and affect. Rather than assuming a priori the existence of a separate researcher and subject, we 'become-with' the data to seek out traces of affects left behind in the *agencement* of heterogenous elements.

Our Encounter with a Video and a Concept

One way to call method into question is to use concepts as a method, defined by Lenz Taguchi and St Pierre (2017) as using concepts, acts of thought, as practices to reorient thinking, undo the theory/practice dichotomy, and enquire into new possibilities. The concept thus orients thinking and images of thought (Gherardi, 2019b) for experimentation. This approach helped us to slow down and experience multiple encounters, many of which occurred while the intra-actions materialized in photograms that affected us. Concepts, writes Jackson, 'do not pre-exist thought (as in Method) but emerge in a dice-throw' (2017, 673). Our dice-throw brought us the concept of 'happy object' (Ahmed, 2010) which refers to how certain objects accumulate positive affective value and generate new bodily horizons to the point that they are perceived as necessary for happiness. This concept emerged in the process of watching, re-watching, and discussing the digital materiality of a video. Rather than starting from an a priori definition about what is digital and what is material, we propose, with Pink et al. (2017), to conceive digital materiality as an emergent process that generates empathetic encounters.

The video was produced in 2018 by a Swedish municipality with which one of the authors (Michela) collaborated in a welfare technology research project. The video is three minutes and 36 seconds long and was distributed on YouTube during a pilot study in order to publicize the municipality's efforts to develop home-help services that guarantee 'a safe, peaceful night's sleep' (as stated in a brochure).

While the video is an artefact that expresses a representationalist logic in which 'reality' (the individual being represented) exists as an entity with clear boundaries prior to, and independent of, the act of representation, we assume that language can be used in such a way as avoid distorting the video, and approach it with a non-representational attitude. Non-representational theory (Thrift, 2007) or non-representational practice (Ingold, 2015), emphasizes pre-cognitive affect and sensation, the materiality of thinking, and ordinary situated practices, spatialities, and things, aiming to study the current of actual everyday life, embodied experiences, affects, and enactments rather than their mere representations (MacLure, 2013). While representationalism obscures the constitutive work being done in the act of representation itself, our attuning to the digital materiality of the video follows the lines of becoming that have neither a beginning nor an end. Thus, the video becomes our research 'subject' that 'speaks' to us by generating reactions that are plugged into our individual (personal as well as professional) experiences.

MICHELA: To understand welfare technology, I needed to look at it from the perspective of the public authority I was working with, together with other colleagues. Then, in my search, I found on YouTube a video produced by the municipality to promote the night camera, which is the main technology implemented in the municipality to monitor older people at home. 'Et voilà', I thought, the first time I watched it, here we are again with the image of an older woman 'in need' of technology to fix her 'problems'. No, I am not so naïve as to think that becoming older does not bring with it any issues, but the association with technology, with a night camera as deus ex machina, is troubling. I was aware that the video was assembled purposely to 'produce' this sense of 'need' in association with the process of 'becoming older', but this 'representation' was troubling me and my research practice in many ways. Let's stay with the troubles—I told myself—and see where they bring me.

SILVIA: The first time I saw the video I had the sensation of something disturbing, even if I had no better words to express why and in what sense the glossy video exuding benevolence made a bad impression. What was 'wrong' with me? What sounds 'wrong' with the video? Weeks later, Sara Ahmed's work came to mind, and I made the connection between her work, her concept of the happy object, and the video. I had the feeling that the video was performing the night camera as a happy object, while my body was reacting and resonating with the image of the night camera as it were in my room, violating my intimacy. I was putting myself in Agnes' shoes, thinking that in fifteen years I will be her age. Once I became aware that attributing a name to the feeling of being disturbed by the video made me feel better, then I became aware of asking: how does the video perform the night camera as a happy object? How is the performative power of the video achieved?

Our conversations about the video, while watching it over and over, flicking the keys back and forth to find what it hid behind what it showed, and asking ourselves *how* it showed and hid or insinuated, became compulsive.

However, the images helped us to slow down and experience multiple encounters. Indeed, the question was not how much time we spent actually looking at the images, but rather to what extent the video occupied our thoughts, feelings, and senses, generating doubts and interrogating the *agencement* of our research practice.

The concept of the happy object created 'a happening' in our research practice *agencement.* In this context, it acquired an intuitive meaning that we grasped even before re-reading Ahmed's suggestion to think of affect as 'sticky', i.e., as what sticks to, sustains, or preserves the connection between ideas, values, and objects. She writes: 'To be made happy by this or that is to recognize that happiness starts from somewhere other than the subject who may use the word to describe a situation' (Ahmed, 2010, 29). Happiness, therefore, turns us towards objects, and in Ahmed's conceptualization happiness is not a state of feeling, but rather a happening: (i) involving affect, since to be happy is to be affected *by* something; (ii) involving intentionality, since to be happy is to be happy *about* something; and (iii) involving evaluation or judgement, since to be happy about something *makes* something good.

We are inspired by her conceptualization to disturb the representation of the night camera in the video as a happy object, and wonder what the video 'does' in order to make the welfare technology good and to forcefully sustain a promise of happiness. We sense how affective and moral judgements are intertwined through a state of promise. Happiness directs us towards certain objects that circulate as social goods, and which accumulate positive value as they are passed around. The more the video is passed around, the more the night camera is made valuable as a social good and is made affective by virtue of its location (*where* I, spectator of the video, experience this or that affect) and its timing (*when* I, spectator of the video, experience and name this or that affect).

The concept of the happy object makes us aware of the moral character of attention, and aware of the fact that we are moved by things and, being moved, we make things. Social groups cohere around a shared orientation towards things being good (what Ahmed defines as sociable happiness), treating them as the cause of delight, because 'they' are delightful.

Our atmospheric attuning to the promise in the video takes place in the research *agencement* of slow seeing, in which the digital materiality of the video performs the night camera as an affective object.

Our Sensing and Becoming-with the Video

MICHELA: You know, Silvia, they told me that this old woman passed away. It is so weird to stay here, watching the video and writing about it.

SILVIA: Rationally I know I'm watching a video, but I can't escape the feeling that a ghost has materialized here between you and me. It's like the past looks me in the face through the eyes of Agnes, who is no longer there, and asks if I, at her age, will be a beautiful lady like her. What promise does the future hold for me?

The promise of happiness is what sends happiness forth, and it is this promise that is staged in the very first photograms of the video, in which the becoming of Agnes's subjectivity flows and we become-with it. We are presented with a good-looking old woman, well-dressed, in what we see is her house; we are informed by subtitles that she is 85 and qualified as an early adapter of a new technology for night supervision. Agnes, who rolls around the house in what seems to be an office chair with wheels, is performed as an intact, self-contained individual who has taken a rational decision, presumably by herself and presumably alone (Figure 2.1).

Fig. 2.1 Agnes's subjectivity represented as a self-in-control

MICHELA: Isn't she in a wheelchair?

SILVIA: It looks like an office chair to me. Let's look again at whether the video shows or proves that Agnes is not self-sufficient.

MICHELA: The video perhaps implies that she is not, but it hides the details.

Both in the video, and in our experience of it, everything is becoming together: the affective, the social, and the material are staged together until they are punctuated in a research practice that separates the body, technology, the researchers, and other potential/excluded participants who spy on and influence the context. We acknowledge how bodies are affectively networked, nevertheless we want to stress 'that the prevailing research methods place and position the researcher on the *exterior of the image* and so at a distance from the image takers. The distance created by the research method *itself* is shaping both how we think about social mediated images of bodies and how we are encouraging other researchers to handle images of bodies' (Warfield & Demone, 2018, 135). To contrast this view from the exterior of the image with an image in relation to it, we are experimenting with a slow seeing of the images of Agnes' body as represented in the video, and how they affect our imagination regarding what a body can do, and what is removed from sight but nevertheless felt in the intensities reverberating between the video and our bodies.

What affect does is a 'wor(l)ding' born from our atmospheric attunement. The images, coming to our mind and felt in our bodies, are 'vital signs', not merely signs for living things but signs *as* living things that have an intrinsic 'vitality' (Mitchell, 2005). If matter is agentic, rather than passive, the materiality of images has a textuality and a narrative agency beyond representationalism. When we unsettle the representational technology embedded in images with the concept of 'transcorporeality' (Alaimo, 2012), which considers all bodies affecting one another and thereby generating intensities, we can read the same photograms in terms of the image of a body that infolds a context and expresses intensity in that context. The digital materiality of the image affects our bodies as we watch it and wonder which experiences resonate in-between the image of Agnes' body and our own bodies, which are bodies of a different age, differently resonating and differently carrying past experiences (an elderly loved one recently passed away), or future experiences (seeing ourselves, or a loved one, in Agnes' situation).

We also consider that other bodies that are present but unseen nevertheless leave a trace in the images we see. These are the haunting bodies (we do not know how many there are) of the operators who recorded the video, who added the subtitles, who translated them from one language to another, and perhaps other bodies that we can only imagine. Maybe Agnes has a cat, or a goldfish, or both. We looked at the video again, again, and again, using imaginative thinking, trying to imagine her life with a cat or goldfish, but excluding the possibility of a dog, considering her impairment. Imagining her life with a companion animal, a pet to keep her company, we felt loneliness. It clashed with the video's spot-on manufacturing of 'the proper atmosphere' for valuing the happy object, visible in the aesthetic choices for transmission cuteness via colours, lights, framing, and objects. Our senses were active in attuning to the representation of 'the proper atmosphere' and we were seduced by the beauty of the nostalgic atmosphere transpiring in the scenes. The physical space is performed as the place someone calls home, and we know the aesthetic, contagious, and reassuring feeling that can affect us since we recognize something familiar, something we share with others, the resonance of 'home'. We resonate at the same time with the ambivalence of the cute, homely atmosphere, Agnes' charm as an old lady, and the sense of loneliness that we previously experienced. Resonant experience has been suggested as a process-ontological heuristic (Revsbaek, 2018) for researchers working abductively with interview data and trying to re-experience interview materials. For us, the video reverberates a vibrant materiality (Brennan, 2004) artfully engineered as an affective atmosphere (Anderson, 2009; Ashcraft, 2020; Cozza et al., 2020), thus contributing to the accumulation of affective value for the happy object under construction.

SILVIA: We are watching this video, discussing, and writing amidst the pandemic, and I can't get my mind off how vulnerability has become the symbol of the human condition. Butler's (2016) words about vulnerability as a condition of receptivity towards outside forces resonate in my mind. Learning to be affected is learning to be vulnerable—to recognize relational vulnerability. This is what we are doing when we look at how Agnes is represented in the video as a sleeping body.

MICHELA: Becoming less uncomfortable with our own corporeal vulnerability to the other's vulnerability, and seeking to put ourselves at risk, can be a productive ethical practice. We are sensing mutual vulnerabilities that require creative attunement.

After staging Agnes' subjectivity as a self-in-control, the following photograms (Figure 2.2) present Agnes's body as a sleeping body, a vulnerable

Fig. 2.2 Agnes's subjectivity represented as a vulnerable body

body whose context infolds an intimate situation. When we see Agnes lying in bed, we also see a hand drawing the sheet over her. It is an iconic
image and familiar in relation to a child being tucked into bed by a parent.
Referring to adults, it suggests a vulnerable body whose capacity to put itself to bed is compromised. It is difficult to see, at first glance, to whom
the hand belongs, and to intuit that it belongs to another human being, in
this context performing the function of a caregiver. Watching the video, we
suppose that a caregiver is made present through the arm helping Agnes
to go to bed. From the image, we cannot guess if a female or a male body
is present, and the bodywork performed by Agnes' caregiver is denied significance in the video, insofar as that person is represented solely by their
helping hand.

Care is excluded from the inter-body relationship between humans and
the curtain is rising on the representation of how the non-human appro-
priates the representation of care. It is Agnes, fully dressed, who speaks
for the night camera, explaining that it works in the following way: 'If I
am in bed on time, it sees that I am present and alive [Agnes laughs with
embarrassment] and that nothing has happened to me.'

SILVIA: A friend of mine who lives alone, and who recently suffered a reduction in her autonomy, described having a remote assistance device at home with the following words: '. . .in case I need help during the night'. It makes me think about how the night is perceived differently by 'able' and less-abled people. I become vulnerable when I imagine the night as a threat, and I feel threatened if I lose my daylight rationality.

MICHELA: You should remember that vulnerable writing is a feminist methodological practice (Page, 2017) and that Helin (2019) suggested writing not in order to overcome vulnerability, but to write through vulnerability as a gift from the dreaming-writing-body. We now are looking at the video through vulnerability and this is how we see the way our bodies depend on each other, and this is how we move away from the dominant patriarchal ontology that perceives bodies as being independent. Look at how Agnes is represented as a monitored body in Figure 2.3.

When we look at the image of Agnes turning off the light on the night table—suggesting that it is the appropriate time to sleep—care passes from exclusively human hands to 'beyond'. The more-than-human caregiver

Fig. 2.3 Agnes's subjectivity represented as a monitored body

(i.e., the night camera) interacts with Agnes through a light that indicates whether the device is active, or inactive outside of the agreed upon appropriate times of monitoring/sleeping. Light helps us to notice the material rhythm of becoming together. Once again, the becoming of Agnes' subjectivity is transformed when the artefact, the 'night camera', comes to the fore. Agnes' body is represented by the digital materiality of a monitored body (Figure 2.3) and the power to perform such a dramatic magic spell comes from framing the camera as a 'naked artefact', that is, an artefact outside a familiar context, stripped of any relationship to other domestic objects. The naked artefact has the function of de-familiarizing the gaze, moving it from Agnes's home to another site, which we understand as participating in the same *agencement* of care practices.

The new site is somewhere downtown, at the headquarters of the home-help staff (Figure 2.3). The video zooms in on an office where a person sits in front of a computer: on the screen appears the image of Agnes, lying in bed at home. A single photogram represents four layers of 'real-IT-y': a 'real' is performed in the interface in-between the operator and the video-maker conversing; a second 'real' is performed at the interface of the operator and the computer; a third 'real' is performed in the digital image that represents the absent body of Agnes; and a fourth 'real' is evoked by the sleeping body somewhere that we imagine to be the origin of all four 'reals'. We can say that one 'real' is activated by the instant representation of several reals, and it is made possible by the intermediation of digital materiality.

In this new site or angle in the research *agencement*, the language spoken at the operation centre, the bodies of the operators evoking competence and techno-power, and the distance from Agnes whose subjectivity is materialized as a monitored body but who is not physically present, allowing others to talk about her, all of these elements also contribute to changing the way in which 'we' are positioned as rational beings, listening to a clinical discussion of how the night camera works as a non-invasive presence. Nevertheless, the images and the words for evaluating the worth of the night camera as a happy object are left to Agnes who, later in the video, says with a shrug: 'It just blinks, that's all!'

Transmitted with these words is not necessarily a feeling, but rather in that moment we share the image and the words spoken by Agnes, that is, an orientation towards that object as good, since it does not disturb, and stays in its corner (Agnes's words). The video composes and promotes an orientation towards happiness neither because the object causes happiness, nor because it affects us in a good way, but because we share an orientation towards it as it promises happiness in return for a reduction of privacy.

These words enact a 'wor(l)ding' in which the happy object promises happiness because it does not invade the intimacy of the human, apart from occasionally blinking. Bodily transformations, like ageing, may transform delightful or threatening experiences so that remote monitoring may be negatively associated with surveillance and subjectification at an earlier stage of life or in conditions where one does not need this kind of support, but the same technology may enact positive feelings at an older age or when specific needs arise. How the ambivalence of the trade-off between surveillance and care affects us as spectators depends on how we position ourselves in relation to the place that the video suggests for us, as well as how we resonate with what we perceive as happening in-between us and the video.

MICHELA: During my fieldwork on this welfare technology, one operator told me that there was an older woman who 'waited for' the light signal on the camera to come on every evening, to wave at people 'beyond' the camera. Don't you think that this kind of war story induces infinite tenderness in listeners? It is told to disqualify the communicative intention of the old woman who, perceiving herself being watched, pretends to establish a social relation with the humans behind the object, thus reducing the asymmetry of the situation: reducing the feeling of loneliness, I would say. The happiness of the object resides in the promise of not being invasive in its control function: is this sufficient to live with this more-than-human caregiver? Wait . . . it cannot be humanized and should not be thought of as a medium for communications, otherwise it loses its pretention of invisibility and betrays its claim to leave solitude somewhat intact.

SILVIA: You are noticing that there is an embedded ethics in the artefact, and we can feel it in the atmosphere of the happy ending of the video.

Agnes, represented as one of the first 'happy customers', concludes her evaluation of the night camera with the following words: '(It) enables me to participate more in society, to feel safe in my home, have a more active lifestyle, and it increases my independence'. We believe her also because we do not know the potential alternatives at her disposal. It is in her actual situation that Agnes evaluates the night camera, while the video-maker zooms on it: 'I sleep very well! The camera does not bother me at all. You do not hear any sounds. It sits up there in the corner and blinks from time to time, to show that it is on. It just blinks, that is all.'

Conclusion

Affect tends to be overlooked because it poses methodological challenges when we refuse to treat it as a 'thing' or to collapse it into emotions. However, there is a diffuse consensus among qualitative researchers that affect is at work 'there', in fieldwork and in writing, and should be addressed—but how? The awareness that affect is 'there' is often expressed by the linguistic artefact 'that special gut feeling' that we have listened to, since it brings to the fore the researcher's body, and makes evident that we produce knowledge through our different bodies, that research is a corporeal endeavour, and that our research methods should express proximity and respect for other bodies, as well as relational vulnerabilities. Our way of writing this chapter is meant to make visible and accessible to the reader our availability to be 'there' with our bodies, exercising their capacities to affect and be affected.

In this chapter we experiment with a research practice that we term 'slow seeing'. It contributes to the family of affective methodologies and is grounded in our previous engagement with affective ethnography as a mode of being in the field, which involves the researcher's power to act, and may be described as a style of being in the field, being with, and 'becoming-with' others (Gherardi, 2019c). We conceive a research practice as an *agencement* of entangled elements that come together and achieve agency in their being interconnected. Researchers are inside the practice they study, together with the epistemic practices they perform; they are entangled with other humans even if humans are not at centre stage, nor the only ones with agency. Materialities of all kinds (air, coal, animals, technology) are entangled with humans, from the bodies that encounter other bodies, to artefacts, to digital materiality, and discursive materialities, to name just a few. In the *agencement* that we have performed in writing, for readers and to enlist readers in the same *agencement,* the heterogeneity of entangled elements can be traced through a video, whose creators are a ghostly absence; through two women researchers whose bodies, biographies, and discourses resonate differently with the video according to their age, previous experience, sensibilities, and other idiosyncratic motives; and through a philosophical concept (happy object) that captures a node of affective forces, thus creating an initial atmosphere for the composition that emerged as the images moved back and forth, and also in creating 'frozen moments of time' through the isolation of single photograms. The writing as well as the reading process is internal to the flow of agency of the 'slow seeing' *agencement*.

The researchers and authors of this chapter have an active presence in the practice of *agencement*, and we both performed atmospheric attuning when we 'became with' the video and while writing, to evoke in readers how we sensed different atmospheric happenings, and to communicate how atmospheric attuning may be learned through reading about it.

Atmospheric attunements have been described by Kathleen Stewart as 'palpable and sensory yet imaginary and uncontained, material yet abstract [...]. They can pull the senses into alert or incite distraction or denial' (2011, 445). Our contribution to her description of ordinary affects consists of theorizing atmospheric attuning as a process, both emergent and deliberate, in which we exercise our bodies' capacities to affect and be affected through movements in which the labour of attuning proceeds in iterations of sensing, becoming, and becoming-with. It may therefore be conceived as a sensory process, a temporal becoming in which the past, the present, and the future are intertwined, and a relational becoming-with the vulnerability of our bodies and others'.

We want to stress how the process of atmospheric attunement is not completely deliberate—it is not a step-by-step procedure—nor is it wholly spontaneous and occasional. Since it takes place in time, and can be defined as a situated knowing (Haraway, 1988; Gherardi, 2017), its becoming has rhythms, tempos, zigzags, and unpredictable improvisational detours or stops. However, all these movements in time and in affective atmospheres leave traces that may be worked on, and we have illustrated how this happens in an encounter with a video and a concept. We call it 'an encounter' and not an object or a topic of study to stress its importance to us not for what it represented, but because of its effect on us and the way it moved us. It was an 'encounter-with' because it was already embedded in our intellectual trajectory, as researchers interested and working on welfare technologies, well-read in affective and non-representational literature, and committed to contributing a chapter to the present book.

Through this encounter, we narrate the beginning of a process of attuning in which we have been affected by the idea of the representation of a night camera as a happy object. Ahmed's (2010) concept of the happy object is presented in our narrative as a guide that pointed us to sense the video's images as the materialization of a promise. A promise enacts an atmosphere in which something good is projected into the future. However, in attuning to this promise, we experienced a wide range of ambivalent sensations and imagined other scenarios of what might be happening. The point is not whether this promise is true or false, or whether the video's representation of the welfare technology is misleading. The point is how the process of attuning creates an inner space where the opposition between representation and reality can be dismissed. This is a cleared space in which we suspend judgment, slow down our looking and feeling, and actively try to enter another 'wor(l)ding'.

In the spirit of experimentation using inventive methods (Lury & Wakeford, 2012), attuning attempts to create a new space for thinking about and imagining what might be happening. The flow of our becoming, in our encounter with the video, is punctuated by moments of conversation, memories coming to mind, imaginings, references to literature, and other moments intertwined with these activities and sensations. This flow has the intricacy of non-linear time, and the rhythm of the video played in reverse and forwards, its stops and starts, changes the atmospheres.

To attend to atmospheres requires more than just representing them from the outside. Thus we engage them from within, sensing their tensions and surging intensities, and our writing became sensitive and evocative. To write about how we experienced atmospheric attunements, we chose three moments of 'frozen time' in which the video represented the becoming of Agnes's subjectivity as a self-in-control, a vulnerable body, and a monitored body. These moments were also specific moments of our attuning to different 'wor(l)dings' and specific moments of our 'becoming-with' them.

We conclude the chapter by recalling Massumi's statement: 'there is no cultural-theoretical vocabulary specific to affect' (2002, 221), since our vocabulary is grounded in structured theories of signification. Moreover, inventing a new vocabulary is neither easy, nor desirable, since that would bring affect into the realm of representation (O'Sullivan, 2001). Instead, we acknowledge the unresolved problem and move on.[2]

References

Abdallah, C., Lusiani, M., & Langley, A. (2019). Performing Process Research. In B. Boyd, T. R. Crook, J. K. Lë, & A. D. Smith (eds), *Standing on the Shoulders of Giants: Traditions and Innovations in Research Methodology*, pp. 91–113. Bingley: Emerald.

---

[2] We would like to thank Antonio Strati for his generous support in preparing the figures.

Ahmed, S. (2010). Happy Objects. In M. Gregg & G. J. Seigworth (eds), *The Affect Theory Reader*, pp. 29–51. Durham & London: Duke University Press.

Alaimo, S. (2012). States of Suspension: Trans-corporeality at Sea. *ISLE: Interdisciplinary Studies in Literature and* Environment, *19* (3): 476–493.

Anderson, B. (2009). Affective Atmospheres. *Emotion, Space and Society*, *2*: 77–81.

Ash, J. & Gallacher, L. (2015). Becoming Attuned: Objects, Affects and Embodied Methodology. In M. Perry & C. Medina (eds), *Methodologies of Embodiment: Inscribing Bodies in Qualitative Research*, pp. 69–85. London: Routledge.

Ashcraft, K. L. (2020). Communication as Constitutive Transmission? An Encounter with Affect. *Communication Theory*, doi:10.1093/ct/qtz027

Barad, K. (2007). *Meeting the Universe Halfway*. Durham and London: Duke University Press.

Beyes, T. & Steyaert, C. (2012). Spacing Organization: Non-representational Theory and Performing Organizational Space. *Organization*, *19* (1): 45–61.

Blackman, L. & Venn, C. (2010). Affect. *Body & Society*, *16* (1): 7–28.

Brennan, T. (2004). *The Transmission of Affect*. Ithaca. NY: Cornell University Press.

Butler, J. (2016). Rethinking Vulnerability and Resistance. In J. Butler, Z. Gambetti, & L. Sabsay (eds),. *Vulnerability in Resistance*, pp. 12–27. Durham, NC: Duke University Press.

Coleman, R. & Ringrose, J. (2013). Introduction. In R. Coleman & J. Ringrose (eds), *Deleuze and Research Methodologies*, pp. 1–22. Edinburgh: Edinburgh University Press.

Cozza, M., Cusinato, A, & Philippopoulos-Mihalopoulos, A. (2020). Atmosphere in Participatory Design. *Science as Culture*, *29* (2): 269–292.

Deleuze, G. & Guattari, F. (1987). *A Thousand Plateaus: Capitalism and Schizophrenia*. (B. Massumi, Trans.) Minneapolis: University of Minnesota Press.

Despret, V. (2004). 'The Body We Care For: Figures of Anthropo-Zoo-Genesis'. *Body & Society10* (2–3): 111–134.

Fox, N. J. & Alldred, P. (2015). New Materialist Social Inquiry: Designs, Methods and the Research-Assemblage. *International Journal of Social Research Methodology*, *18* (4): 399–414.

Game, A. (2001). Riding: Embodying the Centaur. *Body & Society*, *70* (4): 1–12.

Gherardi, S. (2017). One Turn.......and Now Another One. Do the Turn to Practice and the Turn to Affect Have Something in Common?' *Management Learning*, *48* (3): 345–358.

Gherardi, S. (2019a). *How to Conduct a Practice-Based Study: Problems and Methods*, 2nd ed. Cheltenham: Edward Elgar.

Gherardi, S. (2019b). If We Practice Posthumanist Research, Do We Need 'Gender' Any Longer? *Gender, Work & Organization, 26* (1): 40–53.

Gherardi, S. (2019c). Theorizing Affective Ethnography for Organization Studies. *Organization, 26* (6): 741–760.

Gherardi, S., Murgia, A., Bellé, E., Miele, F., & Carreri, A. (2018). Tracking the Sociomaterial Traces of Affect at the Crossroads of Affect and Practice Theories. *Qualitative Research in Organization and Management, 25* (1): 51–62.

Gherardi, S. & Strati, A. (2017). Talking about Competence: That 'Something' which Exceeds the Speaking Subject. In J. Sandberg, L. Rouleau, A. Langley, & H. Tsoukas, *Skillful Performance: Enacting Expertise, Competence, and Capabilities in Organizations*, pp. 103–124. Oxford: Oxford University Press.

Haraway, D. (1988). Situated Knowledges: The Science Question in Feminism and the Privilege of Partial Perspective. *Feminist Studies, 14* (3): 575–599.

Helin, J. (2019). Dream Writing: Writing through Vulnerability. *Qualitative Inquiry, 25* (2): 95–99.

Hultin, L. & Mähring, M. (2017). How Practice Makes Sense in Healthcare Operations: Studying Sensemaking as Performative, Material-Discursive Practice. *Human Relations, 70* (5): 566–593.

Ingold, T. (2011). *Being Alive: Essays on Movement, Knowledge and Description.* London & New York: Routledge.

Ingold, T. (2015). Foreword. In P. Vannini (ed.), *Non-representational Methodologies: Re-envisioning Research*, pp. vii–x. London: Routledge.

Jackson, A. Y. (2017). Thinking without Method. *Qualitative Inquiry, 23* (9): 666–674.

Knudsen, B. T. & Stage, C. (2015). *Affective Methodologies.* London: Palgrave Macmillan.

Latour, B. (2004). How to Talk About the Body? The Normative Dimensions of Science Studies. *Body & Society, 10* (2–3): 205–230.

Law, J. & Mol, A. (1995). Notes on Materiality and Sociality. *The Sociological Review, 43*: 274–294.

Lenz Taguchi, H. & St Pierre, E. (2017). Using Concepts as Method in Educational and Social Science Inquiry. *Qualitative Inquiry, 23* (9): 643–648.

Lury, C. & Wakeford, N. (2012). *Inventive Methods: The Happening of the Social.* London: Routledge.

Lykke, N. (2009). Non-innocent Intersections of Feminism and Environmentalism. *Kvinder, Køn and Forskning, 3–4*: 36–44.

MacLure, M. (2013). Researching without Representation? Language and Materiality in Post-qualitative Methodology. *International Journal of Qualitative Studies in Education, 26* (6): 658–667.

Manning, E. (2013). *Always More than One: Individuation's Dance*. Durham: Duke University Press.

Massumi, B. (2002). *Parables for the Virtual: Movements, Affect, Sensation*. Durham, NC & London: Duke University Press.

Mazzei, L. A. (2013). A Voice without Organs: Interviewing in Posthumanist Research. *International Journal of Qualitative Studies in Education, 26*: 732–740.

Mazzei, L. A. (2016). Voice without a Subject. *Cultural Studies↔Critical Methodologies, 16*: 151–161.

McCormack, D. P. (2015). Devices for Doing Atmospheric Things. In P. Vannini (ed.), *Non-representational Methodologies: Re-envisioning Research*, pp. 89–111. Routledge: London.

Mitchell, W. (2005). *What Do Pictures Want? The Lives and Loves of Images*. Chicago: University of Chicago Press.

O'Sullivan, S. (2001). The Aesthetics of Affect: Thinking Art beyond Representation. *Angelaki: Journal of Theoretical Humanities, 6* (3): 125–135.

Page, T. (2017). Vulnerable Writing as a Feminist Methodological Practice. *Feminist Review, 115* (1): 13–29.

Pink, S. (2015). *Doing Sensory Ethnography*. London: Sage.

Pink, S., Sumartojo, S., Lupton, D., & Heyes LaBond, C. (2017). Empathetic Technologies: Digital Materiality and Video Ethnography. *Visual Studies, 32* (4): 371–381.

Revsbaek, L. (2018). Resonant Experience in Emergent Events of Analysis. *Qualitative Studies, 5* (1): 24–36.

Shotter, J. (2006). Understanding Process from Within: An Argument for 'Withness'-Thinking. *Organization Studies, 27* (4): 585–604.

Stern, D. N. (1985). *The Interpersonal World of the Infant*. Basic Books, New York.

Stewart, K. (2007). *Ordinary Affects*. Duke University Press.

Stewart, K. (2011). Atmospheric Attunements. *Environment and Planning D: Society and Space, 29* (3): 445–453.

St Pierre, E. A. (2011). Post Qualitative Research: The Critique and the Coming After. In N. K. Denzin & Y. S. Lincoln (eds), *The SAGE Handbook of Qualitative Research*, pp. 611–625. 4th ed. Los Angeles, CA: SAGE.

Strati, A. (2009). 'Do You Do Beautiful Things?' Aesthetics and Art in Qualitative Methods of Organization Studies. In D. Buchanan & A. Bryman (eds), *The SAGE Handbook of Organizational Research Methods*, pp. 230–245. London: Sage.

Thrift, N. (2007). *Non-representational Theory: Space, Politics, Affect*. New York: Routledge.

Toraldo, M. L., Islam, G., & Mangia, G. (2018). Modes of Knowing Video Research and the Problem of Elusive Knowledges. *Organizational Research Methods, 21* (2): 438–465.

Vannini, P. (ed.). (2015). *Non-representational Methodologies: Re-envisioning Research*. Routledge: London.

Warfield, K. & Demone, C. (2018). Writing the Body of the Paper: Three New Materialist Methods for Examining the Socially Mediated Body. In Z. Papacharissi (ed.) *A Networked Self and Human Augmentics, Artificial Intelligence, Sentience*, pp. 133–152Z. New York: Routledge.

3

Arts-Based Techniques in Process Research

Learning to See the Forest for the Trees

Ariana Amacker and Anna Rylander Eklund

'What really *exists* is not things made, but things in the making . . .
But put yourself *in the making* by a stroke of intuitive sympathy
with the thing and, the whole range of possible decompositions
coming at once into your possession, you are no longer troubled
with the question which of them is the more absolutely true. Reality *falls* in passing into conceptual analysis; it *mounts* in living
its own undivided life – it buds and burgeons, changes and creates. . . . Philosophy should seek this kind of living understanding
of the movement of reality, not to follow science in vainly patching
together fragments of the result of the dead'
(William James, 1909, 263–264, emphases in original).

Shifting Perspectives by Noticing Differently

We are living in a time of global upheaval, living beyond our resources, with
increasing pollution, climate change, species extinction, loss of biodiversity, ocean acidification, deforestation, soil degradation, overpopulation,
and so on. We read news reports about it on our mobile phones and mo-
tivational quotes posted across panoramic images of exotic places pop up
on our screens. We understand that we need to change the prevailing ways
that we relate to and act in the world around us. But how do we start to
make this change in 'practice'?

To explore these questions, we follow James' appeal in the epigraph above
to shift perspective from an entitative view to a processual view of the
world; to put ourselves *in the making* rather than focusing on the things

Ariana Amacker and Anna Rylander Eklund, *Arts-Based Techniques in Process Research*. In: *Doing Process Research in Organizations, Noticing Differently*. Edited by Barbara Simpson and Line Revsbæk, Oxford University Press.
© Oxford University Press (2022). DOI: 10.1093/oso/9780192849632.003.0003

themselves as James so famously put it. We seek a 'living understanding of the movement of reality' by engaging with the forest as a living organism and ask ourselves how this movement can help us better understand what a processual worldview actually means for us as processual researchers as well as members of nature-society, seeing nature and society as an integrated whole. How can learning to *notice differently* help us make this shift?

In the industrial era, trees have been considered *things*; renewable resources that serve our consumption needs, providing raw material for anything from buildings, paper, packaging, and clothes to biofuel. This functional perspective has led to the clear-felling of forests in Europe and North America as well as the Amazon, making way for tree plantations with monocultures in order to extract as much profit as possible from each piece of land. Such a perspective requires a distanced approach to forests, viewing trees as disposable entities; as input to the production function. However, this perspective is now being seriously challenged. It is increasingly being argued that it is based on flawed assumptions and a short-sighted worldview, with clear-felling leading to a serious threat to biodiversity, releasing carbon dioxide into the atmosphere, making forests more vulnerable to the effects of climate change (e.g. forest fires, storms, and insect infestations) and less resilient in the long term (see e.g. IPBES, 2019). Science is starting to catch up with what ancient forest cultures have always known; the forest is an organism, continuously *in the making*, in which trees collaborate, communicate, take care of each other, learn, and pass their learnings down through generations (Simard, 2021, Wohlleben, 2016).

Acknowledging that our attitudes and practices are inseparable, we examine what a shift in perspective means through our relationships to forests metaphorically, ontologically, as well as practically. We approach noticing differently as something we must actively learn to do—intended to also help us understand what this shift in perspective does or changes practically about our experience with a forest. We have experimented with body-mind techniques, drawn from arts-based pedagogy, for framing our own attention in a small area of forest in the southwest of Sweden. Our aim is to learn to 'see' the forest as well as the trees; to experience the relationality of the forest (in the here and now) by positioning ourselves as part of the forest as a living organism.

We argue that this shift in perspective illustrates a shift we need to make on a far deeper, personal and societal level, regarding our relationship to nature-society. This shift reflects two different worldviews, an atomistic view focusing on trees as separate entities in a production system (things) and a processual view focusing on the relationships in the forest as a growing organism (things in the making), both of which are equally present in our views of organizations, organizing, and of ourselves and others as co-organizers, and reflected in our organizational designs and practices (Rylander Eklund & Simpson, 2020). A shift in perspective calls on us to *notice differently*; to shift what we value, what we pay attention to, and how we understand growth *in the making*.

To understand this shift we draw on Classical American Pragmatism, particularly the work of William James and John Dewey, helping us explore the key elements of an inquiry for noticing differently. Specifically, we build on William James' and John Dewey's anti-intellectualism which calls on us to start our inquiry with direct experience rather than with established concepts. The intellectualist approach, starting from concepts, is guilty of 'the belief that nature is an indifferent, dead mechanism' (Dewey, 1958, 21). 'As long as one remains *talking*, intellectualism remains in undisturbed possession of the field. The return to life can't come about by talking. It is an *act*; to make you return to life, I must set an example for your imitation, I must deafen you to talk, or to the importance of talk. . .' (James, 1909, 290). In making our shift, we therefore need to start from direct embodied experience. We see *noticing differently* as an act that helps us pay specific attention to the role of our senses and imagination in inquiry, supporting us in making the shift.

Developing Body-Mind Techniques to Learn to Notice Differently

Ariana has a background in architecture and dance and has studied a range of embodied awareness practices, many of which are used in theatre and performance pedagogy but are also intended for any 'body'. Anna has a background as a management consultant and organization scholar with a particular interest in creativity and aesthetics and has studied the creative practices of designers trained in art schools. We have worked together since 2012 when Ariana joined the School of Design and Crafts at the University of Gothenburg where Anna was working at the time. We have both always had a strong affinity for Pragmatism, particularly Dewey's aesthetics, which we find strongly resonates with artistic practices and arts-based pedagogy (cf. Eisner, 2002; Jacobs, 2018) as well as our own practice as researchers. We have endeavoured to embody Pragmatist principles in our teaching and research but have become increasingly frustrated with the fixed structures that have come to dominate academia regardless of discipline (detailed study plans and standardized learning goals, publication guidelines, etc.), which force us to adopt an intellectualist stance, starting from objects and established concepts rather than experience. From a Pragmatist and artistic vantage point this is doing things *backwards* (Shusterman, 2002). In this chapter we want to reverse the logic, developing an anti-intellectualist approach that departs from direct experience and relies on artistic practices for learning to notice differently.

Throughout our education we train our habits of perception and thus what we pay attention to. Management and art education train very different ways of noticing. In management education we are trained to focus on abstract concepts—the parts that comprise the whole; we focus on the trees as resources that may be used in the forestry industry. The arts disciplines deal with direct experience and movement as medium; the 'raw materials and energies' (Dewey, 1934) of the world. Art students are therefore trained to pay attention to qualities of experience through material and physical exploration. By focusing on the experience of 'making' art students learn to actively notice the qualitative and relational aspects of experience. By engaging the body and emotion to discover and convey ideas, students also learn to express what cannot be said and uncover the breadth and variety of what humans are capable of feeling (Eisner, 2002). Because learning is individualized, there can be no standardized methods to guide artistic inquiry, instead 'making' progresses through experimenting with, developing, and applying different techniques.

Developing body-mind techniques: Active, voluntary attention cannot be continuously sustained but instead it comes only in beats. It requires physical effort (James, 1890). Therefore, to notice *differently* requires practice, just like any other active physical practice. If we can assume that the repetition of arts-based techniques can result in a 'habitual direction of attention' (James, 1890, 424) we can assume that such techniques can also train types of perception through practice.

Consequently, art as experiential inquiry is supported by the continual practice of rituals and techniques, what some researchers refer to as 'studio habits of mind' (Hetland et al., 2015). Given the reciprocity between art-making and meditative, somatic, improvisational practices it is common for art studio teachers to involve specific techniques from such practices into their art and teaching. Following Dewey (1958) we hyphenate body-mind to highlight their inseparability and refer to body-mind techniques as those techniques that specifically aim at integrating body and mind, action and attention, sensing and imagining, to achieve a state of integrated awareness in the present moment.

In an attempt to synthesize and apply movement in teaching and research, Ariana has engaged with a number of embodied awareness practices over the years including Alexander Technique, contact improvisation, yoga, Butoh, Gaga dance, bodyweather, Feldenkrais method, Jacques Lecoq's actor training, authentic movement, sensory awareness, as well as Vipassana and metta meditation, and neoshamanism. Ariana's experimentation with these practices has been aimed at finding common pedagogical and practical features among them as well as generating her own lexicon of techniques applicable to work and everyday life. Body-mind techniques often have a similar practical foundation for paying attention to how one is moving, noticing habits, and for developing new possibilities in movement and perception. The overarching structure for learning these kinds of practical techniques starts with direct experience—active noticing (as opposed to distanced observation)—followed by verbal reflection, often done in pairs or as a group. Typically teachers physically demonstrate movements and/or verbally guide the experience so that the students can learn the techniques and train their ability to listen to the body-mind while moving. The reflection is a way for them to make sense of their movement experience by trying to put words to it. It helps students become detailed and precise in talking about movement, developing tools (in terms of imagery) and a vocabulary for understanding and describing how movements feel, what and when specific thoughts, emotions, images, or memories come up in the flow of sensory experience, and how and when they change.

Recurring examples of body-mind techniques in embodied awareness practices include simple activities and movements like walking, sketching, embodying visual imagery (ideokinesis), finding ways to release physical tension, trying small movements, changing points of visual focus, speed, rhythm, effort, and physical positions. When these are demonstrated, typically with verbal instructions, it is common for teachers to point out specific sensations to notice, or where to put attention; for example, to use your whole body, the back of the hand, the pelvis, the breath, to shift awareness to the whole surroundings. It is also common for the instructions to involve sense imagery or visualizations to explore while moving, for example to move the spine as seaweed, or to imagine fire on the floor or thousands of eyes on the skin. This technique of using imagery is metaphorical, intended to provoke a felt experience of movement with the understanding that imagery is tied to sensorimotor experiences and can help direct awareness and/or the quality of movement. There is no right or wrong way to move (images are open to individuals' cultural and physical interpretations) so there are typically instructions to let the action be free from judgement and to do what feels easy, with little effort, to be gentle and to not correct movement, but instead to simply notice what happens. For example, students are asked questions while they move to help them track changes in sensation and feeling like: *How does that feel? What do you notice? How do you organize yourself?* This structure of moving-questioning reminds the students of the intention of the exploration while training them to actively notice by bringing their attention to feeling from moment to moment.

The techniques we tested in our trips to the forest followed this basic structure, in particular the ones designed to connect physical and imaginative experience by inviting a mood of playfulness, awareness, and acceptance. Many of the practices Ariana has studied have an aim of accessing and stretching imaginative capacities through physical and sensory play and experimentation. For example, Feldenkrais is practised with the idea that having more flexibility in an individual's movement gives them more choices. This begins with the assumption that a person's self-image and habits condition their perceptions and movement, i.e. sensibilities engrained in neuromuscular structures like holding patterns. So the more individuals can let themselves physically explore and play, the more they can let go of these patterns (for instance moving might bring passing thoughts-feelings that this is strange, uncomfortable, silly, or 'not me') and enable new possibilities of perception, new imagery. The ability to articulate these sensory perceptions in physiological terms is directly anchored to the ability to imagine abstract images (Damasio, 2018).

These body-mind techniques are informally said to be for 'unlearning' since they are not aimed at acquiring a new or specific artistic skill (e.g. relating to expertise in handling a certain material), but learning a flexibility and sensitivity to explore what it could mean to move 'naturally', coordinated, unified. Dewey, who practised the Alexander Technique for twenty-five years as a practical way of becoming aware of, and resisting, his own habits of perception, thought and action, said this practice allowed him to pursue an active, critical, self-directed process of discovery and adaptation that reminded him of childhood learning (Woods et al., 2018). While practising the Alexander Technique had a profound impact on the development of his philosophy, Dewey did not talk much about it as it has to be enacted to be really understood. In his view, we all need to undergo a 'reeducation' of perception to redirect the dulling habits that inhibit us from freeing the capabilities we possess (Jacobs, 2018). How to do this cannot be 'explained' but requires practicing concrete body-mind techniques.

Establishing a Relationship with the Bråta Forest

To train our ability to notice differently, we decided to take some walks in the Bråta forest, with the purpose to build a relationship with this specific forest. The Bråta forest is a small nature reserve located just outside of Gothenburg, Sweden, where we both currently live. We chose Bråta because, as the small sign by the path at the forest entrance explains, it 'has the true sense of wilderness. Or at least something reminiscent of the wilderness.' Indeed, in Sweden there are hardly any old-growth forests left, especially not in the vicinity of major cities. But Bråta has been a nature reserve for a century and now has a rich diversity of species which we found inspiring for our purpose. Anna did a first exploratory walk (in March) and then we did three walks together (two in April and one in early June) during spring 2021. The walks were each very different in character and experience, because of how the forest changed during this period, because of our own states-of-mind, because of how we framed the exercises, and no doubt because of other things we are not aware of.

We decided to do individual walks, come back and write down our reflections individually, as well as do a quick drawing as an alternative mode of expression, all in silence. Afterwards we shared our experiences and reflected together. We followed this basic procedure, but apart from that, allowed our approach to develop as we went along in a very improvisational manner and experimented with various different techniques each time.

To understand how we developed and adapted our techniques we first summarize our practical set-up for exploring what it might mean to notice differently and how we could go about doing it in our visits to the forest. We accepted that we have to learn this through experience so we first committed to letting the process emerge and to discovering possibilities along the way.

Set-up: Our set-up was deliberately exploratory. Before each of our visits to Bråta, we began by discussing our intention for the visit. We both agreed that the underlying theme was to commune with the forest. We were not entirely sure what that meant, but we knew that we cared about establishing a relationship of some form with the place. We spoke about trying to get to 'know' Bråta, treating it like a friend, with respect, trying to be present there as best we can. We would turn off our cell phones.

We had a few intuitions that we tried to initially formalize, for instance, we knew that we wanted a simple, direct approach to experience. We both felt that it was important to try to just 'be okay' with the experience being *wordless* (as a proxy for an anti-intellectual approach). We acknowledged the need for a bodily orientation, wanting to find out what it could mean to perceive and react in a sensory way. Terms like 'instinctive', 'organic', and 'impulse' are used in a practical sense to give ourselves permission to work in ways that feel 'natural', to 'move freely' and to try to not let ourselves be hampered by inhibitions, formalities, or the pressure to produce outcomes that are 'interesting'. We also decided to move, touch, smell, and respond in a free, playful way so we can open ourselves up to a greater range of impressions, thoughts, emotions than we typically do when sitting and talking for example.

We found that part of the technical work for an integrated awareness was the need to 'empty' our interpretations, theories, and content, and our concern for labelling, categorizing what we do. We want to come into a non-judgemental, receptive presence, finding space in our meeting with the forest, with the potential to resonate and empathize with our surroundings. Settling into this receptive presence is done through an active, engaged sensitivity. Concretely the set-up requires a change in disposition, which can physically happen by first opening our bodies up, expanding our limbs and chests, deepening our breath, becoming alert to all of our senses. A simple technique to help with 'clearing' the body-mind is to be silent and bring the breath (inhalation and exhalation) into awareness. This helps us to shift focus to the present moment, avoid getting lost in distanced thoughts, and at the same time release tension. Another simple technique is to begin by standing, however and wherever we happen to be, and notice the contact of our feet with the ground. We try to imagine any stress or worries flowing out into the earth, which gives us a sense of connectedness and grounding. We also remind ourselves to 'listen' and 'cycle through the senses'.

To guide perception we focus on intention, attention and connection. These act as operational definitions (of aspects) of experience that are consciously applied to help us notice differently. They are not meant to divide and analyse but to help us understand what is involved in guiding our direct experience; primarily to remain dedicated to staying in the present and to a sense of unconditional possibilities.

Intention: We see intention as the orientation and guidance of the inquiry. Accepting that inquiry is alive, in motion, our perception is fundamentally through movement. Staying intentional from moment to moment helps to sustain and direct attention. Setting an intention is therefore for practical guidance, it helps give directionality, a path that couples our action and perception. It suggests *a purpose* to explore. It consists of finding words that support our exploration and letting go of other words.

In this case, we use the technique of asking questions that will serve as the point of investigation for each particular site visit to Bråta. We sought open questions using images and metaphors, like in the embodied awareness practices, that frame the basic purpose of the experience but also leave it open to personal perception. For example, in our first field visit we chose to ask the forest, 'Can you show me your spirit?' We are exploring how to relate to the forest in a way that transcends rational interpretation, wanting to reverse the way that we might ordinarily experience the forest by starting with a world of objects. We want to have an aesthetic experience, which we must intentionally give ourselves. Intention is about how we show up to sense 'forestness'. This sentient quality is not based on the conditions of Bråta being a certain way.

Asking the question in this way, speaking to the forest as a being and furthermore inquiring about a spirit opens up avenues for noticing. Attending to an embodied spirit is not to accurately reflect or describe reality; rather it activates sensation and imagination. Our question is playful and straightforward so that the answer can be equally playful and straightforward. The answer emerges through tactile, primary experience, and it is accepted for whatever happens, with nothing added or taken away. We actively stay receptive, trying to stay in the moment with intention, trying not to impose judgement on the situation about the 'right' way to do things or what the outcome should be.

Another technique we used to help set the intention was to imagine a threshold in the forest, like between two rocks or trees, so there is a circumscribed space where we know to shift to an integrated awareness. This imagery emphasizes our entry into the forest with the fullness of our perceptual capacities, one that expands outwards. At the moment we cross this imaginary threshold, we remind ourselves of the intention of the walk.

Attention: We have already described attention as a concentrated awareness that can be enhanced by physical training. In the space and time of our site visits we wanted to direct our attention towards what happens as we engage with the forest. For practical purposes, we can use James's (1890, 416) division of attention along the lines of: first, active or passive and, second, attending to objects of sense ('sensorial attention') or attending to ideal or represented objects ('intellectual attention'). These divisions help us to describe the kind of deliberate 'shift' in attention we were hoping to achieve with our set up. Again, the setting of the intention, as we did through the frame of a question, is to provide a reference point to help us to keep directing our attention towards experience.

The aim was to move from intellectual attention, such as reflecting on past events (for example through a train of images), instead becoming inattentive to outer things, actively placing attention towards a sensorial field of awareness that is extended through our body. The idea was to try to tune into what is going on around us and how we feel (the cold on the ears, the dull whirring sounds of cars far off in the distance, the glimmer of sunlight across the moss, the acidic taste in the mouth). We make it clear that if we think that you have a great insight, something cool to write down, we should let it go in the moment. We also thought about doing sketches during the walk, but then decided not to take notes or anything that would distract us from being present with the forest. We wanted to stop the internal talking.

Sensorial attention is wrapped up with movement and flux, the intricacies of sensory experience as it develops and changes from one moment to another. A basic distinction between sensorial and intellectual attention is that in the latter concentration is placed towards a target of reflection and the former participates in the 'flow' of things. The focus is on staying with the 'flow'. So if we notice our attention drifting from the question we should gently pull it back to the situation and re-ask the question (or restate the intention) in our minds. It helps to stay alert to feelings, what we see and hear, what is tangible and direct. This in turn shapes our perception of the walk and the forest.

Connection: Connection in experience is a perceptual process, a felt quality of immediate experience. For James, this sense perception, or feeling, is essentially somatic (Shusterman, 2011). It is experiential, felt. It cannot be indifferent. As Dewey (1934) points out, a person cannot understand the meaning of art merely through observation, but they have to enter into it, resonate with it. Connection has a sense of *surrender*

(Dewey, 1934). Therefore, connection requires a disposition of inner openness or receptivity, which in a practical way we can describe as being in a 'heart space' rather than a 'head space', by 'a stroke of intuitive sympathy with the thing' as James put it in the introductory epigraph. In this framing we say that the body-mind is already and always expressive of connection, it is immanent and reflects totality. Connection, like intention, is inseparable from movement. James describes a unifying quality of consciousness using terms like *stream* to capture a quality of continual movement. Recognizing movement as a central dimension of life, connection is not just the movement from one position (or state) to the next or one thing to another, but should be understood more like moving with the flux of James's 'undivided life'.

The framing of the situation is all about seeking a connection to the forest. It is a connection to a larger whole, the sense of aliveness, the vital quality, the spirit. Connection is where things merge, edges dissolve. It cannot be held in the mind. One technique related to connection is the use of 'soft focus' where we try not to look directly at things with the eyes, but use the full range of our vision including peripheral vision. This helps us to relax and to not narrow our focus, to receive with the entire body, and to have distributed awareness of our surroundings.

When connecting with the forest, the content of our action, how it feels to move through the forest, is inseparable from the insights that those feelings generate. For example, to talk about how we sense the forest, we inevitably talk about the kind of 'energy' that we feel, and this sense of energy gives the experience an emotional shape or arc, like in a piece of music (emotion is a feeling of energy movement). After our first walk through the forest both of us felt an overall transformation of energy during the course of the walk. For Anna it went from feeling animated, light, joyful in the beginning to feelings of coldness and darkness. For Ariana it was the other way around, the encounter started off feeling hard and unfriendly but then morphed into feeling kind, gentle, even fragile. The emotional energy we each felt gives flavour to the kind of experience of the forest we had, which also led us to more complex interpretations. Anna felt her experience like a closing off while Ariana related hers to feeling 'Swedish'.

To reach connection then, we have to leave a logical, distanced mode where things are held as distinct from one another to enter into an aesthetic, embodied mode that transcends our normal linguistic frames of reference. We no longer have to rely on what seems rational. We soften. We leave behind the dualisms of supernatural-natural, spiritual-material.

We enter into what spiritual practices call a larger field of consciousness. We can start from the assumption that everything is interconnected and alive. We can follow our imagination. We can also dare to be boring. We took inspiration from writers and scientists (notably Simard, 2021 and Wohlleben, 2016) who use terminology and metaphors traditionally applied to human communities for describing relationships within the forest (family, learning, parenting, welfare etc.). This technique fuelled our imagination and helped us connect with the forest. It helped us experience our surroundings as animated, in motion, and relational. When we sat down to reflect in our notebooks, we independently made sense of our walks by generating imagery like 'the trees were dancing', 'the bee was trying to tell me something', 'the rock was listening'. We share these reflections with each other, and there is a construction reminiscent of storytelling. Causal, logical explanations do not aptly describe our experiences; but images are indispensable to our sensorimotor understanding (e.g., Gallagher, 2005). As we let down our trained boundaries of being rational researchers with the discipline of observation, we easily revert to this spontaneous imagery to talk about what happened. It also felt easy and instinctual to enter into one another's stories. They felt honest, human, in between forming ideas, questions, insights, and poetry. We were no longer observers, but co-participants, connected in the production of emergent realities.

These three conditions of intention, attention, and connection help us to articulate our approach and specific techniques. In terms of the development of both of these, we had a few realizations as we went. We can now say that our techniques were done *via negativa*: we did not necessarily know what to do, but we found out through what felt like mistakes. *Via negativa* is also a kind of technique, the point is not to block paths before they are taken, which in turn obliges us to seek many ways forward, also encouraging imagination.

One realization was that we need to give more time-space to the set-up, especially to releasing and 'clearing' away the thoughts of the day, any stress, and just getting out of our heads. We decided that we should make relaxing a more important step, perhaps even shape it into a more formalized ritual as we enter Bråta. Second, we both felt the need to continually remind ourselves to be okay with not having a clear goal (in terms of how we habitually approach research with an intellectual purpose). This helps us to resist the urge to want to see an outcome, and to keep our focus on directly investigating experience. We need to redirect our whole disposition to do this though. We might hope to attain moments of poetry and connection in the space of the site visits to Bråta, but to really connect and value our relationship with the forest, we have to also keep cultivating our capacity and desire to stay present there. This will take time. Third, and interwoven with the other two points, is the decision that the development of our techniques is and will be ongoing. We must commit to learning on our feet and finding out when things do not work or when we feel 'resistance'. For example, on the second walk both of us felt distracted and did not take as much time as on the prior walk to set-up our intention. We accept this as learning and we see it as an opportunity to try new techniques as needed. And although obvious, it is worth mentioning that it is necessary to individually develop our techniques. What might work for one of us does not necessarily work for another.

Embodying Things *in the Making*

Our experiences in the forest helped us sense in a concrete way what James meant with his point in the opening epigraph that it is only things *in the making* that really exist. Specifically, our shift in perspective helped us notice the continuity, relationality, and temporality in the forest. We were struck by the continuity between life and death; by the omnipresence of death, by the necessity of death for life, and by the beauty of life-death. In the forest there is no clear difference between life and death. A tree can live for 300 years, die for 100 years and then stand in the same place dead for another 100 years. Only then does it fall to the ground and slowly, slowly start to decompose with the help of myriad small insects that live in and by dead wood. Everywhere in the forest we see new saplings and trees growing out of dead trees. If something grows on a dead tree, can you really call it dead? Can you even distinguish between life and death?

There were moments during our time in Bråta when the forest truly came alive for us, when we were absorbed by a strong sense of presence and belonging, a sense of connection with the forest. Imagining a group of trees as a family, knowing that they communicate and help each other, collaborate to a greater extent than they compete, nurture and support each other, protect the weaker trees when needed (Simard, 2021), helped us experience the forest as a living organism rather than a collection of trees. Most of the communication and collaboration between trees and other species, notably the mycorrhizas, happens underground and is invisible to humans, and has thus been ignored in modern (industrialized) societies. Only recently has scientific evidence started to catch up with what ancient forest cultures have always known; not only are we dependent on the forest, we *are* the forest, as members of the forest family (see e.g. Davies, 2009; Kohn, 2013). If you know where to look, the signs of the trees' intimate relationships are easy to notice. A family of trees growing out of the same trunk, the entanglements of the stunning diversity of roots covering a bank of a stream as if in a multitude of embraces, saplings growing under the protective foliage of a mother tree. But if we *notice differently* and allow ourselves to regard trees, fungus, and animals as fellow members of the forest family, we may experience their gaze upon us. And their gaze does something to us. It helps us see the forest and ourselves in a new light. It helps us shift perspective.

Finally, our experiences in the forest called for a different sense of temporality. In order to 'see' the collaborative nature of the trees, we have to understand that they also move, just like we do. Trees are in constant movement as they continuously grow and interact with their surroundings. But we move at a speed which is thousands of times faster than theirs. We need to accept this in order to notice the movement. We need to slow down and place ourselves *in the making* to be able to imagine the movements of the forest. On the other hand, the change of the Bråta forest between our second (23 April) and third (10 June) visits was astonishing. In April the forest was just starting to bud, the trees had no leaves, and the soil was bare. It was all different aspects of brown. In June the forest had turned all green with the ground covered in fern and other plants and the trees fully covered in leaves. It felt like a different forest entirely. The kind and speed of growth the Bråta forest had undergone in these seven weeks is equally astounding. The forest has a different temporality than we do in our modern life; it is infinitely both slower and faster than us.

Nurturing Sensuous Imagination

Based on James and Dewey we argue that we can all learn to notice differently. It is a disposition (habits of paying attention, of thinking, feeling and caring) and a (set of) skill(s) that can be trained. How is it relevant to organization scholars engaging in process research?

We have demonstrated how the development and use of arts-based techniques (such as clearing, soft focus, walking, asking questions, imagined threshold, animism, poetic expression, *via negativa*) has helped us train our skills and habits of perception for noticing differently, and how this has helped us free ourselves from our intellectualist habits to better immerse in and understand process ontology through connecting with the forest. We have no doubt that this will influence our future practice as researchers and the theories we continue to develop, just like the Alexander Technique profoundly influenced Dewey and his writing, particularly his views on quality of life, learning, habit, the concept of inhibition, integrated awareness and experience, and body-mind unity. In short, the continuous practice of the Alexander Technique was fundamental for the development of his anti-intellectualist stance.

Drawing on Dewey, we call these skills and habits of perception for noticing differently 'sensuous imagination' (1934, 31) to emphasize the dual aspect of sensing and imagining. Imagination is grounded in the sensory experience of the body, as 'embodiment is the best evidence that can be found of the true nature of the imagination' (Dewey, 1934, 279). This has a direct impact on *how* we relate, since it opens our frames of reference. Imagination is how we extend the present. It is not just about a kind of perception of mind, but it is *enacted* physically so that we can creatively participate in the flow and enhance the experience of living (Dewey, 1934). When we start to give more room to explore sensorial stimuli we discover that the body has many dimensions and layers of sense imagery. As Dewey notes, '"Sense" covers a wide range of contents: the sensory, the sensational, the sensitive, the sensible, and the sentimental, along with the sensuous' (1934, 22). Fuller application of imagination happens when we can abandon outside standpoints and really plunge into immediate experience. Here is a realm that most of us never or rarely experience in a conscious way, one that is open and endless, alive with energy and fullness, mystery, dynamism, uncertainty.

Sensuous imagination, as we see it, is practically about letting go of the tendency to fix attention, which also restricts perception. It is about opening your body-mind to enter into an anti-intellectualist mode. In order to let attention move freely in many (felt) directions, we can explore freedom of movement and the body's holistic 'way of knowing'. Associating inquiry with movement, imagery and metaphors activates different methods for exploration because the focus is on perceptual qualities. We are not suggesting developing a particular kind of sensory state, but rather the capacity to connect with our body and being willing to let go of the habits that we hold onto, like the images we have of ourselves that prevent us from accessing a fuller range of sensations, or doing things in a way that might seem strange. Following the body allows us to access more spontaneous, visceral feelings, intuitions, and rhythms that are already present in us. This inclusiveness of all of experience widens our perceptual experience and thus our capacity to notice and relate differently. It invites sensorial-imaginative participation.

Sensing-Thinking *with* James and Dewey

By highlighting the critical role of sensuous imagination in *all* inquiry, we want to make experience more intelligible and highlight the *continuity* between the aesthetic and the scientific, between direct experience and abstract concepts, as well as between the different world views presented in the introduction to this chapter. An anti-intellectualist stance does not ask us as organizational scholars to choose between an immersive and a distanced approach in research; it calls on us to do *both*, recognizing the centrality of the sensory and imaginative in all modes of inquiry. Indeed, it is the failure to grasp the continuity between direct experience and abstract concepts that leads to intellectualism, reducing and transforming all experience to 'knowledge' that can fit into the available concepts of science.

By developing a perspective where we position ourselves as part of the forest as a living organism, believing this can open up new ways of understanding and relating in our nature-society in general, we share the ambition of 'posthuman' (Braidotti, 2013; Haraway, 2008) approaches to develop a perspective that includes multi-species living, dissolving hierarchies between species. However, with our Pragmatist focus on embodied experience we want to specifically emphasize that we can never escape our bodies-minds. Just as with any other species, the way our sensorimotor systems work defines how we experience the world. This is an inescapable constraint, but it is also where our specific power as human inquirers lies as we engage in sensuous imagination to move productively beyond the conventional bounds of humanism. Acknowledging this possibility-constraint, asks of us to cultivate and harness the human powers of sensing and imagination in inquiry.

With our strong focus on imagination, emanating improvisation, our approach also has similarities to the emerging tradition of post-qualitative inquiry, which suggests that in order to create the 'new' in new forms of inquiry, such as post-qualitative and posthumanist, social science researchers may need to refuse conventional, pre-existing research methodology (St Pierre, 2021). Echoing James and Dewey's anti-intellectualism, post-qualitative inquiry argues that concepts and categories of conventional qualitative research tend to control a study, prescribing particular views of the human being, language, vision and expression that may be incompatible with a processual ontology focusing on movements rather than stable concepts (St. Pierre, 2018). Our practices of inquiry become similarly constrained if we are bound by method, reproducing that which we already know (Mazzei, 2021). Instead, St. Pierre suggests we depart from a philosophy of immanence, focusing on the emergent, engaging in concrete, practical experimentation and the creation of the *not yet* as opposed to repeating *what is* (2019), following 'the provocations that come from everywhere in the inquiry that is living and writing' (2018).

In this tradition, theory, and reading and writing, are essential as we learn to 'think with' James and Dewey (Jackson and Mazzei, 2013), immersing deeply in the literature to allow for concepts to become 'creative and active' rather than merely representative and descriptive (St Pierre, 2018). We have read widely and deeply the classical Pragmatists and texts about them, as well other literature on philosophy, anthropology, the arts and arts based education, social science and, of course, about the forest. We have followed the recent debate on the role of the forest in climate change, for biodiversity and in our economies. We have read scientific, popular and artistic accounts and watched films about the forest. In this sense, theory, and James and Dewey in particular, have been used as a guide for inquiry rather than as a lens for interpreting what we see (St Pierre, 2018). While we acknowledge the critical importance of writing as a mode of inquiry, as is highlighted in post-qualitative inquiry (St Pierre, 2018), we have added a focus on the role of our situated, direct experiences in inquiry. To circumvent intellectualism, James and Dewey remind us, we need to be wary of focusing too much on discourse, and direct our attention to our direct experiences in a particular place. Departing from this premise, we learned to 'sense with' James and Dewey in our endeavours to engage with and connect to the forest.

Conclusions

The epigraph introducing this chapter summarizes what we were aiming to do when going into the Bråta forest—seeking to explore the forest not as a collection of trees (a dead thing), but as a living organism (thing *in the making*), living its own undivided life as 'it buds and burgeons, changes and creates'. By specifically pursuing an anti-intellectualist stance we sought to activate a shift in perspective from a distanced and detached approach, promoted by our training as researchers, to one where 'you place yourself at the point of view of the thing's interior *doing*' (James, 1909, 262). We used the forest both as an embodied metaphor, in the sense of connecting abstract concepts and direct experience, and as a site for experimentation. We developed a set-up to help guide intention, attention and connection, and experimented with and reflected on body-mind techniques, to nurture our sensuous imagination. This helped us achieve the shift on an experiential level, enabling a different relationship to the forest, generating profound insight about the processual nature of reality.

When we learn to notice differently, when we invite imagery and open up for what is imagined and sensed, we open up a world of possibilities. When we give up the trees and the day-to-day goings on, we get moments, stories, insights. When we leave labels, ideas, and references, parsing between roots, trunks, or branches, we step into a timeless place, a place that does not ask anything of us. Our time is infinitesimal. When we go into this other world in this one, the trees are not just trees, but they are nurturers, a family. It is a place where the rocks hold secrets, the beetles rendezvous, the trolls hide, the moss invites you to sleep, and each mushroom holds a spongy mystery. This magical place is brimming with possibilities. If we can notice that the trees are not just trees, what else can we notice? What can we notice about a workplace and how can we relate differently to this social environment? How can we, as processual researchers, nurture our sensuous imagination, our skills of awareness and acceptance, to generate a bigger sense of who we are, a vocabulary that both exceeds us and is connected to the breath and bone? Now that we have sensed a living understanding of the movement of reality, we can no longer be satisfied with vainly patching together fragments of the result of the dead. What will we do with the new possibilities that now open up for us?

References

Braidotti, R. (2013). *The Posthuman*. Cambridge: Polity Press.

Damasio, A. (2018). *The Strange Order of Things: Life, Feeling, and the Making of Cultures*. New York: Pantheon Books.

Davies, W. (2009). *The Wayfinders: Why Ancient Wisdom Matters in the Modern World*. Toronto: House of Anansi Press Inc.

Dewey, J. (1934/2005). *Art as experience* (New). New York: Perigee Books.

Dewey, J. (1958). *Experience and Nature*. New York: Dover Publications Inc.

Eisner, Elliot. (2002). *The Arts and the Creation of Mind*. New Haven, CO: Yale University Press.

Gallagher, S. (2005). *How the Body Shapes the Mind*. Oxford: Oxford University Press.

Haraway, D. (2008), *When Species Meet* Minneapolis: University of Minnesota Press.

Hetland, L., Winner, E., Veenema, S., & Sheridan, K. M. (2015). *Studio Thinking 2: The Real Benefits of Visual Arts Education* (2nd ed.). New York: Teachers College Press.

IPBES (2019). *Global Assessment Report on Biodiversity and Ecosystem Services of the Intergovernmental Science-Policy Platform on Biodiversity and Ecosystem Services*. E. Brondizio, J. Settele, S. Díaz, and H. T. Ngo (editors). IPBES Secretariat, Bonn, Germany. 1148 pages. https://doi.org/10.5281/zenodo.3831673

Jackson, A. Y. & Mazzei, L. A. (2013). Plugging One Text into Another: Thinking With Theory in Qualitative Research. *Qualitative Inquiry, 19*(4), 261–271. https://doi.org/10.1177/1077800412471510

Jacobs, M. J. (2018). *Dewey for Artists*. Chicago: University of Chicago Press.

James, W. (1890/1950). *The Principles of Psychology* (Dover, Vol. 1). Henry Holt.

James, W. (1909/1996). *A Pluralistic Universe: Hibbert Lectures at Manchester College*. Lincoln: University of Nebraska Press.

Kohn, E. (2013). *How Forests Think—Toward an Anthropology Beyond the Human*. Oakland, CA: University of California Press.

Mazzei, L. A. (2021). Postqualitative Inquiry: Or the Necessity of Theory. *Qualitative Inquiry, 27*(2), 198–200. https://doi.org/10.1177/1077800420932607

Rylander Eklund, A. & Simpson, B. (2020). The Duality of Design(ing) Successful Projects. *Project Management Journal, 51*(1), 11–23. https://doi.org/10.1177/8756972819888117

Shusterman, R. (2002). Intellectualism and the Field of Aesthetics: The Return of the Repressed? *Revue Internationale de Philosophie, 220*(2), 327–342.

Shusterman, R. (2011) The Pragmatist Aesthetics of William James. *British Journal of Aesthetics, 51* (4), 347–361. https://doi.org/10.1093/aesthj/ayr030

Simard, S. (2021). *Finding the Mother Tree*. London: Allen Lane.

St Pierre, E. A. (2018). Writing Post Qualitative Inquiry. *Qualitative Inquiry, 24*(9), 603–608. https://doi.org/10.1177/1077800417734567

St Pierre, E. A. (2019). Post Qualitative Inquiry in an Ontology of Immanence. *Qualitative Inquiry, 25*(1), 3–16. https://doi.org/10.1177/1077800418772634

St Pierre, E. A. (2021). Post Qualitative Inquiry, the Refusal of Method, and the Risk of the New. *Qualitative Inquiry, 27*(1), 3–9. https://doi.org/10.1177/1077800419863005

Wohlleben, P. (2016). *The Hidden Life of Trees*. Vancouver: Graystone Books.

Woods, C., Williamson, M., & Eades, J. F. (2018). Dewey and the Alexander Technique: Lessons in Mind–Body Learning. In I. R. Heilbronn, C. Doddington, & R. Higham (eds), *Dewey and Education in the 21st Century*, pp. 83–100. Bingley: Emerald Publishing Limited. https://doi.org/10.1108/978-1-78743-625-120181011

4

Rhythms of Writing

Connecting (with) Words

Charlotte Wegener

Meanwhile

I am writing myself into knowing, and being. Words are my matter (Le Guin, 2016), and to make them matter, I must keep listening—to my body, to the world, to noises, and to silences (Lefebvre, 1992). Processes of writing are hard to share: research texts tend to enter the world as static entities, conveying what *has been done* and what we know *now*. It is said that Western philosophy is focused on substance and that Indo-European languages have a substance bias (Seibt, 2000). Academic texts tend to solidify. Don't blame it on the words. They vibrate as they arrive, carrying multiple resonances (Mol, 2020), making themselves available for us to connect in ever-new formations. Sometimes there are no words, and I must be patient and trust they will return. Meanwhile, I listen to music. On YouTube, I watch bassist and singer Esperanza Spalding perform with her band at The New York Times, and in a break between two songs, a journalist asks: *Do you consider yourself a fusion artist and if so, how would you describe your particular type of fusion?*

Esperanza Spalding replies: *Fusion. What is not fusion? Someone name one thing that is not a fusion of other components? Any identifiable 'genre' is just a snapshot of a phenomenon or a series of phenomena and you just happen to catch them at that moment of their morphing evolution or devolution. So yeah, I am a 'fusion' artist just like anyone making anything. It's in our blood. You're a fusion [points to the journalist]. You're a fusion [points to another]. So, to describe the kind of fusion, it's the kind of fusion that happens to come out of* me. (Lisovski, 2017).

I did not know what I was searching for, but there it was. This is the rhythm of writing.

Charlotte Wegener, *Rhythms of Writing*. In: *Doing Process Research in Organizations, Noticing Differently.* Edited by Barbara Simpson and Line Revsbæk, Oxford University Press. © Oxford University Press (2022). DOI: 10.1093/oso/9780192849632.003.0004

Becoming a Rhythmanalyst

This is a text about paying attention and being patient, about making myself available to the world and to the words as they arrive, and the processes of composing words and sections into a certain arrangement. It is a rhythmic fusion with no beginning and no end, made up to pay tribute to some of my favorite writing-words, to rhythm, to processes of fusing the world's input into textual output, suggesting rather than concluding. My research field is innovation, and one hallmark of innovation is that ideas or objects from previously unrelated domains are brought together (Barley, 2006, among many). I have always needed to do that in writing, too—to continuously bring together words as if they are ideas and objects (which they are) and 'follow the provocations that come from everywhere in the inquiry that is living and writing' (St Pierre, 2018, 603). It is a text about describing the world by keeping it open (Mol & Law, 2002), and about being open to the world, fine-tuning the senses, allowing for resonance.

Writing, to me, is a matter of becoming, a simultaneity of engaging in and creating what I am researching (Lund, 2021). Here, I am doing this as a rhythmanalysis: a composition of experiences that enrich or problematize abstract ideas, texts that 'grasp the excess of specificity that is always present in the actual by making a relation to elsewhere as they make themselves' (Lury & Wakeford, 2012, cited in Chen, 2017, 8). I investigate the rhythmic processes of writing, connecting words and connecting with words to continually sense and understand more nuances and keep asking better questions as St Pierre (2011, 621) reassuringly has taught me:

> I imagine a cacophony of ideas swirling as we think about our topics with all we can muster – with words from theorists, participants, conference audience, friends and lovers, ghosts who haunt our studies, characters in fiction and films and dreams.

With reference to Latour, Chen (2017) says that, instead of defining a procedure and sticking to it no matter what, we 'focus on the objects of concern and then, so as to handle them, produce the instruments and equipment necessary to grasp the questions they have raised and in which we are hopelessly entangled' (p. 9).

Entanglement is a quantum word. In Boje and Henderson's edited book about quantum storytelling, Bonifer uses as an opening quote an excerpt from the novel *Cloud Atlas* about understanding our lives and our choices moment to moment and how 'each point of intersection, each encounter, suggests a new potential direction' (Bonifer, 2014, 11). Reading the editors' introduction, I learn that quantum storytelling interweaves three different kinds of time (Boje & Henderson, 2014). 'Narrative storytelling' is strategic, surveying the past to explain the present and plan for the future. It is a linear logic classifying everything into a three-structure of beginning, middle, and end. 'Living story' is more tactical, proceeding from the middle; it is a matter of coming and going rather than of starting and finishing. It heads in all directions by conjunctions: and . . . but . . . yet . . . The third, the 'antenarrative', connects aspects of narrative time and living story time: 'You could simply say: narrative classifies, living story conjunctures, and antenarratives connect everything differently' (Boje & Henderson, 2014, 4). It is a kind of story that connects time (Chronos) with timing (Kairos) into 'spacetimemattering', say the authors. What is this, *connecting everything differently*? Connecting differently is certainly my way of noticing differently, of inquiring into my topics by keeping them open, and I wonder if it is possible to write a text that *does* that, rather than telling the reader about it. A quantum text? What kind of text would that be? I can only answer that question with Spalding's irreverent reply above: it's the kind of fusion that happens to come out of *me*. This text looks like this because this is the way my mind works. I am noticing differently through connecting differently in writing—it has no name. Yet.

So, here are the words, fragile concepts, serving as headings for short texts about my material and me as we fuse and repel in the empirical field of writing as inquiry (St Pierre, 2018). It is stories about things I experienced, read, or listened to, *my* take on innovation in processes of bringing ideas or objects from previously unrelated domains together in writing. It is a play with the rhythms of sound, and silence. Its aspiration is resonance.

Silence

John Cage is the composer of the piece *4′33″*, which instructs the performer *not* to play his or her instrument for the duration of four minutes and 33 seconds. Cage says that he once visited an 'anechoic chamber' at Harvard University—a room with no echoes due to walls made of special material.

He heard two sounds, one high and one low. He described these sounds to the engineer in charge, who explained that the high one was his nervous system in operation, and the low one was his blood in circulation. On YouTube, we can watch (and hear) a pianist not hitting a key or a conductor guiding an entire symphony orchestra not playing a note. The piece *4'33"* can be performed by any instrument or orchestra (or heavy metal band—look it up).

Is it quiet? Not at all. The piece *4'33"* consists of the sounds of the environment that the listeners make and hear while it is performed. 'There is no such thing as silence. Something is always happening that makes a sound', says Cage (1973, 191). *4'33"* directs our attention to the situation as it proceeds. What is part of the performance and what is not? Are coughing, wind buzzing in the roof structure and that man getting up and leaving the concert hall in anger part of the 'music'? Cage does not tell us that we make classifications all the time; he does not instruct us to reconsider the category 'music'. He makes us do the work. In the foreword to his book *Silence,* Cage explains that his intention is always to say what he has to say in a way that would exemplify it. This means to 'permit the listener to experience what I had to say rather than just hear about it' (Cage, 1973, ix). The form, the arrangement, the way we choose to convey our message, is always part of it. However, this fact only hits us hard when that *way* is different from what we expected. Then, we pay attention.

Wormholes

Something I want to write about but cannot name. It slips through my fingers every time I try to pin it down. Reaching out in time and space, I sense a memory, a premonition. I collect material and place it side by side in ever new formations on the screen. I have always thought of this way of writing as travelling through the wormhole. Googling 'wormhole', I find:

> The wormhole theory postulates that a theoretical passage through space-time could create shortcuts for long journeys across the universe. Wormholes are predicted by the theory of general relativity. But be wary: wormholes bring with them the dangers of sudden collapse, high radiation and dangerous contact with exotic matter.

> (Source: https://www.space.com/20881-wormholes.html)

I imagine these were titles of future papers:

> On Wormholes and Other Shortcuts
> The Danger of Sudden Collapse
> Dangerous Contact with Exotic Matter

Or just:

> Shortcuts for Long Journeys

On long journeys of living, listening, and writing, the wormhole is a passage between previously unrelated material. The passage is theoretical, but writing makes these connections empirical: a text is born. When connecting points in space-time, I create a shortcut that reduces travel time and distance. The points, the material—words, concepts, bits of text—are not new (although they may seem new in an academic context), but the connection is. The text is always in danger of sudden collapse, it may not hold, but when it does, I have created something new in the world. Abandoning simple proximity and writing through the wormhole is an act of irreverence. It is impossible if I aim for linear reasoning, and yet comedians, poets, and children do it all the time. I arrange the material side by side and realize I have created a new, nameless passage. Then I name it.

Stealing and Murdering

Weekend is approaching, and we drive to the fancy grocery store to buy supplies. We need something better than the local budget grocery store within walking distance can offer. She needs frozen edamame beans in their pods, crispy pears, and a larger candy assortment. I need time with her, various organic grains for my breakfast and a non-hangover white wine. At the liquor department, I skip the wine and pick two bottles of spring beer.

> 'So, those are to be consumed directly', she says, making a gesture of binge drinking straight from the bottle.
> 'No, no', I smile reassuringly, 'they will be sipped from a glass. . .'
> 'Mom', she laughs into my face, 'I know you won't be partying tonight, you'll be writing, right?'

Back home, she willingly walks the dog and then leaves with her candy, by bike, in the cold March night. Spring beer or not. . . the snow is swirling as I watch her taillight disappear in the dark. I tell myself that she will be fine, that she will return safely, that no one will ever hurt her. I empty the grocery bags, place the beers in the fridge, arrange leftovers on a plate and pour a glass of water. I finish Philip Pullman's (2017) essays *Dæmon Voices* by the fireplace, my brain crystalline, skipping parts of the last essays, impatiently listening to the words as they buzz in the periphery on their way to my fingertips. I look at the beautiful red hardcover, glossy when the light falls at the right angle, and the raven with a stolen string of words in his beak. The raven, the shiny red, and the words belonging to whomever are all I need for now. I intend to use it all for my own purposes. I open my laptop, and the next thing I know of is her in the doorway telling me it's very late and that she will go straight to bed. How did these hours pass in an instant? I do as I am, implicitly, instructed and go to bed. I dream that I am travelling to South Africa, and a giant horse, twice my height and teddy-bear-like, is getting in my way. I grab my gun and shoot it. I feel some regrets; it was soft and fluffy and somewhat innocent, but after all it was just too large to get past. Saturday is endless, and I can now return and pick up pieces and make use of what Pullman writes about writing. He never starts with the theme of a story. His stories have a theme and they are about something, he says, but he does not know what it is until he is in the process of writing: 'I have to start with pictures, images, scenes, moods – like bits of dreams or fragments of half-forgotten films. That's how they all begin' (Pullman, 2017, 35). Pullman advises everyone to perfect their ability and special gift in writing. What we are good at, we must do over and over; even if we find that what we can do best does not get much credit. We can do something else to fit in, but we will suffer by it. And the writing will, too. I have read piles of books on auto-ethnography and confessional tales and narrative and art-based and post-human and post-qualitative inquiry, and all I know is that I need to start with weekend grocery shopping for beers I don't drink, a black raven on shiny red, and bits of dreams in which I murder Innocence in cold blood.

Passing Through

The songs on Jeff Buckley's first and only studio album, *Grace*, are good, some of them great, but I keep returning to his solo live recording *Live at Sin-é*. He took on these gigs to practise what he found to be his ultimate feat as an artist: unmediated connection to the audience with just his voice and his guitar. No fancy gear, no elevated stage, no entrance fee. *Live at Sin-é* is an intimate concert recorded some afternoons and later turned into an album that became cult. The audience applause is scattered; there are so few people present that you can decipher almost every single handclap. Buckley and I grew into adulthood in the same decade, the 1980s, were raised on the same music, and while he toured and got stoned and felt the pressure of fame and record contracts, I studied music science, partied moderately and had a study job cleaning at a music venue, completely ignorant of him, while critics gradually paid attention and some voiced the thought that he might be the most talented artist of his generation. As I settled into family life, almost drowned in piles of laundry and lack of sleep, trying to make it as a music teacher, and having no clue that irreverent fusion of writing would become my future métier, Jeff Buckley jumped into the Mississippi River with all of his clothes on, thirty years old, while his band were on their way to start recording their second studio album. His roadie, the only witness, told the news reporters that Jeff was on his back, eyes on the evening summer sky belting out Led Zeppelin's 'Whole Lotta Love' until he disappeared (Runtagh, 2019). Nobody believed he wanted to die, and yet he did not resist death. In an interview, he said (Columbia Records, 2010):

Music is endless. And, even though I've heard a whole bunch of music, from so many different places, and fallen in love countless times with all kinds of music, there's still something. I guess it's just called freedom.

Live at Sin-é is an odd collection of his own songs and covers—how many are there, by the way? I google 'Live at Sin-é' and find a short comment by a *Rolling Stone* journalist, who notes that there are imitations and impersonations of artists as diverse as Billie Holiday, Robert Plant, Edith Piaf, Bob Dylan, and the qawwali musician Nusrat Fateh Ali Khan. She continues (Schoemer, 2003):

Buckley seemed to believe that the entire history of twentieth-century popular music needed to course through his veins. Blues, R&B, folk rock, acid rock, classic rock and grunge were just the beginning.

All this material neither represented a *genre* nor suggested a new one. And yet, he made it fuse in some strange way powerful enough to still resonate. It is all entirely his, and at the same time, he gives it all away.

Oscillation

The Zen practitioner and writer Natalie Goldberg (2005) has taught me to go to a café and write, so I do. There is a free barstool at the high table with a street view, and for the next hours I intend to immerse myself here, coffee, croissant, and laptop within reach, while moving on with this manuscript. The editors liked my abstract, so this should be straightforward, right? Just produce a text about the rhythm of writing, connecting words, and creating resonance. I write the following:

I want to write more about resonance, and the very thought makes my whole system tremble. There is too much information out there, and too much aspiration in here, and it all sort of rattles and clatters in unpleasant gusts, and it is very unnerving. The whole world resonates in me. This morning, I called my friend, who is 2,850 kilometres away, heartbroken, and made her stop crying. What did I say? I said: 'I'm here, right next to you.'

Resonance is effort and trust, touch and retraction, recognition and surprise. I have written about resonance before (Meier & Wegener, 2017), but I need to look it up as if for the first time. Zen practitioners call it Beginner's Mind. Resonance:

> Frequencies at which the response amplitude is a relative maximum are also known as **resonant frequencies** or **resonance frequencies** of the system.[3] Small periodic forces that are near a resonant frequency of the system have the ability to produce large amplitude oscillations in the system due to the storage of vibrational energy.
>
> (https://en.wikipedia.org/wiki/Resonance)

This is *exactly* why I don't do this very often. It is far more information than my system can handle. I get carried away by Frequencies and click one link, then the next. I read about natural frequency: the frequency at which a system tends to oscillate in the absence of any driving or damping force.

I know! My natural frequency needs a reset, and the world keeps driving and damping its forces on me! Resonance frequencies, response amplitude and small, seemingly innocent words sneak in to suddenly produce amplitude oscillations and vibrational energy far, far beyond my will. Wait a minute: due to the storage? Is there a *place* somewhere? A free archive named 'Mine' with endless rows of steel drawers filled with brown cardboard index cards, and deep down between the narrow rows a minia-ture firetruck with a never-ending ladder transporting me effortlessly up and around to fetch everything I need for my writing? And the raven is there, too. His name is Rave; I know him very well. He picked up this and he picked up that and he keeps collecting and rearranging my world, re-naming the drawer labels to keep it all in the proper categories, perpetually. He tells me to take a break and watches over me in my dreamless rest, then wakes me up with new strings of words in his beak, telling me it's time to go to work:

'There is no template', he croaks, 'just keep writing'.

Refreshed, I pick up the strings and write on, to the distant sound of amplitude oscillations.

Quality Time

I am interrupted by a happy, surprised voice: 'Hallo Charlotte, so you are working here at the café today.' While wondering if this kind of writing counts as work, I tell my acquaintance that I am here while my house is being cleaned. To be honest, I feel both guilt and pleasure at paying a poor student to do the dirty work on a Saturday when she was supposed to be studying or dressing up for a party while I am tapping the keyboard with clean fingers, sipping a double-shot cappuccino with a delicate milk foam heart on top. All through my university studies, I cleaned offices before morning lectures, and at weekends I cleaned at that music venue. Backstage was the filthiest, though the toilets were bad, too. One time, backstage, a banknote to the value of a month's pay was floating in the midst of beer puddles, cigarette butts, sooty tin foil, and vomit. At first, I assumed it had fallen out of a musician's pocket, and I felt lucky until I realized it was for me, the invisible cleaning maid—and shame flooded in.

I congratulate my acquaintance on her pregnancy: 'I am happy for you, a third kid after some years is such a delight', I say, and she sweeps her coat tails and long scarf to the side and displays a twenty-four-week stomach. 'I will come to terms with it, eventually', she says, 'this was not planned, in fact, but you reap what you sow, and we were irresponsible.' I say OK and wait. 'Now we just have to cope with it, start over and make the best of it.' I know her husband is busy writing books, doing interviews and taking care of jetlag. He is funny, though, and good looking; money is not an issue. She directs her attention to the bread on display, and I to the screen. Start over. . .

I write for some time, not that absorbed anymore, then pay for the coffee and head home by bike, pedaling with healthy legs, transporting the cold spring air into my lungs. My heart insists on beating, and I willingly accept. The body.

Back home, I listen to Esperanza Spalding's album *12 Little Spells* and read that it is 'a significant departure from all her previous work. It's a combination of highly experimental space jazz with odd meters and melodies that are cleverly woven together with a breezy charm and panache' (Campbell, 2020). High on odd meters, I resume writing about *fusion*:

Writing is the making of connections over and over and leaning into the trust that we, at times, manage to catch a phenomenon or a series of phenomena at a moment of their morphing evolution or devolution and make it into something read-worthy to others. 'Life comes without headings', I once concluded an unsuccessful attempt at organizing my ethnographic data into neat categories (Wegener, 2014), and, in producing that sentence, I fused defeat and triumph. I could not organize my material about innovation into piles fitting precise headings, but I could write a sentence that rang true. Life comes without headings. What we do as researchers is to invent headings and organize material, thus justifying the findings, the conclusions, the implications. It can be done. I can do it. But it feels so ephemeral, more like a moment of truth I am lucky enough to catch. It feels true to keep categories fragile. I like them this way. Writing at the café did not reset anything at all: imagination running off (a living story from the middle?), the memory of shame while dealing with other people's dirt and being tipped for it in my youth, my soft and clean fingers on the laptop keyboard, the baby in the womb who will grow to the beat of her mother's heart day by day until she arrives, unplanned and even unwanted as she may be (a three-structure story of past-present-future?). Her mother was stunning, more than ever before, obviously grown up enough to handle the arrhythmia of taking care of a baby again even though she had other plans. In an interview in one of the magazines filled with recipes and diets and features about men and women with lots of kids and great careers and big houses, I recall her husband praising 'quality time' and claiming that being a good parent has nothing to do with the amount of time you spend with your children—it's about being *present*. It seems that he chose first and picked Kairos, which leaves her with Chronos. I wonder if they will manage to connect time with timing in a *spacetimemattering* parenthood. All I can do is write us all into my text.

Lefebvre, whom I consulted to become a rhythmanalyst, wrote that rhythmanalysis is an embodied endeavour of experimenting empirically with 'how rhythms are lived' (Alhadeff-Jones, 2017, 182). Being in rhythmic transaction with the world involves all of our senses, breath, heartbeats and use of one's limbs. In rhythmanalysis there 'is a constant oscillation between theorising the method of rhythmanalysis and conducting empirical research' (Chen, 2017, 16)—'it allows an "arbitrariness", which suggests a freedom rather than badly designed research'. Chen is a historian, working in the archives (I had to invent my own, imaginary one) yet the same is true of me: by writing this piece, I allow for arbitrariness and suggest connections I did not know of beforehand. The different parts of the text are nothing new, just ordinary stuff, intense and fragile enough to vibrate towards each other, even oscillate. I cannot conclude what I now know, but I can keep writing simply because writing is my preferred way of thinking and being—combining memories and things and ideas with each other. Will this resonate with any reader? I cannot know.

I may, someday, reap what I have sown. Some embryos lie dormant to suddenly sprout in surprising ways, at surprising times. I may reap something I did not sow, and a sprout I nonchalantly flung away may grow into a sunflower in front of somebody else.

Impact

I have a postcard from my dentist announcing that he is closing down and that I will be transferred to his colleague nearby. He says thank you to us all for having been his patients. He really enjoyed the years; however, he has finally given in to his long-time passion: root canal treatment. He is looking forward to fully immersing himself in his new practice. I once had a root canal treatment, and it never occurred to me that this could be the passion of the person at the other end of this activity. If we want to do great writing, we must seek to convey passion, and nothing is too inferior for passionate writing. Why do we fall in love with certain concerns? Often, because someone has infected us with their passion. We do not take in the message of a text because the writer dictates to us how important it is. We take it in because we trust that writer, because we sense a truth in what this person says. In an interview with Charlie Rose, the late author David Foster Wallace talks about David Lynch and other great artists: what they do, he says, is to be entirely themselves; they have their own way of 'fracturing reality, and if it is authentic and true, you will feel it in your nerve endings' (Rose, 1997).

When we are impacted by the passion of another human being, we expand our capacity for passion, in life and in writing. We may all, knowingly or not, be that someone who impacted another human being with our passion. We cannot force this to happen, but as researchers we, too, must strive to be great artists, fracturing reality in our own way and writing our way to truths. I never cared much for my dentist, but I will keep his postcard forever. It feels so good to know he is out there passionately performing root canal treatments, completely unaware that he made me write about impact.

Arrhythmia

Saturday night, I cook for him, and after dinner he tells me that the irregular heartbeat has lasted for several hours now. He asks me if I can hear it, and I put my ear to his chest and hold my breath. His heartbeat comes and goes, like a crazy dance, revealing to me no pattern. I have never heard anything like this before. I am leaning into arrhythmia. This is temporal complexity beyond metaphor.

I leave him with the dishes and read that arrhythmia doesn't necessarily mean that your heart is beating too fast or too slow; it's just out of normal rhythm: 'It may feel like your heart skipped a beat, added a beat, is "fluttering", or is beating too fast (which doctors call tachycardia) or too slow (called bradycardia). Or you might not notice anything, since some arrhythmias are "silent"' (Beckermann, 2020). I also read that arrhythmias can be harmless, or an emergency. How do we know?

Too fast is not resolved with too slow. I remember reading a paper about 'Slow Ontology'. I look it up (the ongoing clatter and plash from the kitchen tells me not to hurry back) and read that alternative rhythms of inquiry are needed to resist a fast-paced fabrication of articles, chapters, books, and monographs: 'Given that much of the academic life cycle is predicated on writing, it provides a potential site of intervention for those who desire to produce research differently, reimagine impact, or write to something other than the rhythms of the clock' (Ulmer, 2017, 202). Alhadeff-Jones

(2016) writes that rhythm is constitutive of 'those phenomena through which people aim at finding and following a particular rhythm, where individual freedom is understood as the conquest of one's own rhythms' (pp. 166–167). What *is* one's own rhythm? And what if one's rhythm is arrhythmic? Can you fuse your own arrhythmia with another person's arrhythmic crazy-dance-pattern and experience a kind of synchronization? Emancipation requires some irregularity—you need to break free from your well-known patterns, but it seems to me that this builds on the idea of a 'true', inner rhythm. Alhadeff-Jones refers to Sauvanet's use of the term *syncope,* its meaning close to words such as kairos, crisis or leap. These words describe rhythmic experiences that may have freeing effects because they momentarily liberate us from a pattern of strict repetition. A syncope requires a capacity for sorting, separating, organizing, deciding, and judging 'what has to be done' (p. 168). So far, so good. Freedom involves the ability to go with one's own flow, be that discursively, corporeally or socially. You can provoke a syncope to resource or reinvent yourself and break free from a life lived too monotonously (Alhadeff-Jones, 2016). Is this obsession with writing throughout the weekend a liberating syncope, is it increasing (or challenging) my capacity for sorting and deciding, or is it maybe a proof of my ability to go with my own flow? Is it harmless? I know the term syncope as referring to an off-beat or suspension in music, but when I look it up, a homepage about heart attacks and strokes tells me it means 'fainting'. Oh no. I rush to the kitchen and offer my assistance, but the coffee is already brewing, heartbeats regular he says, all smiles. The music flowing from the stereo is fully unfamiliar.

Listening

This text is becoming an assemblage of different sites of rhythmic production (Chen, 2017), a purposeful experimentation (Highmore, 2018), a performative text that seeks to connect the nearby and the far away, the everyday and the conceptual, necessarily fragmented and uncertain (Pelias, 2014). It is a process of weaving 'a simultaneity of "stories-so-far"', as Massey (2005) said (quoted in Speedy, 2012, 351). It is not a text *about* rhythms of writing, and not at all about how to conceptualize innovation. It is writing my way to the words, writing as listening, writing at the café, it is in the making, arriving in arrhythmic patterns. I seek help in Annemarie Mol's writings because she is not invested in stabilizing the words (or the world) but insists on letting the simple co-exist with the complex:

> The texts that carry academic stories tend to organize phenomena bewildering in their layered complexity into clean overviews. They make smooth schemes that are more or less linear, with a demonstrative or an argumentative logic in which each event follows the one that came before. What may originally have been surprising is explained and is therefore no longer surprising or disturbing. Academic texts may talk about strange things, but their tone is almost always calm.
>
> (Mol & Law, 2002, 3)

Lefebvre (1992) writes that the rhythmanalyst will listen to his body and learn rhythm from it and then he 'will listen to the world, and above all to what are disdainfully called noises, which are said without meaning, and to *murmurs* [rumeurs], full of meaning – and finally he will listen to silences' (p. 19). I am listening to my body, and it provides me with strange information. I listen harder, and there is almost a silence, a pause deep down in the sea of noise. I listen. Dewey (1934, 179) says: 'A pause in music is not a blank, but is a rhythmic silence that punctuates what is done while at the same time it conveys an impulsion forward, instead of arresting at the point which it defines'.

I am inquiring into rhythms of writing, molding lived matter into textual matter, yet I have no mold—the form must emerge as I write. I listen to Jeff Buckley for remembering pasts, and to Esperanza Spalding for imagining futures. Jeff Buckley died way too young. This is just the way it is. The music is here, though, and so are the words. I too listen to all kinds of music, but I don't sing. I write. I *have* to, because only what is written stays with me. It has to course through my veins. What I read, reflect upon and talk about tends to disappear. Taking notes won't suffice. Theory and life lived must be consumed and spat out, fingers on keyboard, in sections, sitting side by side, juxtaposed chunks of words, sections soaking up significance from each other. In an interview during his Australian promotion tour of *Grace* (Cobain, 1995), Jeff Buckley talks about 'catching the moment very raw'. The interviewer asks him how he manages to create these transcendent moments on stage, and he replies that he is not trying to be transcendent at all:

*What I am trying is to sing what comes to my body, in the context of the song. And
if you go by the emotion of the song, you know, it's almost like stepping into a city
and the city has certain customs and rules and laws, and laws you can break. And
that's what I was doing.*

Buckley sang because his body was full of music and because he could
sing. He was not *managing* anything in particular. The music wanted to
pass through him, and he made himself available to it and to the audience,
obeyed rules, and broke some. He did not forge connections or fuse genres; he just performed the music he liked, and it turned into a fascinating
composition unmistakably *his*.

Music, for Lefebvre, was exactly that; it requires three conditions for its
existence, he says. 'First: it must have rules. Second: it must escape those
rules. Third: as it escapes, it must be received by our bodies' (Dayan, 2019,
27). Rhythmanalysis is a call for research that situates itself *amidst* social phenomena and transgresses disciplinary boundaries. It is a call for
research that collapses social fields and explores 'the connection of experiences' (Chen, 2017, 7). It is the body, silent, sensitive, and vibrational
enough to make room for resonance. The rhythmanalyst must be able to
receive and make it into words, handle fragile concepts irreverently, with
passion.

Attention

Rhythm is a meta-sense that invites new vocabularies (Chen, 2017). The
rhythm of a text is the effect of the patterning of material, rhythms are
produced by the way words and sections are placed, side by side, and each
intersection, each encounter, suggests a new potential direction, as Bonifer
quoted from *Cloud Atlas* and as quantum theory teaches us. As this text
emerges in front of me right now, on the screen, I know it is an assemblage
of things that do not fit (Mol, 2020). Not yet. I am the one to make it fit,
and still be bold enough to keep it open, don't squeeze too tight, don't issue
any orders but keep listening. Writing this way is topological, it is a composition of moments to identify and create rhythms: 'It is the push-and-pull
relationships of the abstract and concrete that characterise the modes of
attention of rhythmanalysis as a methodology' (Chen, 2017, 15).

This writing is ongoing attention to the process of bringing ideas or objects together. I must connect and tear apart and include and discharge
material until it turns into a text that cares for equivocations (Mol, 2020).

'While connecting with material, in writing, a writer organizes instants in space and time into a subjective system of instances', says Alhadeff-Jones (2017, 180), referring to Bachelard. While preferring some words, some instants and some organizing principles over others, we organize our world, create a place to comprehend, reflect and rest for a while, a place from where we can experience not only instants but also the very processes of connecting them into some kind of intermediate whole.

Zero Gravity

We are on the couch, each of us with our laptop. Eyes on the screen, she says:

> 'Mom, do you want to be a space sheriff or an intergalactic smuggler?'

After some thought, I decide on the intergalactic smuggler, and that turns out to be a good choice:

> 'You just have to keep prepared and when they make contact, you must transport contraband from one galaxy to the other. These are just things that people need elsewhere, so your job is to make connections.'

The next two days I do not need to work, because I am waiting for my space capsule to be built. Meanwhile, I work out and sign up for practicing zero gravity.

> 'That space capsule really takes up a lot of space in the backyard', she says and then interrupts herself, 'Oh, you can make prank calls!'

While one of the other Simmers makes a prank call to her mom, I unobtrusively enter the space capsule, take off and disappear.

> 'Oh no, you didn't take your time to practice zero gravity', she says. 'I hope you'll make it.'

Truths

Academics are supposed to take control of words, use them for specific purposes and express *what we know*. We perform control in a variety of ways: we define, explain, categorize and conclude. We refer and paraphrase and cite. We arrive at our laptop keyboard with stolen strings of words in our beaks to compose a new story. For this text, I stole and murdered, I listened to Esperanza Spalding and Jeff Buckley, went to the café and returned home to read about quantum storytelling, and write more. I read Pullman and a number of academic texts about rhythm, rhythmanalysis and writing. I cooked for someone I like very much, and I entered a space capsule in my daughter's Sims game. It is a three-structure narrative of weekend approaching, of Friday, Saturday, and Sunday night, which will arrive in a moment. It is a tactical, living story proceeding from the middle of a writing aspiration heading in all directions, but arranged into a whole by the concept of rhythm. It is an antenarrative composed by me, with words chosen by me to experiment with the experience of writing. I performed control by placing these words into a certain pattern making a rhythmic suggestion, a tale that might ring true. Placing them otherwise would suggest other truths.

Presence

Writing this way is a delicate balance between a private, self-absorbed I and a plural I that aims to create a space for resonance and familiarity (Pelias, 2005). It is performative writing with 'no separation between mind and body, objective and subjective, cognitive and affective' (Pelias, 2005, 418). Experience in itself is not scholarship, as Pelias points out: performative writing is highly selective, and much is left on the editing floor. Everyday experience, then, is not scholarship, but the shaping of everyday experience into resonant tales can be.

Much was left on the editing floor.

My oldest son drops by to pick up the bike helmet he left here the other day. I finally managed to persuade him to buy one. I equipped him with my credit card when he needed a new tire and told him to buy anything he needed for the bike as long as it included a helmet. I ask him if he knows Jeff Buckley and he says: 'Of course, everybody my age does, he is cool.' I ask how, and he says we just do. We listen to (and watch) *Lover, You Should've Come Over* (Buckley, 1995). 'It's never over, she's the tear that hangs inside my soul forever.'

I look at him across the table as he finds new songs and adds them to my playlist. I fetch the remaining ice cream from the freezer, extending the moment, just a bit. We laugh, for no reason.

I let all these kinds of material pass through my veins and tried to make them into a text with threads clearly visible (Mol, 2020). I did it as a *suggestion* by letting the text itself say what I have to say in a way that would exemplify it, as Cage taught me. It is a process text, in the making; it seeks to *do* innovation. The live recordings of Jeff Buckley's gigs and interviews show a complex young man, elusive, ambitious, just a few years older than my son today. Buckley is my age and my son's age at the same time. That is quantum, isn't it? He connects that young girl cleaning at the music venue, lost in a sea of noise, with this mature researcher, finally listening to silence. She and I can now fuse, for good or for a little while, as I can now fuse noises and silences of my life, defeat and triumph, into writing—life comes without headings; I made them up.

My son leaves with his helmet, and I put on Buckley's version of 'Don't Let the Sun Catch you Crying' (Buckley, 2016). It's a live version recorded in 1993, and it ends with him stating: 'I just like that song.'

So do I.

This Sunday night, writing arrives, shines its light on the whirling of the world, the twirling of the words, spat out from my fingertips. Working the keyboard with ease, hovering time, I can lay it all out and allow the world's impact to fuse into some kind of whole made up of encounters, each suggesting a new potential direction.

Initially, I asked the bass player and singer Esperanza Spalding, or rather, I let the journalist who was actually *present* ask her:

'Do you consider yourself a fusion artist and if so, how would you describe your particular type of fusion?'

It was Innocence asking, and it was well asked—it allowed Spalding to shoot, ever so gently, to defy categorization and claim freedom of expression, for everyone. She may not need to say it because she is already free it seems, but I needed to hear it. Along with her music. New listeners can start here: 'I Know You Know' (Spalding, 2009)

I can't wait to read the kind of fusion that happens to come out of *you*.

References

Alhadeff-Jones, M. (2017). *Time and the Rhythms of Emancipatory Education: Rethinking the Temporal Complexity of Self and Society*. Oxon: Routledge.

Barley, S. R. (2006). When I write my masterpiece: Thoughts on what makes a paper interesting. *Academy of Management Journal, 49*(1), 16-20.

Beckermann, J. (2020, June 01). Arrhythmia. https://www.webmd.com/heart-disease/atrial-fibrillation/heart-disease-abnormal-heart-rhythm#1

Boje, D. M., & Henderson, T. L. (Eds.). (2014). *Being quantum: Ontological storytelling in the age of antenarrative*. Cambridge Scholars Publishing.

Bonifer, M. (2014). Quantum Cowboy. In: Boje, D. M. and Henderson, T. L. (eds), *Being Quantum: Ontological Storytelling in the Age of Antenarrative*, pp. 11–39. Newcastle-upon-Tyne: Cambridge Scholars Publisher.

Buckley, J. (1995). Lover, You Should've Come Over (from Live in Chicago), Jeff Buckley YouTube Channel https://www.youtube.com/watch?v=vLHcHWDvgfQ.

Buckley, J. (2016). Don't Let the Sun Catch You Cryin (Audio), Article I, Jeff Buckley YouTube Channel https://www.youtube.com/watch?v=yPZs WzdDeNg

Cage, J. (1973). *M: Writings' '67–'72* (Vol. 635). Wesleyan University Press.

Campbell, C. (2020, October 22) https://wdet.org/posts/2020/10/22/90190-at-36-esperanza-spalding-is-just-getting-started/

Chen, Y. (2017). *Practising Rhythmanalysis: Theories and Methodologies*. London: Rowman & Littlefield.

Cobain, Sol (1995, 31 August). Entrevista Australia. https://www.youtube.com/watch?v=yEULzVTturE

Columbia Records (2010, 11 July). Jeff Buckley - The Making of Grace (Part 1). https://www.youtube.com/watch?v=56Ijh8lu93I

Dayan, P. (2019). How Musical Is Henri Lefebvre's Rhythmanalysis? In S. L. Christiansen & M. Gebauer (eds), *Rhythms Now: Henri Lefebvre's Rhythmanalysis Revisited*, pp. 17–32. Aalborg: Aalborg University Press.

Dewey, J. (1934/2005): *Art as Experience*. Penguin Group: New York, NY

Goldberg, N. (2005). *Writing Down the Bones: Freeing the Writer Within* (2nd ed.). Boston & London: Shambhala. Retrieved from https://books.google.com/books?hl=da&id=9v5ZOh3liu0C&pgis=1

Highmore, Ben (2018). Aesthetic Matters: Writing and Cultural Studies. *Cultural Studies, 32*(2), 240–260, doi: 10.1080/09502386.2017.1298641

Le Guin, U. K. (2016). *Words Are My Matter: Writings about Life and Books, 2000-2016 with A Journal of a Writer's Week*. Easthampton, MA: Small Beer Press.

Lefebvre, H. (1992). *Rhythmanalysis: Space, Time and Everyday Life*. London: Bloomsbury Academic.

Lisovski, A. (2017). Esperanza Spalding live at The New York Times 16/05/2017, Andrew Lisovski YouTube channel, https://www.youtube.com/watch?v=6gYkXMG7RtM

Lund, P. C. (2021). Prolonged Grief Disorder: An Implementation Gone Awry and a Researcher Going Gonzo. *International Journal of Qualitative Methods, 20*, doi: 16094069211020176.

Massey, D. (2005). *For Space* Sage.

Meier, N. & Wegener, C. (2017). Writing with Resonance. *Journal of Management Inquiry, 26*(2), 193–201. doi:10.1177/1056492616673911

Mol, A. (2020). Not Quite Clean: Trailing Schoon and Its Resonances. *The Sociological Review (Keele), 68*(2), 385–400. doi:10.1177/0038026120905489

Mol, A. & Law, J. (2002). Complexities: An introduction. In J. Law & A. Mol (eds), *Complexities: Social Studies of Knowledge Practices* (pp. 1–22). Durham and London: Duke University Press.

Pelias, R. J. (2005). Performative writing as scholarship: An apology, an argument, an anecdote. *Cultural Studies ↔ Critical Methodologies, 5*(4), 415–424, doi:10.1177/1532708605279694

Pelias, R. J. (2014). *Performance: An Alphabet of Performative Writing*. Walnut Creek, CA: Left Cost Press. Retrieved from http://site.ebrary.com/lib/aalborguniv/reader.action?docID=10838700&ppg=8

Pullman, P. (2017): *Dæmon Voices: Essays on Storytelling*. Oxford: David Fickling Books.

Rose, C. (1997). *David Foster Wallace*. Charlie Rose (Director). (1997). [Video/DVD] PBS and Bloomberg TV. Retrieved from https://charlierose.com/videos/23311

Runtagh, J. (2019, 23 August). Jeff Buckley's 'Grace': 10 Things You Didn't Know. *Rolling Stone*, Retrieved from https://www.rollingstone.com/feature/jeff-buckley-grace-things-you-didnt-know-867539/

Schoemer, K. (2003, 8 October). Live At Sin-E, *Rolling Stone*8/10/2003, https://www.rollingstone.com/music/music-album-reviews/live-at-sin-e-189351/.

Seibt, J. (2000). Process Philosophy, *The Stanford Encyclopedia of Philosophy* (Summer 2020 Edition), Edward N. Zalta (ed.), https://plato.stanford.edu/entries/process-philosophy/#Bib

Spalding, E. (2009, 23 July). 'I Know You Know / Smile Like That' (Live in San Sebastian, 23 July 2009 - 3/9). Esperanza Spalding YouTube Channel https://www.youtube.com/watch?v=2aRC3YY3svs.

Speedy, J. (2012). Collaborative Writing and Ethical Know-how: Movements within the Space around Scholarship, the Academy and the Social Research Imaginary. *International Review of Qualitative Research*, 5(4), 349–356, doi:10.1525/irqr.2012.5.4.349

St Pierre, E. A. (2011). Post Qualitative Research. The Critique and the Coming After. In: N. K.Denzin & Y. S. Lincoln (eds), *The SAGE Handbook of Qualitative Research*, 4th ed., pp. 611–635. Thousand Oaks, CA: SAGE.

St Pierre, E. A. (2018). Writing Post Qualitative Inquiry. *Qualitative Inquiry*, 24(9), 603–608, doi:10.1177/1077800417734567

Ulmer, J. B. (2017). Writing Slow Ontology. *Qualitative Inquiry*, 23(3), 201–211, doi:10.1177/1077800416643994

Wegener, C. (2014). Writing with Phineas: How a Fictional Character from A. S. Byatt Helped Me Turn My Ethnographic Data into a Research Text. *Cultural Studies* <=> *Critical Methodologies*, 14(4), 351–360, doi:10.1177/1532708614530306

5

Diffractive Inquiring, or How I Came to Care

Anne Augustine

Diffractive Inquiring and Fidelity to Experience

This chapter explores the ongoing and generative interplay of diffractive inquiring (DI)—an experimental, difference-oriented noticing of affect (noticing differently, as a verb) and effect (noticing difference, as a noun)—in the interwoven and performative processes of reimagining, analysing, theorizing, and writing up my doctoral thesis about practising caring.

Diffraction explores how processes can be understood through the effects created by their difference (Keevers & Treleaven, 2011). DI diffracts difference through a whole-bodied 'rupturing of indifference' (Barad, 2012), or compassionless action. It is enlivened here in three vignettes, comprising encounters from my fieldwork, re-told as 'speculative fabulations' (Haraway, 2011), transdisciplinary fables rich with possibility.

The vignettes show how, in noticing differently (affect), caring emerges through everyday social experiences, including emotions and relationships, leading to consequential collaborative action, or change. Theorizing practising caring (noticing difference, effect) affords an ontologically processual counterpoint to entitative theories of Care Ethics with their dyadic focus on vulnerability, power, and the normative practice(s) of care (work):

1. A provocative and troubling dyad: conflictual emotions about colleague(s) became the catalyst for understanding how being touched by our feelings is a pre-requisite for generative collaborative action.
2. Breaking bread together: cultivating collaborative responsiveness through everyday practices like sharing lunch breaks, extending the boundaries of caring actors to include non-human participants.

Anne Augustine, *Diffractive Inquiring, or How I Came to Care*. In: *Doing Process Research in Organizations, Noticing Differently*. Edited by Barbara Simpson and Line Revsbæk, Oxford University Press. © Oxford University Press (2022). DOI: 10.1093/oso/9780192849632.003.0005

3. Becoming one of the girls: sharing experiences about the workplace effects of the menopause and hormone replacement therapy, reimagining the researcher's entanglement with participants.

A tentative and partial articulation of DI as an abductive noticing of affect and effect offers promise as an alternative to ways of seeing/knowing that 'valorise sameness' (Mazzei, 2014). At the same time, DI calls upon us to acknowledge the ongoing ethical consequences in our instrumentality, as our agentic noticing (re)makes worlds.

DI—in its fidelity to experience—has resonance in inquiries where organizations and organizing are understood as emergent, dynamic, and fluid. In the pursuit of a different way of knowing, where everything is 'in the making' (James, 1909), data is 'transgressive' (St Pierre, 1997), and beyond categorization in most qualitative research.

Diffracting Diffraction

Diffraction, as a way of noticing the effects of difference, was proposed by Donna Haraway as a 'narrative, graphic, psychological, spiritual, and political technology for making consequential meanings' (1997, 273), and expanded by Karen Barad as 'not merely about differences, and certainly not differences in any absolute sense, but about the entangled nature of differences that matter' (2007, 381). Both acknowledge Trinh T. Minh-ha (1989, 1998), filmmaker and scholar, in challenging them to think differently about difference, as a duality that does not necessarily lead to separatism. For Kathrin Thiele (2014), diffraction is more than finding better differences in our inquiries: it is also about changing our engagement with difference. It is a provocation to how we gaze as much as where and at what, foregrounding entanglement, co-creation, and the relational dynamics of practising (Keevers & Treleaven, 2011).

Diffraction in feminist technoscience—distinct from its meaning and use in physics—departs from the optic metaphor inherent in reflexive practice (Barad, 2007; Mazzei, 2014). While Constructionist scholars situate reflexivity within a relational ontology, others—from an ontology of immanence—suggest reflexivity perpetuates an ontology of separateness. Of inter-subjectivity (entities exist prior to connection) rather than intra-action (how we become, entangled and material), as well as reifying discursive (and human) practices over messier, more entangled, embodied, and more than human ways of experiencing and knowing. These contrasting understandings have implications for what we think of as data in our inquiries, a point I will come on to.

My understanding and use of diffraction as a way of inquiring—with acknowledgement to Minh-ha, Haraway, Barad, and Thiele—is that it is both (verb) process (affect) and (noun) result (effect) in dynamic relation, rather than categorically separate. Diffraction ongoingly influences a phenomenon (including ourselves) and is also unfolding as a result or change. What this means to me in practice is that diffraction exemplifies an inferential, or abductive, logic (Simpson & den Hond, 2021), re-tuning our sensitivities towards previously unnoticed dynamics in situations. Diffraction enables us to become speculative and experimental. In organizations and organizing, diffractive entanglement can help us not only notice what is unfolding but also map the effects of practices, interferences, and interventions (Keevers & Treleaven, 2011).

Diffracting Care

For Joan Tronto (1993), care involves taking action in personal, social, moral, and political life; and our interdependent care relationships are what make us human. This definition has been applied to care as paid and unpaid work, at home, in a marketplace, and in the caring / care giving professions. Care Ethics is a socio-political movement and scholarly discipline (Vosman, 2020), situated within a relational ontology. Care is theorized as a practical, situational, and relational ethic (Gilligan, 1982), or practice(s). On the whole, these literatures associate care with vulnerability, pain, and dependency (Brugère, 2014a), typically for the cared-for in the care dyad, but also at times for the one caring.

However, there are wider organizational and societal (human and beyond-human) resonances—to questions of kinship, stewardship, justice, solidarity, growth, participation, and democracy. Jane Addams (1902, 1911), Milton Mayeroff (1965, 1971), Barad (2007, 2014), Haraway (2011, 2016), John Shotter (2015, 2017), Mary Parker Follett (1919), and John Dewey (1929, 1939), are helping me see the potential of care not only as contested practice(s), moral sentiment, or set of values, but as an ethos, transformative relational dynamics we perform ongoingly and collaboratively.

Caring—as a verb or action—is central to all social experience, not limited to professions such as health and social care, and certainly not limited to women's work, and/or other undervalued types of paid or unpaid labour. Caring is embodied and developmental (involving the whole person and not simply the mind or body, sense or reason), of becoming in relationship with (an)other(s) that develops and deepens over time (Mayeroff, 1965, 1971). It takes the needs and concerns of others as the basis for action (Barnes, 2012, 8), where we might respond with tenderness and a feeling of oneness (Mayeroff, 1965, 464). For Mayeroff, this other may be a person, or it could be an idea, an ideal, a community, or a living non-human entity. What is significant for him is that that this other is always specific, unique, and irreplaceable, and never a generalized other. In our caring relations, we must be able to understand this other and their world as if we were inside it.

In *A Fortunate Man* (Berger & Mohr, 1967), John Berger recalls shadowing a GP[1] who—through his relationships with his patients and participation as a member of the local community—strove to become his patients so that he could better understand them and how they might find comfort.

In diffracting ideas about care and emotions, I am learning that we are 'opened up to the other from the "inside" as well as the "outside"' (Barad, 2012, 216). Thiele and Barad help me understand that inquiring into caring is less about calculating who is responsible and for which (typically, human) other, and what good care looks like, the pre-occupations of most studies about care. In caring, we are collectively and ongoingly transforming problematic situations, responding to and reconfiguring our entanglements as Patti Lather (2016) says.

The vignettes below comprise Deweyan 'situations' (1939), that is a 'contextual whole' comprising environment, conversation, social relations, events, pre-cognitive and felt uncertainty, and more. Inquiry for Dewey is a collaborative process of transforming these problematic or 'indeterminate' situations such that new insight and action may follow.

This understanding of the totality of a situation is helpful because it enables us as researchers to widen our noticing of data beyond the dialogic or discursive—a focus for interpretivist scholars—to also include the 'ordinary affects' of relations, scenes, contingencies, and emergences (Stewart, 2007) in all its transgressive multiplicity and the 'troubling subjectivity' of dreams, emotions, and sensory experience (St Pierre, 1997, 2011). These everyday relational and situational dynamics unfolding within quotidian tasks, activities, and preoccupations are overlooked

---

[1] A GP is a General Practitioner, or family medical doctor.

by many organizational scholars. And is this not where the interesting stuff actually happens?

Vignette 1: A Provocative and Troubling Dyad

Despite an acknowledgement that we cannot care without feeling for the other (itself an asymmetrical or dyadic perspective typically emphasizing the carer's emotions, whether those feelings are compassion and/or disdain), indeed we cannot be human(e) without emotions, some care ethicists suggest care is in need of desentimentalizing (Brugère, 2014a), or categorizing so that we can highlight the emotions that motivate good care (Pulcini, 2017).

My doctoral research about collaborative leadership and organizational learning within a Health and Social Care Partnership in Scotland ended abruptly during the first COVID-19 lockdown, less than halfway through its planned duration. This coincided with my doctoral supervisor entering an extended period of sickness absence. Without supervisory guidance or access to organizational participants, and with a perceived paucity of relevant empirical data, a crisis ensued.

During those weeks of rumination, two troubling moments from the supervisory dyad that comprises Esther[2] and me, came back into focus. In diffracting those recollections with the care literature I was now reading, I began to see that what was unfolding in my inquiry was a whole-bodied discomfort about caring—how we become entangled by the transformative effects of noticing feelings of shame, tenderness, and empathy.

'The Logic of Care' and the Women's Strike (March 2020): *The third week of the industrial action affecting UK universities, and the day of the Women's Strike. I am joining the picket line, dressed in red for solidarity with those taking part, and specifically for Esther and Tanya. My bag is packed, so much so that standing hurts my already tender menopausal lower back and hips, as I head off to my 'writing retreat'. The problem with looking at pictures of picket lines on social media is that they don't convey the noise, even with what looks like a small group of protesters. I arrive at the meeting point, the picket under cover as it looks like it will rain, but the acoustics of the space amplify the sounds of the whistles, drums, instruments, and voices. I am already agitated by the weight of my backpack and the walk to*

---

[2] All empirical participants have been given pseudonyms for these vignettes.

the picket line, and the realisation that I am not dressed warmly enough to stand outside for several hours. I see Esther and Tanya, but I don't go over to them. I stand by a pillar, placing my bag on the floor. Esther has a banner and is waving it at cars passing by. She sees me and comes over. She is talking at me but all I can hear is drums and whistles. I can feel my back tense and I make a smile at her. The noise is going right inside me, I suppose that's the idea. Esther leans into me, holds onto my forearm, and begins to enthuse about a book she has started reading, 'The Logic of Care' by Annemarie Mol. It sounds intense, she describes it as profound. I ask Esther why she is reading it and she looks surprised. I am not interested, not because I am not interested but because I am so fucking distracted by the noise and the cold and my back pain. As we are standing there, I check Amazon on my phone and order the book, to appease her. I might read it, sometime.

How should I care? (April 2020): *I am sitting with a load of guilt at the moment. Guilt of not doing enough, not noticing enough, not caring enough. Esther is signed off work for several weeks due to illness. She was telling me for weeks something was not right, not directly, but in her talk about workload, in us not talking about supervision matters during supervision, her feeling unwell, and even on one occasion actually saying she could feel something crisis-like developing that hadn't happened for a long time. I heard all of that, and I saw all the ways she didn't look right, and didn't act right, and I didn't ask her outright what was wrong. Why was that? Because I feared crossing yet another boundary I didn't know existed, by not knowing my place. And now with my research participants I feel like I am deserting them in their crisis too. They need to act; they need to respond to the COVID-19 health crisis and how it unfolds. They also need to pay attention to their own resilience – individually and collectively – and rather than me doing my bit to help them, to show solidarity, I am withdrawing into my own headspace. Both of these things feel shameful. That my response to both those situations, as well as my own health and need to shield from the virus, might be appropriate and proper, isn't good enough. I am knowingly walking away from people experiencing pain.*

I did read *The Logic of Care* (Mol, 2008), several weeks after that encounter with Esther on the picket line. The book focuses on the clinical and relational processes involved in the giving of medical care, where the patient is not only the object but a principal actor. Mol was talking about a different kind of collaborative ethos. It had relevance for my doctoral inquiry, and the Primary Care[3] sites implementing the National Clinical Strategy

---

[3] GP practices, GP surgeries, and Doctors' surgeries are terms used interchangeably to denote the community-based 'frontline' or first point of contact in the National Health Service (NHS), the

(NCS); one of many transformational changes to healthcare strategy, leadership, and delivery in Scotland. Realistic Medicine—one of the goals of the NCS—seeks to situate the care receiver at the centre of decisions made about their needs to facilitate shared decision making, guided by the vision of careful and kind care.

But why does talking about the possibility that we might feel caringly about others, maybe even in a caregiving context, feel risky and decidedly un-scholarly? Perhaps emotions arising from heartfelt concern for another's well-being collide with professional expectations to maintain appropriate detachment (Lindebaum et al., 2017, 653). Words (and the messy emotions behind them) like compassion, love, and kindness—particularly in Western leadership and organizational research—still seem perilous to explore in policy and academic contexts. And yet organizations are emotional places, where conflicts, anxieties, and passions are woven into the relational dynamics of performing, organizing, and leading.

I feel trapped between a rock and a hard place, not knowing how to be a friend to Esther, whether that would even be an appropriate or welcomed gesture, or how to show solidarity with my research participants. I stopped myself from acting on my overwhelming feelings—partly for professional reasons. I also began to rethink—with the help of Mol, Addams, and Follett—whose feelings, agency, and needs were being served by my taking action when my concern, and possibly relevant insight, wasn't asked for. To react could be perpetuating the unequal and dualistic one-caring/cared-for dyad, taking away agency, dignity, and expertise. Doing nothing can be caring, however uncaring it feels (Mayeroff, 1965). Addams and Follett tell me this is not nothing, but a generative space for experimentation, capability, and knowing to emerge and flow among all participants.

If I feel so viscerally, perhaps this caring dynamic exists within my participants' workplace encounters too: the GP who knows they are powerless to relieve the suffering of patients who can't help themselves because their socio-economic circumstances militate against their efforts to sustain resilience against many complex health needs; the organizational development manager who designs a suite of leadership development interventions for staff for which there is limited take up despite an expressed need for more interventions; the nurse who feels ambivalence about her official

---

UK's healthcare system. These frontline services—comprising GP practices, pharmacies, dentists, and optometrists—are collectively called 'Primary Care'.

ID staff pass that allows her to bypass queues for the supermarket during the first lockdown, a privilege she knows nurses employed directly by GP surgeries do not enjoy; the administrators who resist adapting to a new workflow process because they are fearful of the consequences for patients if they get it wrong.

Barad (2012, 216) explains to me that perhaps it takes encountering our inhumanity—who and how we other—before caring can emerge, to rupture our 'in-difference'. They speak of 'com-passion' (Barad, 2012, 216): suffering together with, participating with, feeling with, being moved by. More than a response to another's vulnerability, pain, suffering, and dependency, it seems to me that in caring relations we are responding to a mutual desire for justice, growth, and change. Iris Murdoch (1970) says that although scholars might talk of justice or freedom, they rarely talk of love, which is how we come to know others. Such a morality is about movement, bringing about change in the world.

Barad says this is troubling we need to stay with, for troubling is at the root of caring. Realizing that caring might become a creative line of inquiry in my research was a breakthrough in helping me see that my research participants may also be experiencing conflictual feelings as caregivers, colleagues, and friends, in discerning how to respond caringly in vexatious situations.

Vignette 2: Breaking Bread Together

In diffracting the relational ontological assumptions of Care Ethics, where care is theorized as a human endeavour, I am noticing how caring unfolds as more-than-human and quotidian action, here through shared experiences of eating together. And in these shared experiences, how kinship and trust can emerge in spaces that allow for the sharing of food and the airing of differences, cultivating collaborative responsiveness.

I am reading Line Revsbæk and Lene Tanggaard's (2015) paper. They write about the process of analysing as an interpretive practice where the researcher makes sense of their past experiences (gained through a process of inquiry) while analysing in the present, dealing with specific empirical materials on hand. Sitting on a train travelling through the Scottish Lowlands, my phone's music library plays the song *Ndofara* by Zimbabwean band Machanic Manyeruke and the Puritans. I am struck by the parallel between Revsbæk's experiences of evoked recollections prompted by listening to cherished music—interpreting past situations to understand the present situation—and what is happening here and now.

I remember hearing *Ndofara* for the first time, back in the late 1980s, its gloriously uplifting rhythmic guitar and the backing singers. My friend Martin, a psychiatric social worker, and I dancing in a field at a music festival. I recall our time working together in a Social Services office, as well as our friendship, which endures although we rarely see each other nowadays. Martin was insistent that all staff—social workers, admin, team leaders, the home care staff who popped in from time to time, and the security guard who oversaw our safety from potentially disturbed visitors—should sit and eat lunch together while the office was closed to the public. It was an exceptional practice. I did not know how to appreciate the rarity and importance of these shared moments of decompression and connection—as well as sustenance—back then.

I pay attention to the staff groups I am with—the busyness, the prevalence of multiple forms of communication (smart phones, laptops, landlines, etc.), the junk food lunch on the go, or the unimaginative and unhealthy piles of sandwiches and crisps that the caterers prepared hours before they even arrived in our meetings, the resulting isolation even when people are sat around the same table. I re-value Martin's efforts to make us sit together and 'break bread'—talking about the clients who had come into the office and the characters we dreaded or sat and laughed with, what we had done the night before and were going to do after work, what we had brought in to share or were persuaded to share or had just bought from the market traders outside our office. This deliberate investment in relationships and community seems so starkly in contrast to what I typically experience today, even if—as is the case with one of the doctors' surgeries I am spending time with—there is a large communal staff room. People sit in their gaggles of teams. Or stand alone by the kettle or microwave for the three minutes it takes to heat up whatever they've brought. And the doctors have their own break room. Perhaps lunch is skipped or hurried, at one's desk, eaten while attending to correspondence.

When I am at Dr Gail's surgery over a lunchtime, I notice that even if everyone is sat doing their own thing, responding to emails, checking their phones, there are at least a few minutes when everyone is acknowledged and brought into a shared conversation, even if it's to ask who wants a cup of tea in the minutes before reception opens again. I am told that during the summer months, and when the surgery is closed for lunch, the practice team will go to the roof of the health centre and eat lunch together in the sun.

I am reminded of a conversation at a Primary Care transformation programme board staff development day months before. There was discussion about how you know when a group of staff is beginning to bond, to which the answer that caused the greatest amount of laughter, but also seemed to resonate, was that a new staff member would be invited to join everyone for the Christmas party. Someone said the real test would be whether that new staff member actually came along.

Llewellyn Vaughan-Lee (2020) writes of embracing reality through what is most simple and ordinary, such as baking bread and cooking soup. It is precisely through the disappearance of these rituals, or practices, that Byung-Chul Han (2020) says we are experiencing a 'crisis of community'. Rituals that serve as processes of embodiment—physically and emotionally experienced—and a form of communication and community building (Han, 2020, 11), if they exist at all, now lack the symbolic potency to bind people together. And yet these practices, Haraway says (2016), are how we are 'rendered capable' as kin.

During the first COVID-19 lockdown, one of the most striking caring acts was how the general public helped provide lunches for key workers (health and care staff, and others whose jobs are vital to public health and safety during the lockdown, such as food chain and supermarket staff, transport operators, utility workers, and public services) via online donations to restaurants and caterers or by volunteering to prepare and deliver fresh food. As restaurants and the hospitality sector closed, some businesses turned their operational focus into preparing meals to be delivered to NHS staff, paid for by donations.[4] One such model, Food4Heroes, extended its service to also feed families dependent on food banks. It mobilized communities to care for others, with unemployed chefs offering to cook meals. They shared the fear and reality of hunger experienced by others whose livelihoods were disrupted by the virus, because they had been furloughed, were in precarious work, or lost their livelihoods, as well as by those who were already struggling.[5]

It seems to me that how food is given significance—in its omission or attention—within the various groups and meetings where I spent time, reveals something of the value placed on kinship and kindness, on taking time for relationships to develop, as well as how we ongoingly nurture our caring for each other. The sharing of food can be

---

[4] https://www.independent.co.uk/news/uk/home-news/help-hungry-restaurants-feed-key-workers-nhs-coronavirus-lockdown-a9528396.html
[5] https://www.xero.com/blog/2020/05/food4heroes-feeding-nations-nhs-workers/

regarded as an informal catalytic practice (Ferguson & Thurman, 2019, 11), where food is imbued with the potency to facilitate a more informal and comfortable environment that builds trust, relationships, and kindness.

Perhaps food is a relational actor, and not just a practice. The Graeco-Christian word 'agape' means love feast, eating together to celebrate kinship. I remember the years spent working in the Gulf States and the importance of offering your guest a drink of water. A simple gesture of kindness towards a stranger. I wonder if taking time to break bread enables the airing of differences and the capacity to continue working together—as a diffractive act—in an environment that was more conducive to patient care. That difference can be tolerated because there is a basis of kinship and trust.

I see too how food can be used cynically—in the case of Dr Gail asking Louisa to order lunch for a local leadership meeting in the hope that attendance might increase if food is provided—as an unthinking practice, at the townhall style meetings I attend where a buffet lunch is provided, curled up sandwiches, unhealthy snacks, made by outside caterers on a budget, where food is expected but not to be enjoyed. I see the times when lunch was ordered and it didn't arrive, such as when Eleanor was embarrassed that the buffet she had thoughtfully chosen never made it to the meeting, or as an afterthought when we were told to bring our own lunches to an all-day offsite workshop, but for those who didn't there was nowhere to buy anything, and no-one offering to share, to the time Jenny offered to buy me lunch during her trip to the shops, being offered cups of tea, other times sitting in a stuffy room with no offer of a drink and nowhere to get a glass of water. Literally gasping, both for air and a drink, in a hostile meeting.

Vignette 3: Becoming One of the Girls

In diffracting norms about the position and ethics of researcher objectivity I explore the effects created by difference from my position as observant and entangled participant and research instrument. A knowing becomes possible that would have otherwise remained hidden to me as I shadowed these participants. And this knowing changes the situation. Following Lather, not only does diffraction enable us to notice difference/differently in our inquiries, but also to feel our way as we reconfigure ourselves as researchers, as we are 'pulled out of shape' in our embodied encounters (2016, 127).

I am shadowing a group of administrators at a doctors' surgery. This team is called 'the girls'. I find that term demeaning and patronizing—that admin is not even women's work, but so simple even girls can do it. My irritation is crystallized in a mental picture redolent of the distinctive paintings of the artist Beryl Cook. Extraverted and outrageously behaved girls on nights out—in pubs and clubs and day trips to the shops or the seaside. Predatory older women moving in packs, with whom I don't feel any affinity. I look, sound, and feel out of place. Even calling them the admin team rather than the girls signifies me as not from around here.

The girls are talking about how warm the admin room was. I joined in because I was overheating too. I was distracted by the radio, not because it was on but because it was a radio station I didn't like. I was irritated by someone for no reason. I was thirsty. My focus wasn't on the girls but on my own irritable [dis]comfort. I am so easily irritated these days.

Sensitivity to heat is perhaps the stereotypical representation of the menopausal woman. The menopause is a natural transition for all cisgender women (and some transmasculine, intersex, and non-binary people).[6] Perimenopause is the time leading up to the cessation of menstrual cycles (the menopause), and it is a phase that can last for many years. During this time the levels of hormones produced by the ovaries fluctuate and progressively decrease—hormones that have a direct link to physical, cognitive, social, and emotional functioning and wellbeing. It is a time of profound uncertainty and change, with beginnings and endings that can only be identified retrospectively. You only know you are going through the menopause *in media res*—when you are going through the menopause.

Practitioner studies in the UK highlight how hormone deficiency can have a significant impact on attendance and performance at work. For example, a study by the Chartered Institute of Personnel and Development (Suff, 2019) found that for every ten working women experiencing menopausal symptoms, six said it had a negative impact on their work. These impacts included less patience with clients and colleagues, more anxiety and stress, and impaired concentration. Women like the girls. Women like me too.

---

[6] I hope queer kin will understand that while I write here about 'women', you are also in this conversation.

But as Germaine Greer (2018, 2) says, 'The irrational certainty that the womb was the real cause of the ageing woman's anger or melancholy effectively obscured the inconvenient possibility that she had genuine grounds for feeling angry or sad.'

After years of not noticing or understanding what was happening to me as I experienced worsening perimenopause symptoms, and then a refusal to consider medical treatment once I understood what was happening, I eventually agreed to start hormone replacement therapy (HRT), three months into my fieldwork.

Now when I look at 45–55-year-old women, I wonder about them too, looking for signs of overwhelm and anxiety, the stiffness in our bodies as we move, flashes of recognition as we feel each other overheating and the laughter as we strip off layers, opening the window as someone crawls under the desk to turn off the radiator.

After a meeting ended and the girls had left the room, Dr Elsa and I began to chat. The conversation quickly turned to the menopause. It turns out she has recently just started using HRT too. We agree how much it is transforming our lives for the better and how frustrating it is to know so little about the menopause.

I was stunned at how uninformed she was, as a doctor! Not being able to make sense of her symptoms, unable to talk about it, and her own doctor telling her she was suffering from burnout because neither of them connected her distress and incapacity to her hormones. I now know that GPs don't learn about the menopause at medical schools in the UK. So much for careful and kind care in this transition that all women go through, whether they experience it as debilitating, or it passes unnoticed, or even as a liberation to a time of contentment and potency, challenging stereotypes about ageing and feminine fragility.

In another conversation that becomes about the menopause, I am told of a time when Helen, a senior manager, walked around the grounds of a hospital unable to find the right building where a meeting was taking place, despite having been there many times before but feeling confused and overwhelmed. Of being embarrassed to walk into the meeting late and flustered. The feeling of isolation, not being able to say she felt lost.

In those moments, I became one of the girls, entangled as kin, no longer distinguished by my difference as the researcher or the spy from head office, but another older woman struggling with her own increasingly alien body and mind while feeling we are (were?) so much more than this. Bernard Rimé (2007), a psychological scientist, suggests that when individuals respond to events by communicating and sharing their emotions with others, this can strengthen social bonds, positive affect, and also generate collective memory.

I am reminded of the words of Alice Walker, that what feels like intense pain and confusion is, in fact, a process of change and growth. Of enlargement. I now see these girls, not solely as administrators, but accomplishing changes that would be otherwise difficult to achieve.

What I experience from the inside are nurturing feelings of kinship and knowing. Verónica Montes and María Dolores Paris Pombo (2019) argue that through collective actions caring is enacted—practices based on trust, reciprocity, and solidarity. I now notice the pivotal role that the girls play in care networks and peer groups—other admins from other doctors' surgeries, pharmacy staff, and care workers—as knowing and well-connected nodes with technical (self-taught and learned on the job) expertise. Signposting.

I got invited to lunch with the girls. As we stand up to leave their office, Liz jokes about me being part of the team now and finding some work for me to do. I am one of the girls and it feels good.

Diffractive Inquiring, Abductive Practising

Diffraction is more than about finding better differences in our inquiries but is rather changing our engagement with difference (Thiele, 2014). Crucially for my study, 'diffraction attends to the relational nature of difference' (Barad, 2007, 92), illuminating differences as they emerge rather than as pre-defined subjects or objects within an inquiry.

What this means to me in practice is that diffraction exemplifies an inferential, or abductive, logic (Simpson & den Hond, 2021), of noticing differently (affect) and noticing difference (effect), re-tuning our sensitivities towards previously unnoticed generativity in situations. This offers richer possibilities in our engagements and theorizations, for novelty and practical relevance.

Karen Locke, Karen Golden-Biddle, and Martha Feldman describe abduction as the 'search for possible explanations to an experienced anomaly' (2008, 908), where the situation is characterized by feelings of doubt and uncertainty. It is enacted through spontaneity and what-if thinking in response to the continuous unfolding of events, travelling to new and unexpected places, and to different knowing.

I mentioned above how Vosman opines care ethics is a socio-political movement and a scholarly discipline, where its practice focus is on the actors (who) and the actions (what) of giving good (normative) care. Most scholars theorize care ethics by extending its political philosophical scope, rather than exploring its application for practical action (Engster, 2015). Much as this chapter is attempting to exemplify, care ethics need practising. This (how) focus is the contribution that I hope DI will make to my doctoral inquiry.

Thomas Lawrence and Sally Maitlis (2012) suggest that feminist literature offers the potential to see care as an ongoing central dimension of relationships, experienced in the quotidian. This shifts care from being anchored in caring professions to loving (although still dependent) relationships. Mayeroff reminds me that caring is not solely positive intention or felt emotion but requires expression through action.

Mol and her colleagues (Mol, Moser, & Pols, 2010; Mol, Moser, Piras, et al., 2010) suggest that such care is a matter of tinkering, where knowing is fluid and people and technologies interact in uncertain, adapting, practices. Within these collectives, they say, individual expertise and unique insight is still needed, but they are understood to be part of an ongoing caring process involving the care receiver as an active and knowing participant.

In my study, noticing differently moved me from seeing care as a normative activity to also considering the possibilities of practising caring as emergent social process unfolding in quotidian happenings in organizations and organizing. This is less about perpetuating a dualistic or binary separation of seeming opposites—of cared-for vs one-caring, care vs caring, ethic(s) vs ethos, noun vs verb etc.—but bringing more depth, nuance, and generativity in different knowing. By noticing difference and noticing differently, situated within a processual rather than a relational ontology.

In addition to the inferential possibilities in diffraction, DI calls upon us to acknowledge the ethical consequences in our instrumentality, as our agentic noticing (re)makes worlds. As researchers, we make choices about what we see in the field, analyse, and then theorize. We are world-making, for abduction is a 'consequential process' (Locke et al., 2008, 913). This is an ethical matter, involving the entangled past and the future. My organizational participants were not temporally involved in this diffractive inquiry, and yet they are, because these caring encounters emerge from their actions, and our interactions. I speak because of them, but not for them. I am making what Barad calls an 'agential cut' (2007, 2014), creating a semantic boundary around a phenomenon, as well as what Haraway

(2016) describes as 'speculative fabulation'—a mode of attention, a theory of history, and a practice of worlding.

The predominantly first-person telling of these empirical experiences in this chapter, the fluidity in my use of pronouns and tenses, are not intended to reify my authority or knowing as researcher and author, but to express 'witness speaking' (Shotter, 2006), the speaking made possible when I think within these encounters, where knowing emerges through the unfolding of embedded and embodied experience (Braidotti, 2019).

Resonances When Performing Processual Research

I have raised many questions about the doing of processual inquiries—how we perform process research, where are the boundaries of our inquiries (in terms of temporality, experience, and participation) and who gets to say where, what constitutes data and how we gather, analyse, and theorize what we discern. The vignettes illustrate how data garnered for one research purpose, or not even considered data, became the source for a different inquiry when engaged with inferentially and speculatively. I was not in the field to study care, or caring, but in noticing differently and noticing difference, I found a more complex, uncertain, and agential engagement with emergence that matters.

Process studies are rooted in an ontology of becoming, of constant change and emergence. They focus our inquirings on how phenomena evolve over chronological as well as 'vertical time' (Helin, 2020), adding contours to (past) experiences that are still unfolding by going deeper into ourselves as a way of connecting to something that matters. This fluidity is true not solely for the phenomenon under study, but for the inquiry process too. Diffraction, in its dynamic performativity, enables us to 'travel with' (Simpson et al., 2018), notice, and engage in unfolding action rather than bringing experience to a standstill.

A processual ontology, then, affords the potential to see DI as more than an alternative to interpretive analytic practices that seek out, group and valorize sameness in the quest for order and stability, which also essentialize human (and only human) experiences in the process of representation (Jackson, 2013; Mazzei, 2014). DI offers possibilities for a different kind of knowing, where everything is moving and 'in the making' (James, 1909); and where data is mutable, fallible, and beyond categorization in most qualitative research.

Andrew Pickering encourages me to act out an ontology of becoming. Such a shift in our ontological awareness, he says, would inevitably lead to shifts in our ways of conducting ourselves in the world, to experimentation, to 'imaginatively and critically explore the open-ended spaces of the world's possibility' (Pickering, 2008, 12). I take this to mean fidelity to experience, to guide my participating, inquiring, and theorizing.

For organizational scholars, consultants, and practitioners, diffractive noticing means shifting our attention from discrete things like leadership and management, to agentic processes 'emerging within material intra-actions occurring within the flow of activities occurring out in the world at large' (Shotter, 2015, 75).

In DI separating what might be considered methodological from theoretical concerns is difficult (and unfruitful), as they comprise a duality—alternate ways of being in, and knowing about, the world, rather than being in opposition to each other (Simpson & den Hond, 2021). This chapter has explored the methodological potential of diffraction, but perhaps practising caring is itself diffractive. A way of noticing, a way of theorizing, and a way of social relations all mobilized by making a differ-ence. In diffracting care within these situations, I suggest, caring is about becoming aware of difference, diffraction is a way of seeing dynamic differ-ence, and practising caring ongoingly makes a difference. Brugère (2014b) reminds me that caring begins through an apprehension of differences.

Pausing, Not Concluding, on How I Came to Care

Diffractive inquiring is not a thing—method, methodology, or practice—in any normative sense. This chapter is not a how to, but rather a how I. What it offers is an alternative perspective on empirical experiencing—of diffractively noticing—that might speak to those who find intrigue in what is so often suppressed or overlooked, who think qualitative data can be far wider and even more nuanced than the spoken and written word, and who believe that our world-making responsibilities as researchers are an urgent, ethical matter.

In coming to care, I am learning how noticing and practising caring is critical, particularly when it is seemingly 'out of place, superfluous or even absent' (Puig de la Bellacasa, 2011, 93). Have the stakes ever been higher—to embody a different humanity, to care differently?

References

Addams, J. (1902). *Democracy and Social Ethics*. New York: Macmillan. DOI: 10.2307/3401957.

Addams, J. (1911). *Twenty Years at Hull House*. Pantianos Classics.

Barad, K. (2007). *Meeting the Universe Halfway: Quantum Physics and the Entanglement of Matter and Meaning*. Durham: Duke University Press.

Barad, K. (2012). On Touching—the Inhuman that Therefore I Am. *Differences*, 23(3): 206–223. DOI: 10.1215/10407391-1892943.

Barad, K (2014). Diffracting Diffraction: Cutting Together-Apart. *Parallax, 20*(3): 168–187. DOI: 10.1080/13534645.2014.927623.

Barnes, M. (2012). *Care in Everyday Life. An Ethic of Care in Practice*. Bristol: Policy Press.

Berger, J. & Mohr, J. (1967). *A Fortunate Man – The Story of a Country Doctor*. Edinburgh: Canongate Books.

Braidotti, R. (2019). A Theoretical Framework for the Critical Posthumanities. *Theory, Culture and Society, 36*(6): 31–61. DOI: 10.1177/0263276418771486.

Brugère, F. (2014a). *Emotions as Constituents for an Ethic of Care*. Oxford. https://www.ageing.ox.ac.uk/events/view/209.

Brugère, F (2014b). Pour une société du care. *Études*, 7: 61–72.

Dewey, J. (1929). *The Quest for Certainty: A Study of the Relation of Knowledge and Action*. New York: Minton, Balch & Company.

Dewey, J. (1939). *Logic, The Theory of Inquiry*. New York: Henry Holt and Company.

Engster, D. (2015). Introduction. In: D. Engster, *Justice, Care, and the Welfare State*. Oxford: Oxford University Press, pp. 1–33.

Ferguson, Z. & Thurman, B. (2019). *The Practice of Kindness. Learning from the Kindness Innovation Network and North Ayrshire*. Dunfermline.

Follett, M. P. (1919). Community Is a Process. *The Philosophical Review*, 28(6): 576–588.

Gilligan, C. (1982). *In a Different Voice: Psychological Theory and Women's Development*. Cambridge: Harvard University Press.

Greer, G. (2018). *The Change – Women, Ageing and the Menopause*. London: Bloomsbury.

Han, B-C. (2020). *The Disappearance of Rituals*. Cambridge: Polity.

Haraway, D. (1997). *Modest_Witness@Second_Millennium. Female-Man_Meets_OncoMouse: Feminism and Technoscience*. New York: Routledge.

Haraway, D. (2011). Speculative Fabulations for Technoculture's Generations: Taking Care of Unexpected Country. *Australian Humanities Review*, 50 (May): 95–118. DOI: http://doi.org/10.22459/AHR.50.2011.06.

Haraway, D (2016). *Staying with the Trouble. Making Kin in the Chthulucene.* Durham: Duke University Press.

Helin, J. (2020). Temporality Lost: A Feminist Invitation to Vertical Writing that Shakes the Ground. *Organization*. 1–16. Online First DOI: 10.1177/1350508420956322.

Jackson, A. Y. (2013). Posthumanist Data Analysis of Mangling Practices. *International Journal of Qualitative Studies in Education*, 26(6): 741–748. DOI: 10.1080/09518398.2013.788762.

James, W. (1909). *A Pluralistic Universe*. Gutenberg. DOI: 10.2307/1412963.

Keevers, L. & Treleaven, L. (2011). Organizing Practices of Reflection: A Practice-Based Study. *Management Learning*, 42(5): 505–520. DOI: 10.1177/1350507610391592.

Lather, P. (2016). Top Ten+ List: (Re)thinking Ontology in (Post)Qualitative Research. *Cultural Studies – Critical Methodologies*, 16(2): 125–131. DOI: 10.1177/1532708616634734.

Lawrence, T. B. & Maitlis, S. (2012). Care and Possibility: Enacting an Ethic of Care through Narrative Practice. *Academy of Management Review*, 37(4): 641–663.

Lindebaum, D., Geddes, D., & Gabriel, Y. (2017). Moral Emotions and Ethics in Organisations: Introduction to the Special Issue. *Journal of Business Ethics, 141* (4): 645–656. DOI: 10.1007/s10551-016-3201-z.

Locke, K, Golden-Biddle, K. & Feldman, M. S. (2008). Making Doubt Generative: Rethinking the Role of Doubt in the Research Process. *Organization Science*, 19(6): 907–918. DOI: 10.1287/orsc.1080.0398.

Mayeroff, M. (1965). On Caring. *International Philosophical Quarterly*, 5(3): 462–474. DOI: https://doi.org/10.5840/ipq1965539.

Mayeroff, M. (1971). *On Caring*. Harper Perennial, New York.

Mazzei, L. A. (2014). Beyond an Easy Sense: A Diffractive Analysis. *Qualitative Inquiry*, 20(6): 742–746. DOI: 10.1177/1077800414530257.

Minh-ha, T. T. (1989). *Woman, Native, Other*. Bloomington: Indiana University Press. DOI: 10.1057/fr.1987.1.

Minh-ha, T. T. (1998). Not You/Like You: Postcolonial Women and the Interlocking Questions of Identity and Difference. In: A. McClintock, A. Mufti, & E. Shohat (eds), *Dangerous Liaisons: Gender, Nation, and Postcolonial Perspectives*. Minneapolis: University of Minnesota Press, pp. 415–419.

Mol, A. (2008). *The Logic of Care: Health and the Problem of Patient Choice*. Oxford: Routledge.

Mol, A., Moser, I, Piras, E. M., et al. (2010). Care in Practice. On Normativity, Concepts, and Boundaries. *TECNOSCIENZA Italian Journal of Science & Technology Studies*, 2(1): 73 86.

Mol, A., Moser, I. & Pols, J. (eds) (2010). *Care in Practice. On Tinkering in Clinics, Homes and Farms*. Transcript.

Montes, V. & Paris Pombo, M. D. (2019). Ethics of Care, Emotional Work, and Collective Action of Solidarity: the Patronas in Mexico. *Gender, Place and Culture*, 26 (4). Routledge: 559–580. DOI: 10.1080/0966369X.2018.1553854.

Murdoch, I. (1970). *The Sovereignty of Good*. London: Routledge.

Pickering, A. (2008). New Ontologies. In: Pickering, A. & Guzick, K. (eds), *The Mangle in Practice: Science, Society and Becoming*. Durham: Duke University Press, pp. 1–14. DOI: 10.2307/j.ctv11smg5w.4.

Puig de la Bellacasa, M. (2011). Matters of Care in Technoscience: Assembling Neglected Things. *Social Studies of Science*, 41(1): 85–106. DOI: 10.1177/0306312710380301.

Pulcini, E. (2017). What Emotions Motivate Care? *Emotion Review*, 9(1): 64–71. DOI: 10.1177/1754073915615429.

Revsbæk, L. & Tanggaard, L. (2015). Analyzing in the Present. *Qualitative Inquiry*, 21(4): 376–387. DOI: 10.1177/1077800414562896.

Rimé, B. (2007). The Social Sharing of Emotion as an Interface Between Individual and Collective Processes in the Construction of Emotional Climates. *Journal of Social Issues*, 63(2): 307–322.

Shotter. J. (2006). Understanding process from within: An argument for 'withness'-thinking. *Organization Studies* 27(4): 585–604. DOI: 10.1177/0170840606062105.

Shotter, J. (2015). On "Relational Things": A New Realm of Inquiry. In: Garud, R., Simpson, B., Langley, A., et al. (eds), *The Emergence of Novelty in Organizations*. Oxford University Press. DOI:10.1093/acprof:oso/9780198728313.003.0003.

Shotter, J. (2017). James, Dewey and Mead: On What Must Become Before All Our Inquiries. In: A. Langley & H. Tsoukas (eds) *The SAGE Handbook of Process Organization Studies*. London: SAGE Publications, pp. 71–84.

Simpson, B. & den Hond, F.(2021). The Contemporary Resonances of Classical Pragmatism for Studying Organization and Organizing. *Organization Studies*, 43(1): 127–146. https://doi.org/10.1177/0170840621991689.

Simpson, B., Tracey, R. & Weston, A. (2018). Traveling Concepts: Performative Movements in Learning/Playing. *Management Learning*, 49(3): 295–310. https://doi.org/10.1177/1350507618754715.

St Pierre, E. A. (1997). Methodology in the Fold and the Irruption of Transgressive Data. *International Journal of Qualitative Studies in Education*, 10(2): 175–189. DOI: 10.1080/095183997237278.

St Pierre, E. A. (2011). Post Qualitative Research. The Critique and the Coming After. In: N. K. Denzin & Y. S. Lincoln (eds), *The SAGE Handbook of Qualitative Research*. 4th ed., pp. 611–625. Thousand Oaks: SAGE.

Stewart, K. (2007). *Ordinary Affects*. Durham: Duke University Press. DOI: 10.1515/9780822390404-002.

Suff, R. (2019). Majority of Working Women Experiencing the Menopause Say It Has a Negative Impact on Them at Work. Available at: https://www.cipd.co.uk/about/media/press/menopause-at-work (accessed 31 May 2021).

Thiele, K. (2014). Ethos of Diffraction: New Paradigms for a (Post)humanist Ethics. *Parallax*, *20*(3): 202–216. DOI: 10.1080/13534645.2014.927627.

Tronto, J. C. (1993). *Moral Boundaries*. New York: Routledge.

Vaughan-Lee, L. (2020). A Ghost's Life. Available at: https://emergencemagazine.org/op_ed/a-ghosts-life/ (accessed 28 December 2020).

Vosman, F. (2020). The Disenchantment of Care Ethics. A Critical Cartography. In: Vosman, F., Baart, A., and Hoffman, J. (eds), *The Ethics of Care: The State of the Art*. Leuven: Peeters Publishers, pp. 17–66.

6

Seeing and Hearing in the Poetics and Cinematics of Process Research

Wandering Through a Sea of Fog into a Blizzard of Black Snow

Stephen Linstead

'Art does not render the visible; rather, it makes visible'.

Paul Klee (2013/1920) *Creative Confession*

Noticing differently seems to have two prominent characteristics—first, the ability to see and hear what others do not notice even when it is in front of them; second, the ability to develop one's own discernment, to notice today what was overlooked before. These often appear together, linked by a reflexive capability, and in the case of studies of organizing the researcher has been characterized with great sophistication as a 'detective' reading clues (Goodall, 1989), or as a 'connoisseur', sensing unvoiced subtleties, halftones, aromatics, overtones, and nuances, knowing what lies between the lines of analysis (Turner, 1988). In Klee's sense, the researcher in doing this is not a social scientist but an artist. Sims (2010) argues that such heightened sensitivities should extend to leaders being required to be an organizational 'poet-in-residence', bringing out unseen shades of organizing (Parini, 2008). To make his point, he invokes Midgley's (2001, 3) image of the drunk who has lost his house key at night on the street, but is looking for it under the lamppost because that's where he can see better. For Sims, developing poetic and aesthetic sensibility is necessary to get us looking in the right places, rather than just the bright ones. In this chapter I will look more deeply into what such a suggestion might entail. I will discuss other treatments of the poetic in organization studies and social research,

Stephen Linstead, *Seeing and Hearing in the Poetics and Cinematics of Process Research* In: *Doing Process Research in Organizations, Noticing Differently.* Edited by Barbara Simpson and Line Revsbæk, Oxford University Press.
© Oxford University Press (2022). DOI: 10.1093/oso/9780192849632.003.0006

then place the poetic moment in the context of complementary aesthetic, ethical, and political moments, which are the source of power in work that moves us to see and hear the world differently. These moments take us beyond methodological triangulation towards a multiplicity of horizons, clouds, and crystals. I'll conclude with examples from a short film, *Black Snow*,[1] about the Oaks Colliery Explosions in Barnsley, South Yorkshire, still England's worst mining disaster, and although the worst in the world in the nineteenth century, almost forgotten for 150 years. But I will begin with the work of a German Romantic painter whose work is currently enjoying renewed resonance.

In Caspar David Friedrichs' painting 'Wanderer above a Sea of Fog' (1818) (Figure 6.1) we see an iconic Romantic voyager poised atop a Bohemian peak having burst through the cover of river fret that masks the earth below into clear, pure air. This Ruckenfigur has his back to us as we gaze, with him, upon the ambivalent prospect. Friedrichs (1774–1840) was born on the Baltic coast but later moved to Dresden, and the landscape is a creative reconfiguration of the Bastei in the Elbsandsteingebirge, sandstone mountains on the banks of the Elbe to the southeast of the city. The undecidability of the scene is neither accidental nor naïve: one of Friedrichs' other paintings, 'Two Men Contemplating the Moon' (1819) (Figure 6.2), was identified by the legendary Modernist playwright Samuel Beckett as the inspiration for *Waiting for Godot*, which begins: '*A country road. A tree. Evening*'. This is the exact setting of 'Two Men'. The image is referenced elsewhere in the play, and even in Beckett's notes for his own direction of it in Berlin in 1965 (Knowlson, 2003, 53–54). The troubled line launched by Friedrich's romanticism passes directly through Beckett's modernism and delivers us to Stewart Lee's postmodernism.

Lee (2019) restaged 'Wanderer' recently in live performance, the painting's landscape forming a backdrop to *March of the Lemmings*, but replacing the Wanderer's spatzierstock with a selfie-stick. Lee, with his back to the audience, assumes the part of the Ruckenfigur as the performance concludes and spins round at the climax of the piece to turn a nineteenth-century contemplation of metaphysical mystery into a twenty-first-century obsession with self-regarding simulation, returning the landscape to a role as a functional backdrop to the elusive search for personality. Lee's critique

---

[1] The explosions occurred in December, and reports suggest that the weather was frosty with a thin dusting of snow at times. However, when the pit exploded, soot and ash ejected from the two main shafts rose high into the air, forming clouds that spread over a distance of five miles and deposited 'black snow' as they cooled.

Fig. 6.1 Caspar David Friedrichs *The Wanderer above the Sea of Fog* (1818), also known as *Traveler above the Mists*.

of contemporary consumption is more savagely politicized by the knowledge that the 'mountain' upon which he stands on stage is made from heavily discounted copies of his competitors' live DVDs, which he picked up from the Internet.

Fig. 6.2 Caspar David Friedrichs *Two Men Contemplating the Moon* (original 1819, this version 1825–30).

The tense relationship with nature was re-envisioned by Friedrichs in a slightly later painting, originally commissioned as *Northern Nature in the whole of her Terrifying Beauty* by Johann Gottlob von Quandt. When first shown in Prague in 1824 it was titled *An Idealized Scene of an Arctic Sea (with a) Wrecked Ship on the Heaped Masses of Ice*, then *The Polar Sea*. By 1826 it had become *The Sea of Ice*, and later assumed the title *The Wreck of (the) Hope* (actually a title of one of his lost works) (Figure 6.3).[2] However Friedrichs' radical interpretation of the commission caused von Quandt to reject it and it remained unsold until after his death. Yet the eyes of early-twentieth-century critics and the 1920s Expressionists saw it differently. It inspired Diagonalism, a movement resurgent in the 1970s, several other

---

[2] The theme of a wreck among the ice also appeared in a work from 1798 *A ship in the Ice Sea* or *A Wreck in the Polar Sea*. In 1787, at the age of 13, Friedrichs had fallen through an ice-sheet and almost died. He was saved by his brother, who was then unable to get out himself, and drowned, with Caspar too weak to assist and only able to watch. His struggle with the depression that resulted was lifelong and is a constant presence in his art.

Fig. 6.3 Caspar David Friedrichs *The Sea of Ice/Das Eismeer* (1823–4) or *The Polar Sea* (title used after 1826). Also mistakenly known as *The Wreck of (the) Hope.*

artists including Paul Nash, Lawren Harris, and Guy Larramèe, and the architect Thom Mayne for whom architecture and landscape are in a dynamic relationship. It is also one possible inspiration for Jørn Utzon's Expressionist Sydney Opera House.[3] The painting shows a scene of an ice sheet, dramatically punctured by fractures and faults rising to jagged towering peaks, pinnacles, and pyramids surrounded by slabs and shards. Tucked away and just visible, partially crushed by the movements of the ice sheets, is a naval vessel, given the name of HMS *Griper*, a citation[4] of one of the ships in William Edward Parry's 1819–20 exploration and search for the North West Passage on whose accounts Friedrichs drew, along with his own studies of drifting mountain ice-floes on the Elbe.[5]

---

[3] Utzon began the design by evoking opening shells, organic rather than simply fractured, but this posed major problems as to how they could be constructed. He eventually came up with the idea of a deconstructed sphere where diagonalism deconstructs the cube—a solution that transcended style and explored the alternate geometry of the sphere for architecture, design and engineering.

[4] Rather than a depiction—Griper was not lost although it had a torrid time and was trapped for 10 months, cf Deveaux (2019)

[5] 'Parry First Expedition.' Princeton University Library. Accessed 26 June 2021. https://library.princeton.edu/visual_materials/maps/websites/northwest-passage/parry-first.htm.

Our interest in this painting is particularly current given the recent (2021) BBC2 re-broadcast of the first season of Ridley Scott's 2018 AMC TV series *The Terror*, about the loss of Captain John Franklin's *HMS Erebus* and *HMS Terror* with all crew in the Arctic in 1845–8[6], both ships having been discovered only recently (*Erebus* 2014; *Terror* 2016). What is most important about this painting is its challenge to see and think differently. Although the painting is still, its message is turbulence, power, and powerlessness, and the eye is drawn into this in a struggle for perspective. As James Greene puts it in a comment on Moritz (2012) 'If we stay and look more closely, we have to make *an effort to look differently...* it is as if we have got to start from scratch to learn to see nature in its own terms ...' (emphasis added). Even perspective is radically questioned, as our capacity to see definitively is repeatedly frustrated in the face of the Arctic mountains of ice.

The ice painting offers us little clarity and even less control, extending the conundrum faced by the Wanderer but adding a darker side. In his call for the greater integration of the arts into the social sciences, *Imaginative Horizons*, Vincent Crapanzano (2004) delivered his message by using *The Wanderer* for the cover. Friedrichs' mountain quest fits Crapanzano's title perfectly. Whilst it remains buoyed by its aspiration to see beyond or through, the observer's commanding position is as illusory and unstable as Lee's pile of plastic is slithery and wobbly. There are no firm foundations for either going forward. As Wallace Stevens (1997, 476) also put it more than a century later in 'July Mountain' (1954):

> We live in a constellation
> Of patches and of pitches,
> Not in a single world - -
> Thinkers without final thoughts
> In an always incipient cosmos,
> The way, when we climb a mountain,
> Vermont throws itself together.

Crucially here, we don't perceive Vermont more completely by our ascension to a better place. There is no point of vantage. Vermont is always slipping away from us, changing with the light by the second, and no day

---

[6] Based on the eponymous fact-based supernatural fiction by Dan Simmons (2007/2018). The many more strictly factual treatments of the mystery include Beattie and Geiger (2004), Hutchinson (2017) and Palin (2019).

is ever exactly the same, as any filmmaker or photographer knows. Stevens (1997, 435) becomes even more self-reflexive in another similar, if desk-bound, late poem 'The Poem that took the Place of a Mountain' (1954). Here he extends Friedrichs' fog metaphor towards seeing the mountain itself as a poem, in which 'reality is a process, and all one can do to understand it is to find a solid position and observe the ever-changing images produced by the metamorphoses of the world' (Prohászka-Rád, 2015, 60). Nevertheless, the solidity of that position remains questionable.

Poetry as a Way in to Difference

But other than provide metaphors for intellectual introspection, however powerful, can poets and painters intervene in our own research craft? Norman Denzin (2014, 86) argues that 'the poet makes the world visible in new and different ways, in ways that ordinary social science writing does not allow. The poet is accessible, visible, and present in the text, in ways that traditional writing forms discourage.' But whilst the self is to be discovered, revealed, expressed, and shared, this is not enough (Pelias, 2011; Prendergast, Leggo & Sameshima, 2009). For Kathleen Stewart (2005; 2007), the world both takes shape in real time before us and creeps up behind us, catching us by surprise. This 360° world needs both sound and vision in order for us to begin to experience it more fully. Poetry is insufficient if it stays on the page, its music unvoiced. It needs to be embodied if it is to fully realize its affective potential, its power to move us (Todres & Galvin, 2008).

But using unfamiliar non-textual and non-prosaic media does not stop at changing the way we feel. It also reconfigures our thinking processes. The means by which we apprehend the world can become a constraint for us—as Aldous Huxley (1954, 97) wrote, in order to live a more genuine, more authentic human experience, as human beings we need to 'intensify our ability to look at the world directly, not through the half-opaque medium of concepts which distort every given fact into the all too familiar likeness of some generic label or explanatory abstraction'. Unfamiliar media can serve this quest because as Eisner (2005, 181) argues 'as we learn to think within the medium we *choose* to use' (emphasis added) rather than those conventionally available to us, 'we also become more able to raise questions that the media themselves suggest'. For Sean Wiebe, in an editorial dialogue on poetic inquiry with John Guiney Yallop and Sandra

Faulkner), 'each medium, each form, has within it *a slightly different kind of thinking*' (Guiney Yallop, Wiebe, & Faulkner, 2014, 6 emphasis added), and as Jacques Rancière (2004) demonstrates, such a repartitioning of sensibility has political as well as aesthetic implications. So using different media makes researchers more attuned to elusive processes, politicized or not. Heidegger (1977, 252) alerts us to the magnitude of this challenge, in echoing T. S. Eliot's (1942) 'Little Gidding':

> the most difficult learning is to come to know actually and to the very foundations what we already know. Such learning demands dwelling continually on what appears to be nearest to us.

Accordingly, Guiney Yallop (Guiney Yallop et al., 2014, 3) felt the need to shift from his everyday somnambulism and 'woke up the poet to become a researcher. I am reminding myself to stay awake and to keep waking up. Academic life, if one is not careful, can put one to sleep; it can kill (or dull) the spirit by constantly pulling it away from itself.' (see also Guiney Yallop 2010). This is a point I make in discussing the aesthetic moment, when the patterns and rhythms of the surface of experience can draw us away from responding to significance (Linstead, 2018, 328). As he later elaborates (Guiney Yallop et al., 2014, 3):

> Poetic inquiry is a way in for me. There are other ways in, but for me, I had to reawaken the poet to become a researcher (Guiney Yallop 2005), or at least, to continue to become the researcher I needed to become in order to do the work I needed to do, that is to explore my own identities and the communities in which those identities were located (Guiney Yallop, 2008).

Sandra Faulkner responds that the way in is also a communicative way out:

> I consider poetry an excellent way to (re)present data, to analyze and create understanding of human experience, to capture and portray the human condition in a more easily "consumable", powerful, emotionally poignant, and open-ended, non-linear form compared with prose research reports (Faulkner, 2009). Poetry constitutes a way to say things evocatively and to say those things that may not be presented at all.
>
> (Guiney Yallop et al., 2014, 3)

And continuing the dialogue Sean Wiebe similarly concurs that poetry is interstitial and responsive to the world's metamorphoses.

Poetic inquiry invites me into the in-between space between creative and critical scholarship. Such a space is reflexive and critical, aware of the nexus that is both self and other, both personal and public.

(Guiney Yallop et al., 2014, 3)

Looking for what we might call a particularly poetic moment that offers both entrance and exit in Friedrichs' paintings, a punctum that energizes the artwork and engages the viewer, rather than simply poetic elements that convey some transcendent quality, is easier in some than others. Perhaps the easiest is in *The Sea of Ice*, where the fragmentary partial glimpse of the crushed vessel speaks so powerfully of the insignificance of humanity helplessly pitted, for all our cleverness, against elemental power. *The Wanderer* might offer the figure itself, unconventionally turned away from us, as this catches our attention unexpectedly, or perhaps it is the fog, obscuring a vista that remains ambiguous for all its magnificence. But another candidate, and I think perhaps the most compelling, is the walking stick. Whilst a typical device of a mountain hiker, even today, it is not conventionally deployed. Indeed one might expect a real hiker to have put the stick aside, to relish the absolute freedom of having reached the summit. But the stick remains to ground the figure, to cement that link between the body and the material world. The wanderer is not yet ready or capable to decipher the truth of the mists, and the stick both anchors and restrains him in the face of the mystery. Finally, *Two Men Looking at the Moon* might seem to be the simplest, but had this been so it would hardly have inspired Beckett. Friedrichs' composition and his use of colour convey a restlessness about the scene—the reflected moon, present but not present, the off-kilter intimacy of the shapes of the two bodies, but most striking perhaps is the tree. The two men, and in one of his own variants of the painting a man and a woman—are waiting: for the night, for the stars, even for the dawn, looking at the sun indirectly reflected towards them, knowing all is in motion, yet, as Beckett grasped, they are voyeurs, as it is not in motion *for* them. It is a distraction from the once again fractured landscape they inhabit, split by the ground-become-figure of a partially uprooted tree, with its broken and incomplete branches—is it dead? Is it a willow? Is the death of a willow the end of its existential sadness, as Vladimir and Estragon speculate in *Waiting for Godot*? In the "man and a woman" version, the smaller tree on the left is more clearly identifiable *as* a willow, and the evergreen pines in the faintly illuminated right distance are more numerous. A sign of hope? The tree frames the enigma, and holds it, unsolved, materially still but metaphysically restless.

The Poetic in Practice

There are several experiments and exercises available for developing poetic sensibilities as well as technique, and many of these can be accessed online, or via workshops led by networking and training organizations such as *The Poetry Business*. One poet, Ian McMillan, who has a weekly writing show, *The Verb*, on BBC Radio 3 and appears regularly on TV, as well as being a columnist and author, embodies a useful exercise on his Twitter feed. Every day he goes for an early morning walk, and tries to come back with a line or two, not in rhyme, that simply express something he has seen, however simple, on his walk, in a metaphor or simile that presents them in a different aspect. Recent tweets include:

> A bird flies across the sky like a series of tattoos.
> Builder's sand wishes it was a tropical beach.
> A baby's dummy comforts a patch of unsettled grass.
> For a moment morning looks back to darkness.
> Air still as unbroken glass.
> A cockerel daubs primary sonic colours across Sunday.
> Rain's comforting rhythms on my hood. These puddles have
>   appeared overnight like popup tear farms.
> The dentist's lights shine toothily.
> The air is undercoated with damp.
> Each tree points to a particular patch of sky.
> A bird flies as fast as time does; then it lands and settles,
>   which time doesn't.
> A security light illuminates the everyday miracle of a spider's
>   web.
> Bulbous, knotty clouds.
> A branch waves spikily from a skip.
> The sky is a wide open mouth full of clouds.
> I wish I spoke the language of fallen leaves. A passing taxi
>   monetises time and distance.
> The cool breeze is autumn's outrider. That watercolour sky.
> The eastern sky tries on new shades of vivid.
> A gate creaks open symphonically.
> A curled rubber band like a malleable ammonite.

These are not reworked or polished—he tweets them at the end of his walk. These little fragments are literally exercises in seeing differently, and in some of them quite explicitly new directions and turns of thought also emerge, making unexpected connections. It's possible, too, to do a similar thing with a phone camera. Rather than simply point and shoot, experiment with composing the elements of the shot, then disturb the balance of that composed image by focusing on one element and rebuilding the shot around that. Then try another. I had been trained to photograph architecture and streets by slowing the shutter speed to remove moving objects (mostly people). But a professional street photographer showed me how to use the people I was erasing to tell different stories about the place or the moment. Different bodies establish different relations to what's around them, and may draw our attention to what we are customarily overlooking, making the photograph epistemological, rather than just an image. The face and body of a subject communicate with their objective context.

Moving closer to the poetic in the analysis of action, Cunliffe (2002) offers a succinct summary of a range of approaches to language, including varieties of discourse analysis, narrative and conversation analysis, in outlining her take on a term—social poetics—as developed by Shotter from work by Andersen (1991). A useful critical discussion is also offered by Kuiper (2007; see also Thomas, Cole & Stewart, 2012). Cunliffe alludes to the origin of the term poetry in the Greek poesis, which means to create, yet neglects the development of the noun 'poetic' meaning an account or justification of one's creative practice, a literary term with a long history but adopted by Richard Harvey Brown in his landmark *A Poetic for Sociology* (1977). Cunliffe's social constructionist argument draws on Bakhtin (1981) and Wittgenstein (1953) as interpreted by Katz and Shotter (1996). She looks at the use of figurative technique—metaphor, simile, allusion—in research-driven discussions (not naturally occurring conversation) to look at how illumination is achieved and built on in communication. Poetic moments in this account relate to the use of illustrative figurative language to create some new connection, importantly with some overall purpose even if not fully realized to generate or convey a narrative, or cultural sense of meaning beyond the utterance and its immediate context. Paying attention to this rather than structure or function is an important means of noticing and acknowledging productive imaginative difference in accounts rather than simply the ordering 'work' of language in interaction. Cunliffe's etymological line is different from that of Nowak (2020) who draws on the work of Langston Hughes (1947). Where 'social poetics' for Cunliffe originates in social interaction, that is enhanced by social actors using poetic figures of speech rather than poetry itself, Hughes and Nowak start with poetry that *becomes* social when it transcends the reflective individuality of the lyric form and voices common cause with others, attracting inevitable censure. Social poetics here is activist rather than expressive, collective rather than interpersonal. As Hughes (1947, 205) confessed

> The moon belongs to everybody, but not this American earth of ours. That is perhaps, why poems about the moon perturb no one, but poems about colour and poverty do perturb many citizens. Social forces pull backwards or forwards, right or left, and social poems get caught in the pulling and hauling.

The ethics and the politics here tend to socially occlude the aesthetics and poetics, and as Hughes (1947, 205) further observes the stakes can be high:

> I have never known the police of any country to show an interest in lyric poetry as such. But when poems stop talking about the moon and begin to mention poverty, trade unions, colour lines, and colonies, somebody tells the police.

Nowak (2020) who is one of the United States' most innovative political poets takes this inspiration into working-class poetic activism, and in *Coal Mountain Elementary* (2009) he takes the poetic across genres combining verbatim testimony from West Virginia miners and rescue teams, the American Coal Foundation's curriculum for schoolchildren, newspaper accounts of mining disasters, and full-colour photographs of Chinese miners, an effort which has been lauded for regenerating the rich tradition of working-class literature (Rapport & Hartill, 2012) My own usage of the term poetic moment is strongly resonant with this approach, but more specific, and perhaps more dramatic, though grounded in mundane occurrences. From my perspective, noticing differently can be theorized as an outcome of four possible interacting potential orientations towards four 'moments'—the aesthetic, poetic, ethical, and political (appearance, significance, moral responsibility and power). A 'text'—any weave of symbols, signs and representations in any mode—is effective in moving its audience by creating an interplay between these 'moments' to generate what might be called a form of empirical 'art' (see Linstead 2018 for a full account). There is a dual sense of 'moment' here—it can be both a *point in time* (especially in narrative, symphonic, epic, or cinematic forms), and a *point of leverage*, providing energy and opening up changes in direction, especially in poetic and lyric forms. The *aesthetic* moment is where the reader or viewer is drawn into the surface of the work, its appearance and surface, whether that is beauty or horror, and becomes forgetful of self and significance. In *The Wanderer* this is exactly what the Wanderer himself is doing, contemplating the vast, ambiguous, partially veiled landscape. Even more so, *The Sea of Ice* presents us with a dramatic and dazzling landscape in which human presence is all but forgotten, and *Two Men Looking at the Moon* is bathed in strange light (and ethereal colour). The *poetic* moment—that is the moment that language becomes poetic by doing whatever is distinctive of poetry whatever the medium in which it is found—is a moment of breakthrough of one 'reality' (narrative level or intertextual arc) into another, where the distinction is such that direction may change or stop altogether, where significance, though not necessarily clear but no longer sidelined by aesthetics, rushes back in, almost taking the breath away in some instances. As Lyotard (1991) argued, it is more powerful to the extent that it is unresolved, and evokes a sense of incipience. This has two aspects. One is of something *about to happen*, the 'not yet' of event and our condition of 'not-knowing' (Heidegger, 1971a; b); the other is of some event *having happened*, but we are not sure what, a condition of *reflected* or *retro*-incipience. In both we become involved in a more active search for meaning: for the first 'what is going to happen' in *Two Men*, and for the second 'what happened' when we notice the tiny, partially obscured boat in *Sea of Ice*. The poetic moment is eventful in that it changes what comes after it—we do not see the world in quite the same way again having been struck by it. The *ethical* moment is a new realization of our moral position, and the *political* moment is more purely of power, although these are invariably co-emergent. It is not accidental that there are two people looking sidelong at the moon—the ethical relationality of a common predicament mutually experienced is different from that evoked by the central Wanderer with his back to us, blocking our view, standing *for* us rather than *of* us. That Friedrichs composed an alternate version featuring a man and a woman was not trivial either—it was another invitation to see differently. But even more pointedly, *Sea of Ice* focuses us on the hubris of a particularly male form of engagement with the world.

The glimpse of the Wreck surges with the futile masculine effort that created the situation—the challenge to nature, the pointless heroics, the disastrous urge to over-reach—and of course the crushed naval vessel had no women on it. The British Navy was quite rigidly masculine in its disciplines and methods of operation and control, as well as being institutionally sexist and to a considerable degree racist. Whilst the men on the boats died, not too far away from them indigenous communities, the Netsilik Inuit, survived (Eschner, 2018). It was not for the Navy to ask how and learn though, if it meant abandoning rules and standards—rather than fully absorb local knowledge and learn to hunt with the natives, they unwittingly slowly poisoned themselves with faulty tinned rations (Swanston et al., 2018). Friedrichs' critique of man's arrogance towards nature is a point that Graham Ibbeson also makes with his sculpture at the heart of the film *Black Snow*. Graham did not want to celebrate, however poignantly, male heroic sacrifice—he wanted to draw attention to the moral and political place of those men in their communities, and the consequences for others who had to take up the mantle and sustain those communities after disaster occurred. By displacing the disaster (it occurs 'off-stage') and the victims (placed below the main female figure), community, caring and social struggle become centred (see Figure. 6.4). Between the ice-field and the coalfield there is an arc of continuity that insists on seeing our moral and political relation to each other and nature differently.

Returning to poetry, seeing the environment differently is a challenge addressed by French Oulipian writer Jacques Jouet (2001), who seeks to develop 'creative constraints'—arbitrary rules that by restricting specific options inspire creativity in other areas (Maréchal & Linstead, 2010; Motte, 2020). Jouet's invention—'metropoems'—were in the moment, composed in the head between stations and written down only whilst the train was standing in the next station, the journey being predetermined. He actually sets down the rules of the metropoems in a metropoem.

> A metro poem is a poem composed during a journey in the metro.
> There are as many lines in a metro poem as there are stations in your journey, minus one.
> The first line is composed mentally between the first two stations of your journey (counting the station you got on at).
> It is then written down when the train stops at the second station.
> The second line is composed mentally between the second and the third stations of your journey.
> It is then written down when the train stops at the third station. And so on.

Fig. 6.4 Oaks Colliery Disaster Memorial (photo: Stephen Linstead).

> You must not write anything down when the train is moving.
> You must not compose when the train has stopped.
> The poem's last line is written down on the platform of the
>   last station.
> If your journey necessitates one or more changes of line, the
>   poem will then have two or more stanzas.
> An unscheduled stop between two stations is always an
>   awkward moment in the writing of a metropoem.

This generic format is, Maréchal and Linstead (2010) argue, capable of being adapted to other environments because it enables the taking of a position that neither turns inward towards the ethnographer's self nor outward towards an empathic relation with the ethnographic other. It is focused in the moment, in place, and in motion—on action rather than reflection or representation. The discipline it imposes is derived from a specific activity, which embodies the rhythms, time, sounds, and space of that activity. It demands attention to technique, and craft, which underlines the processes by which other knowledge texts are crafted. Despite being practically, empirically, and metaphorically enformed by the mobility of contemporary urban social experience—based around the metropolitan commute—it provides a methodology that can adapt to other forms of organized life. The poetry may not be great poetic work, depending on the poet—and Jouet argues that the poet does need to be a master of their craft—but for research it is the novel sensitization to context that is invaluable. It forces the poet to see differently by forcing them to write differently.

More generally, of course, any poetic form imposes some constraints that can be potentially enabling—the sonnet, the haiku, senryu, tanka (Furman & Dill, 2015) or haibun (Ledgard, 2020), the villanelle, and the sestina for example—but it usually does so through setting the poet challenges that are abstract and formal, rather than having any connection with context. Their value lies in what they enable, and what the poet is able to do with them. One might not know what a villanelle is, for example, but will instantly recognize how right that form is to convey the complex emotional intensity of Dylan Thomas' 'Do not go gentle into that goodnight', his gift to his dying father with a lesson for never settling for the banal in one's work for the rest of us. Rich Furman and LeConte Dill (2015) use the tanka form to perform qualitative 'data reduction'—a subjective and interpretive counterpart to quantitative data reduction delivering affective intensity. Mel Ledgard (2020) movingly uses the haibun form (a combination of blank verse and haiku verse) to pay tribute to her working artist friend who died of cancer whilst isolated during the Covid pandemic. Social anthropologists Lauren Berlant and Kathleen Stewart (2019, 8) set themselves the 'productive restriction of form' of 100 'prose-poems' of 100 words, in order to 'make theory descriptive' (p. 44), to counteract 'evaluative critique . . . a mental habit of demagnetizing things for the sake of clarity' (p. 120) and 'expand capacities for sensing'.

But what happens when the constraints of research point the researcher away from the moment towards the past, towards recollection, reports, memory, history, and archives (Guiney Yallop, 2010)? Can a poetic awareness sensitize us to unacknowledged genealogical dynamics whose affect is filtered and diffracted? Can we notice what lies between the lines?

Sound and Cinematics

One of the problems in dealing with textual and archival sources is the loss of actual dynamism that is found in real life. This does not have to entail drama, but as Kathleen Stewart (2007) argues, signs, symbols, stories, and action circulate rather than transmit, evoke rather than represent, surround rather than appear in an ocularcentric frame. They sneak up on you from all sides, jostle for attention, distract, and attract, in what she calls 'cultural poesis' as we try to distil or impose some meaning, however contradictory, fragmentary, ambiguous, or temporary, on this non-linear reality (Burrell, 1997; Thrift, 2007). Film has the advantage that movement can be recorded in two (and if the resources are present three) dimensions, although this is not yet a realistic possibility for research. We do experience surroundings via touch (including atmospherics like breeze from a door opening), smell (a sense undervalued in social research largely due to its unrepresentability as Riach and Warren [2015] argue), taste (connected with smell but requiring intimate contact with its object) and sound, which is and can be used as an evocative proxy for the others (an important sense for Derrida, 1988). When creating film, the effect of greater dynamic range and immersion is what is regarded as 'cinematic', and sound recording and design are an important part of enabling audiences to notice and anticipate elements that would otherwise remain static, unvoiced, or backgrounded. It also enables the juxtaposition of time and place within narrative arcs, and the effects of history and memory, repetition and recall. It's also possible to create other worlds that may be realistic or fantastic. And at a more mundane level, the technical demands of relating to subjects through a lens, or taking into account all the elements of a natural soundscape (as all silences are different) don't stop there—you become more sensitized to both what's in front of you and what's around you when 'off set'.

One example would be how sound and vision were used at the beginning of the short documentary *Black Snow* (Linstead, 2017) to integrate the four moments—aesthetics, poetics, ethics, and politics—into a sense of history, whilst problematizing that history. The film was made for the 150th anniversary of an almost forgotten disaster, the Oaks Colliery explosions of 1866, in which at least 361 men and boys died, telling the struggle of the surviving community, led by women, to survive and rebuild. It also told the story of the struggle by volunteers, including the internationally respected sculptor, Graham Ibbeson, to establish a permanent memorial, and by extension, the modern struggle of a devastated post-industrial community to survive economic disaster.

The opening sequence begins in darkness, with a hubbub of voices gradually building. This is an aesthetic moment as the voices are not discernible—we know there are people, there is concern, and because the sound was recorded inside a large building, we can tell that without seeing it. But the initial affect is of a response to people, to collective humanity—an important note to strike. The first scene is a visual flyover of the Palace of Westminster (Houses of Parliament)—movement being sweeping and panoramic, evoking power and the political moment, as the hubbub gives way to an MP questioning the House on how the Oaks Disaster will be remembered. As he does so, he points out the deaths involved, particularly of children, thus invoking the ethical moment. As the voice dies away, the tracking shifts to the site of the disaster, now overgrown or overbuilt, which shifts to another panoramic shot of a person walking over the former spoil-heap (in the same direction as the Parliamentary pan, so maintaining continuity with the sweep of history) which then blends into a virtual reality reconstruction of the original pit top, as the walk continues. Music specially arranged of a song written by a Northern miner accompanies the beginning of the walk, exhorting a miner's wife to 'guard her man well' while she has him at home, safe from the dangers he faces every day. This poetic intervention is then layered by the voice of a miner's wife (an authentic local accent) using the words of original testimony from the 1867 inquests and reports culminating in an explanation of why the pit was so full that December day—'they all went down, for t'bairns, for Christmas'. And in that poetic moment, the irony of the sacrifice and its spiritual dimension offer a powerful closure to that section, having set in train however briefly the major threads that will develop and weave together in what follows. Setting aside the technical dimensions of this deceptively simple but layered minute of film, the four moments have been activated and the audience is alert to a span of topics from personal loss to historical memory, the gendered nature of working-class community struggle to the political economy of the nation. And drawing on original testimony, we hear the poetic sensibility of that socially brutalized and marginalized voice.

Another approach to noticing differently is through the juxtaposition of styles and narrative arcs. Currently many broadcast documentaries and fictional series play with technique in ways that do little more than confuse—time leaps that have little rationale or integrity and often serve to make a relatively simple story appear more profound—or become formulaic in that the mode of storytelling is determined by the need to showcase technical aspects and becomes rather predictable as a result. It can be that constraints on technology available bring out greater strengths in other areas of a documentary filmmaker's art.

In making *Black Snow* producer Andy Lawrence and myself were undertaking an exercise in challenging those who saw it to see history differently, as the sculptor Graham Ibbeson had a very clearly articulated aim, fully subscribed to by the National Union of Mineworkers who commissioned his work, that unlike many other memorials it would not be a tribute to an iconic industry, nor to the tragic heroism of the Miners. It would be a tribute to community. The bearers of that community, who ensured that it survived after almost the total male working population of the village was wiped out, were women. So rather than a statue of a muscular male with pick in hand, the statue featured a troubled mother, with a babe-in-arms. Ibbeson was a master of conveying natural motion, and the woman, with an anxious expression, was hurrying somewhere—we would assume towards the pit, and indeed the memorial was sited looking in the exact direction of the original colliery. As the woman's hair cascaded down her back it became a shower of coal that eventually tumbled into the slopes of a mining village at her feet. Below that, below the surface of the ground, there is a miner—her husband perhaps—who hacks away at the coal, pick in hand, on his side, with his back to us. The parallels and differences from the Wanderer are striking: our middle-class romantic (and according to critics' accounts ex-military) explorer has time to travel and reflect, to reach open spaces and ponder over the vision that unfolds. Our working-class miner has no such options: where the Wanderer stands erect, he is forced to crawl; the Wanderer's supporting stick becomes the miner's pounding pick; the Wanderer's stylish mountain outfit becomes the miner's earth-bound sweated nakedness. Yet both have no faces for us, and what they see is both natural yet unclear, whether the Wanderer's white clouds or the blackness of the coalface. And for each there is potential danger in what they confront.

Whilst it might seem that the motion in the statue follows the cascade from top to bottom, there can be seen a simultaneous motion upwards (see Figure 6.4). From the point where the miner hacks away at the future, the community is built from the coal and the spirit of the people, embodied in the mother and her child rising from the coal heap. Then

Fig. 6.5 Graham Ibbeson's Mother and Child Sculpture (photo: Stephen Linstead).

comes the powerful juxtaposition that confirms this direction of travel— a large entirely abstract stainless steel hoop that enframes the woman's head and shoulders, madonna-like, and lifts her upward and forward, to- wards an unknown future (see Figure 6.5). Ibbeson had tried out the idea of incorporating a traditional pit wheel into his design in various early sketches, and even the first maquette, but found the effect lacked the dynamic quality he was trying to capture. By simplifying and abstract- ing with the 'halo' in a contrasting lighter and brighter material, he was able to symbolize the community more broadly (South Yorkshire was a steel area, and there were foundries and engineering works in the town) and inject some light, hope, and aspiration into the work. This forward motion was also inscribed onto the rear of the work, where subsequent generations of women up to the present day were depicted. From the cinematic perspective, I wanted to use the statue to provide a fulcrum for the distinctly feminine voices of these women, articulating it in ways that allow them to be properly heard—and fully noticed—within the film's narrative.

This was possible because so much testimony of the time was from the women who survived themselves. Of course, this still needed properly scripting to bring out its poetic qualities, and supporting with appropriate voicing (we used women with authentic local accents), music (we used an original composition and a special arrangement of a lyric written by a miner), sound effects (I used a combination of existing sound effects, extraction from footage, editing, and layering in creating the right atmospherics) and visuals. We were fortunate in having an ex-miner who could create virtual reality environments to help with building authentic underground and overground landscapes with traverses, accompanied by explosive special effects, to interlace with illustrations from the time, our footage from a coalface of the same period that was still open as part of the National Coal Mining Museum for England (NCMME), and our soundscapes, to enable us to take the viewer down the pit and through the experience of an explosion. Whilst we wanted to be entertaining, our deeper purpose was to carry the argument embedded in the sculpture and turn it into a new way of seeing for the audience—a means of noticing how history, laminated around them, lived on in its communities. The aesthetics and poetics were entwined with the politics and ethics, emerging from the archive and connecting to the present as seamlessly as possible. Dramatic effects were not used simply for dramatic effect—they were only used where we had strong evidence in the contemporary accounts that there was a dramatic experience at the time. Noticing differently does not stop with the researcher—creative researchers seek to share this by creating the conditions for an affective event in which their audiences will notice the world anew.

Conclusion: The Poetics and Cinematics of Taking Notice

At the beginning of this chapter I suggested that researchers tend to become very good at making discoveries that further illuminate already familiar fields, the bright places, but often struggle to break out of their comfortable habits of thought and perception to recognize that the bright places are not always the right places. Often overlooked, there is a poetics at work in everyday life and everyday speech that can energize reflection and change. The specific view taken by social poetics from the conversational perspective sees communicative language constructing a form of life that is characteristically intersubjective. But the more material poetics of Friedrichs and Stevens decentres conversation in favour of relations and movement in the environment, which is no longer a mere backdrop providing context, but a space where *interobjectivity*—which is not limited to the relations between humans and non-human objects but extending to object–object relations and networks, such as the shifting relations between clouds and mountains, ice and boats—opens up a wider mystery that need not succumb to idealism or vitalism (Knox, 2020; Latour, 1996). The social poetics of activism exceeds intersubjectivity, which tends to take place between members of functionally, phenomenologically or socially related groups (managers and management researchers, for example) that are relatively depoliticized though not unethical and not incapable of addressing power issues. By contrast it pursues *transcollectivity*, where issues common to a wider range of groups potentially unite those groups via common concerns and experiences as a result of non-functional characterizations—race, class, ethnicity, gender, sexuality, belief—that lead to real immediate and historical disadvantage yet are rarely voiced without facing delegitimizing responses, if not ignored. The broader poetic and cinematic practices I am advocating in this chapter increase our ability to notice, and continue to notice, a broader range of material, contextual, environmental, ethical, and political shades that transcend the poetic and aesthetic dimensions of the dialogic enformation between language and forms of life. This opens up to the potentially meaningful, the semiotic, rather than the meaning-saturated, the symbolic: it is an open text, a perpetually inconclusive event, an existential glissement, a shape-shifting mystery, in process and in play across time. As Knox (2020, 271) expresses it, what is on offer are 'new forms of reflexivity and responsiveness' to 'reconsider the past in the light of a troubling future that awaits us' because 'the present becomes eternal through a constant reflective practice and a recognition of its own incessant incipience' (Pierce, 2013, 54).

References

Andersen, T. (1991) *The Reflecting Team: Dialogues and Dialogues about the Dialogues.* New York: Norton.

Bakhtin, M. M. (1981). *The Dialogical Imagination: Four Essays*, ed. M. Holquist Austin TX: University of Texas Press.

Beattie, O. & Geiger, J. (2004) *Frozen in Time: The Fate of the Franklin Expedition.* London: Bloomsbury

Berlant, L. & Stewart, K. (2019) *The Hundreds.* Durham, NC: Duke University Press.

Brown, R. H. (1977) *A Poetic for Sociology: Toward a Logic of Discovery for the Human Sciences.* Chicago IL: Chicago University Press.

Burrell, G. (1997) *Pandemonium: Towards a Retro-organization Theory.* Beverley Hills, CA: Sage.

Crapanzano, V. (2004) *Imaginative Horizons: An Essay in Literary Philosophical Anthropology.* Chicago IL: Chicago University Press.

Cunliffe, A. L. (2002) Social Poetics as Management Inquiry: A Dialogical Approach. *Journal of Management Inquiry* 11, 2: 128–146

Denzin, N. K. (2014). *Interpretive Autoethnography* (2nd ed.). Thousand Oaks, CA: Sage.

Derrida, J. (1988) *The Ear of the Other: Otobiography, Transference, Translation.* Lincoln NE: University of Nebraska |Press.

Deveaux, D. (2019) The Sea of Ice *Sartle: Rogue Art History.* https://www.sartle.com/artwork/the-sea-of-ice-caspar-david-friedrich. Accessed 23 June 2021.

Eisner, E. (2005). *Reimagining Schools: The Selected Works of Elliot W. Eisner.* New York, NY: Routledge.

Eliot, T. S. (1942). *Little Gidding.* London: Faber and Faber.

Eschner, K (2018) Tales of the Doomed Franklin Expedition Long Ignored the Inuit Side, But 'The Terror' Flips the Script, *Smithsonian Magazine.* 6 April https://www.smithsonianmag.com/arts-culture/heres-how-amc-producers-worked-inuit-fictionalized-franklin-expedition-show-180968643/

Faulkner, S. L. (2009). *Poetry as Method: Reporting Research through Verse.* Walnut Creek, CA: Left Coast Press.

Furman, R. & Dill, L. (2015) Extreme Data Reduction: The Case for the Research Tanka. *Journal of Poetry Therapy: The Interdisciplinary Journal of Practice, Theory, Research and Education,* 28(1): 43–52.

Goodall, H. L., Jr. (1989). *Casing a Promised Land: The Autobiography of an Organizational Detective as Cultural Ethnographer.* Carbondale: Southern Illinois University Press.

Guiney Yallop, J. J. (2005). Exploring an Emotional Landscape: Becoming a Researcher by Reawakening the Poet. *Brock Education, 14*(2), 132–144.

Guiney Yallop, J. J. (2008). *OUT of Place: A Poetic Journey through the Emotional Landscape of a Gay Person's Identities Within/Without Communities.* Unpublished doctoral dissertation. University of Western Ontario, London, ON.

Guiney Yallop, J. J. (2010). *Of Place and Memory: A Poetic Journey.* Halifax, NS: Backalong Books.

Guiney Yallop, J. J., Wiebe, S., & Faulkner, S. L. (2014) Editorial: Poetic Inquiry in/for/as, *in education, 20*(2), Autumn, 1–11.

Heidegger, M. (1971a) *On the Way to Language.* New York: Harper and Row.

Heidegger, M. (1971b) *Poetry, Language, Thought.* New York: Harper and Row.

Heidegger, M. (1977). Modern Science, Metaphysics, and Mathematics. In Krell, D. F.ed., *Martin Heidegger: Basic Writings.* New York: Harper Torchbooks, pp. 243–282.

Hughes, L. (1947) My Adventures as a Social Poet, *Phylon*, Vol. VIII, No. 3, Third Quarter, 205–212.

Hutchinson, G. (2017) *Sir John Franklin's Erebus and Terror Expedition: Lost and Found.* London: Adlard Coles.

Huxley, A. (1954). *The Doors of Perception / Heaven and Hell.* London, UK: Chatto & Windus.

Jouet, J. (2001) Metro Poems, tr. Monk, I. *AA Files*, No. 45/46 (Winter), pp. 4–14.

Katz, A. M. & Shotter, J. (1996) Hearing the Patient's 'Voice': Toward a Social Poetics in Diagnostic Interviews. *Social Science and Medicine, 43*, 919–931.

Klee, P. (2013/1920) *Creative Confession.* London: Tate Enterprises.

Knowlson, J. (2003) *Images of Beckett.* Cambridge: Cambridge University Press.

Knox, H. (2020) *Thinking Like a Climate: Governing a City in Times of Environmental Change.* Durham, NC: Duke University Press.

Kuiper, C. (2007) *The Eventmaker: The Hybrid Art of Performing Professionals, Work-setting Rehabilitation.* Amsterdam: Lemma

Latour, B. (1996) On Interobjectivity. *Mind, Culture and Activity, 3*(4): 228–245.

Ledgard, M. (2020) Charlottes and Garlands. In Linstead, N. and Linstead, S. (eds), *Viral Verses: Art in Exceptional Times.* York, UK: Borthwick Press, p. 209.

Lee, S. (2019) *March of the Lemmings: Brexit in Prose and Performance 2016-2019.* London: Faber and Faber.

Linstead, S. A. (2017) *Black Snow.* Documentary film Written and directed by S. A. Linstead produced by A. Lawrence and S. A. Linstead Barnsley: bellebete productions 22'30. Accessed at https://vimeo.com/299841616

Linstead, S. A. (2018) Feeling the Reel of the 'Real': Framing the Play of Critically Affective Organizational Research between Art and the Everyday. Special Issue on Organizational Creativity, Play and Entrepreneurship, *Organization Studies* 39, 2–3, pp. 319–344.

Lyotard, J-F. (1991) *The Inhuman* (trans. G. Bennington and R. Bowlby). Cambridge: Polity Press.

Maréchal, G. & Linstead, S. A. (2010) Metropoems: Poetic Method and Ethnographic Experience, *Qualitative Inquiry, 16*(1), 66–77.

Midgley, M. (2001) *Science and Poetry* London and New York, NY: Routledge

Moritz, R. dir. (2012) *Masterworks: Hamburger Kunsthalle, Caspar David Friedrich - The Sea of Ice* documentary film, produced by RM Arts, in *Masterworks: Hamburger Kunsthalle* (Germany: ArtHaus Musik, 2012), 10 mins. Accessed on 23 June 2021 at https://search.alexanderstreet.com/preview/work/bibliographic_entity%7Cvideo_work%7C2098100

Motte, W. (2020) Oulipian Mathematics. In Robert Tubbs, R., Jenkins, A., and Engelhardt, N. *The Palgrave Handbook of Literature and Mathematics.* Switzerland: Palgrave, pp. 226–242.

Nowak, M. (2009) *Coal Mountain Elementary.* Minneapolis, MN: Coffee House Press.

Nowak, M. (2020) *Social Poetics.* Minneapolis, MN: Coffee House Press.

Palin, M. (2019) *Erebus: The Story of a Ship.* London: Arrow.

Parini, J. (2008) *Why Poetry Matters.* New Haven, CT: Yale University Press.

Pelias, R. J. (2011) *Leaning: A Poetics of Personal Relations.* Walnut Creek, CA: Left Coast Press.

Pierce, G. B. (2013) Contemporaneity and Antagonism in Modernist and Postmodern Aesthetics. *The Comparatist*, 37, May, pp. 54–70.

Prendergast, M., Leggo, C., & Sameshima, P. (2009) *Poetic Inquiry: Vibrant Voices in the Social Sciences.* Rotterdam, NL: Sense Publishers.

Prohászka-Rád, B. (2015) Homeward Journey through Poetry: Wallace Stevens's The Poem that Took the Place of a Mountain. *Acta Universitatis Sapientiae, Philologica*, 7(1): 55–63.

Rancière, J. (2004). *The Politics of Aesthetics: The Distribution of the Sensible.* London/New York: Continuum.

Rapport, F., & Hartill, G. (2012). Crossing Disciplines with Ethnographic Poetic Representation. *Creative Approaches to Research*, 5(2), 11–25.

Riach, K., & Warren, S. (2015) Smell Organization: Bodies and Corporeal Porosity in Office Work. *Human Relations, 68*(5): 789–809.

Simmons, D. (2018). *The Terror.* New York NY: Bantam (original Little, Brown and Company 2007).

Sims, D. (2010) Looking for the Key to Leadership under the Lamppost. *European Management Journal, 28,* 253–259.

Stevens, W. (1997) *Collected Poetry and Prose.* Des Moines IA: Library of America.

Stewart, K. (2005) Cultural Poesis: The Generativity of Emergent Things. *Handbook of Qualitative Research,* 3rd edition, eds. Norman Denzin and Yvonna Lincoln. Sage, pp. 1027–1042.

Stewart, K. (2007). *Ordinary Affects.* Durham NC: Duke University Press

Swanston, T., Varney, T L., Kozachuk, M., Choudhury, S., Bewer, B., Coulthard, I., Keenleyside, A., Nelson, A., Martin, R. R, Stenton, D R., & Cooper, D.M.L. (2018) Franklin Expedition Lead Exposure: New Insights from High Resolution Confocal X-Ray Fluorescence Imaging of Skeletal Microstructure. *PLoS ONE, 13*(8): e0202983. August 23.

Thomas, S., Cole, A., & Stewart, S. (eds). (2012). *The Art of Poetic Inquiry.* Halifax, NS: Backalong Books.

Thrift, N. 2007. *Non-representational Theory: Space, Politics, Affect.* London: Routledge.

Todres, L., & Galvin, K. T. (2008).Embodied Interpretation: A Novel Way of Evocatively Representing Meanings in Phenomenological Research. *Qualitative Research,* 8 (5), 568–583.

Turner, B. A. (1988) Connoisseurship in the Study of Organizational Cultures. In Bryman, A. (ed.), *Doing Research in Organizations.* London: Routledge, pp. 108–122.

Wittgenstein, L. (1953) *Philosophical Investigations.* London: Macmillan Publishing Company

7

Noticing Colour

Shades of a Chromatic Empiricism

Timon Beyes

'Adults, productive persons find no footing in color; for them color is possible only in relation to law. They have a world order to provide (. . .)'.

(Benjamin, 2011a, 2012)

'Others tried to align words to the conceptuality of ordinary things, to build muscles of response to the suggestion of a color or tone'.

(Berlant and Stewart, 2019, 44)

'You might want to reach out and disturb the pile of pigment, for example, first staining your fingers with it, then staining the world. You might want to dilute it and swim in it, you might want to rouge your nipples with it, you might want to paint a virgin's robe with it. But you still wouldn't be accessing the blue of it. Not exactly.'

(Nelson, 2009, 4)

Situated in the multiple tints and shades of colour and organization, this chapter is dedicated to colour as process, and to the implications of colour as process for noticing differently in the context of organization and organizing. This might begin with the rather simple if consequential assumption that the study of organization, itself largely chromophobic (Batchelor, 2000), should notice colour. Then, noticing colour *as process* implies keeping one's distance from perceiving colour as merely a provider of managerial order, as if colour would only be imaginable in relation to laying down the law, as Walter Benjamin warns us. (Benjamin's early fragments on colour already entail what I am trying to develop here). This, in turn, means that accessing and stabilizing the blueness of blue, or the redness of red, is one such way of laying down the law. Noticing colour as

Timon Beyes, *Noticing Colour*. In: *Doing Process Research in Organizations, Noticing Differently*. Edited by Barbara Simpson and Line Revsbæk, Oxford University Press. © Oxford University Press (2022).
DOI: 10.1093/oso/9780192849632.003.0007

process is more akin to diluting it, or swimming in it, and building muscles of response to it, as Maggie Nelson, Lauren Berlant, and Kathleen Stewart write. (For learning how to swim in it, and to build muscles of response to its suggestions, please read Nelson's *Bluets*.)

There is precious little on colour in process approaches, aesthetic approaches, embodied and affective approaches, neo-material approaches, spatial and atmospheric approaches, even in visual approaches to organization. So this chapter tries to formulate an invitation to learn how to swim in colour, as scholars of organizing. I first discuss the intimate relation of colour and organization and present colour as organizational force. I then follow Benjamin into the ontological and epistemological strangeness of colour and colour experience. From there, it is but a step back to the foundational text of a modernist sensibility of colour movement, Goethe's *Theory of Colours*, first published in 1810. Guided by Goethe's notion and practice of tender empiricism, I evoke the shades of—or perhaps compile a preliminary palette of—what I suggest calling 'chromatic empiricism' through the notions of situation, scene, attunement, estrangement, montage, and poetics. Returning to colour as in-between order and disorder, the chapter ends with a brief note on old and new theories, immanent critique, and the tyranny of the drawn line.

Towards a Chromatics of Organizing

Colour is ubiquitous and constantly, and deeply, affecting. Organizational sense-making, to reference a foundational notion of organizational process studies, is predicated on the aesthetic making of sense, on producing or altering what can be sensed, perceived, and felt (Holt and Cornelissen, 2014). In organizational terms, the making of sense thus implies the everyday 'distribution of the sensible' and its 'material conditions', 'modes of perception' and 'regimes of emotion' that shape patterns of cognition, categorization, and interpretation (Rancière, 2013, x). In shaping everyday modes of perception and regimes of emotion, colour is a primary organizational force (Beyes, 2017). As such, it is at the heart of industrial modernity, and of the forms and processes of organization it engendered. The rise of commodity capitalism is predicated on the artificial production and standardization of colour, what the business historian Regina Lee Blaszczyk (2012) has called 'the colour revolution'. Colour is 'the commodity's commodity' (Taussig, 2009, 234): a commodity and industry in its own right, yet one that provides goods with an aesthetic and profitable surplus value.

Beyond yet including the world of business and formal organizations, the ubiquity and availability of colour in the late nineteenth and early twentieth century ushered in a reorganized human sensorium, a 'colour sense' (Gaskill, 2018): a way of experiencing and feeling colours and an acculturation of the senses to be organized, trained, and practised. As Michael Rossi has shown with regard to the US, this was about the 'administration of perception (...) as a precondition for managing productivity and safety' (Rossi, 2019, 14). Cautioning against well-worn theses of the disenchantment and de-aestheticization of industrial modernity, '[s]ensation, perception, sensibility, and sensitivity came increasingly to be included alongside modes of manufacture, finance, and legal and business information as substrates for the rational and productive ordering of society' (Rossi, 2019, 15), which included the eugenic measurement and ordering of skin colour, with colour as 'organizing principle' of racial classification (Gilroy, 2005, 37).[1] For instance, colour became wedded to principles of Tayloristic ordering so as to subject functional colour to rational management routines of 'managing the palette' for production and consumption. Perhaps colour even became 'the ultimate tool of scientific management' (Blaszczyk, 2012, 229).[2]

Such is the multiplicity of colour as organizational force. A chromatics of organization encounters colour in social ordering and control across and within organizations, in the aesthetic distribution of what can be sensed and how (thus organizing the human sensorium), in the dressage and liberation of human bodies, in commodity capitalism, and in the lure of countless digital colours (Beyes, 2017). Yet all of this is predicated on colour's processual *force*: on its permanent and endless capacity for chromatic differentiation.[3] Consider how any attempt to turn colour into

---

[1] As an everyday technology of ordering, colour serves to represent, support, and solidify social codes and to symbolize communicative purposes or purposes of interpellation in no uncertain 'terms' (van Leeuwen, 2010). Colour in this sense is an erstwhile marker of racialized identity, and relating differences in skin colour to discrepancies in capacities constitutes the folly of enlightenment reason. The construction of a dualism of 'blackness' and 'whiteness' is of course one way of stilling and fixing colour ascription and meaning, and a catastrophic one (Gilroy, 2005, 42). Yet understanding colour as processual organizational force would imply tracing the unmaking of racialized (in the sense of colour-coded) bodies.

[2] The intimate relation between colour and processes of social ordering is echoed in bleak assessments of 'color after digitalization', where commodified colour regimes have become a prominent site of 'biopolitical management of commercial novelty and governed predictability' (Cubitt, 2014, 150–151).

[3] Force is here understood aesthetically as an ongoing 'play of expression and concealment', 'an endless generation and dissolution of expressions, an endless transformation of one expression into

a managerial tool of commerce, manufacture, control, entertainment, and education is confronted with its perennial unruliness. The imagination of a rational and productive ordering of society through colour is confronted with the latter's uncanny capacity to evade all efforts to be systematically captured and coded (Riley, 1995). Colour seems in-between organization and disorganization, flitting between colour management and unmanageable substance. In other words, '[a]n eye for colour requires a mind for process' (Gaskill, 2018, 246). If thinking organization in processual terms implies recognizing 'a more general force which includes us in its perpetual movement between order and disorder, certainty and uncertainty', as Robert Cooper remarked (1998, 154), then colour is to be recognized and apprehended as a primary aesthetic force of organizing and disorganizing. '[T]o bring colour again into credit', Goethe wrote more than 200 years ago (1840, xlvi), is 'to awaken the conviction that a progressive, augmenting, mutable quality, a quality which admits of alteration even to inversion, is not fallacious (. . .)'. With Goethe, this is an awakening to what might be called a methodological sensibility attuned to the protean and recalcitrant force of colour, a *chromatic empiricism* shaped by a situated attunement to colour's endless movements and mutations.

A trace of this chromatic sensibility can be found in the introduction to the voluminous *Oxford Handbook of Process Philosophy and Organization Studies*. Here the editors signal that colour is at the very heart, and at the very start, of modern process thought. For they begin their reflections on process and organization with colour, as encountered in a Cezanne painting, Montagne Sainte-Victoire, experienced as a performance of process: 'Apparently fixed, isolated objects begin to burst through their edges, colours flow within one another, as greens are pulled into more distant purples and pinks, which themselves are pulled back into occasional foreground details, hesitant to comply with the form-giving order to recede.' This way, the image 'upsets entirely the conceits of any neat organization of the world by allowing movement and insubstantiality equal voice amid a democracy of presence' (Helin et al., 2014, 1–2).

For another trace of chromatic sensibility in the study of organization, consider Connellan's explorations of white (in the rooms and corridors of hospitals, churches, parliaments, prisons, universities) as both suppressing and uplifting: as materialized and embodied ambivalence of colour that

something different' (Menke, 2013, 44). It designates 'pure' relation, since it exists in the relation, in connecting, and is expressed through the succession of 'connectings' (exceeding any particular expression or form).

cannot be stilled into a technology of domination and sameness (Connellan, 2013). And this is only about white! Colour fundamentally dissolves the logic of solids (to use Bergson's term), against which the process view of organization has been constructed. As ubiquitous organizational force or 'polymorphous magical substance' (Taussig, 2009, 40), colour's fleetingness and volatility seems like a gift for process-minded scholarship. Yet it also unsettles implicit or explicit assumptions that seem to shape extant process approaches. In fact, colour's unsettling quality, its instability, fleetingness, and evanescence, might be to blame for the chromophobic history and present of social and organizational theory, suggesting a fear of colour's perennial deceitfulness, and/or a displacement and denigration of its otherness, of what is considered (too) queer, or childish, or tender, or oriental, or even pathological (Batchelor, 2000). For one, the movement of colour is visual and spatial—one might say its shimmering is atmospheric—before it is linguistic. To posit language and communication as an a priori of organizational analysis already misses out on 'colour sense' and helps reproduce 'the great swindle of modern thought (. . .) at the price of embodied experience and the colourful world it reveals' (Gaskill, 2018, 11). Sensemaking here literally means the making and remaking of sense experience, and not (or not primarily) a process of talking and writing organization into existence. And noticing the organizational force of colour calls for a kind of speculative thought, for (writing) experiments with a poetics of organizing and for a kind of 'tender empiricism', to use Goethe's term (on which more later): a chromatic empiricism that pushes at the limits of empirical research on processes of organizing.

Colour as Process

Shortly before the First World War, in Berlin (and later in Switzerland, to avoid the war) the young Walter Benjamin was pondering how colour unsettles, and helps reimagine, notions of experience and imagination and their Kantian a prioris of space, time, and the distinction of objects and subjects (Caygill, 1998). For colour confounds these distinctions and assumptions. In Benjamin's early writings, like *Dialogue on the Rainbow* and *A Child's View of Colour*, colour is described as 'something winged that flits from one form to the next' (2011a, 211). Colour affects objects and subjects and can be reduced to neither of them. Hence, '[c]olours see themselves, (. . .) and they are [seeing's] object and organ at the same time' (2011b, 218). The foundational distinction between observer and observed, perceiver and perceived, is suspended in the experience of colour; and not space or time but colour becomes the fluid medium of intuition and imagination, 'precisely because it is quality alone; in no respect is it substance or does it refer to substance' (p. 218). And colour for Benjamin, following Goethe and positing Goethe against Kant, is endlessly variable. After all, a given colour takes on intensity and meaning in association with, or contrast to, other colours, entering into indefinite, and indefinitely shifting, configurations. While perpetually being captured and fenced in by form, it is colour's infinity and malleability that becomes the processual a priori of experience, shaping its spaces, allowing for spatial surfaces and lines yet itself not predicated on any spatial surface. Colour, we might say, is pure process: the 'medium of all changes, and not a symptom', 'full of movement' and 'arbitrary' (Benjamin, 2011a, 211–212).

Emphasizing that colour precedes form, that it is not a symptom of larger forces, and that it resists categorization along object- and/or subject-based lines of inquiry also means that Benjamin's colour sensibility is resolutely opposed to psychologizing or spiritualizing what colour does. There is no direct path to a kind of colour spiritualism, which in impoverished form is echoed in opinion polls, market research, and design manuals—if not in altogether empty claims—about the affects conveyed by the choice of specific colours. Likewise, there is the reduction of specific colours to the vulgar psychological promotion of an individual's creative capacities. Blue is marketed as promoting creativity, or green, or how about even purple: Pantone's choice of 'ultra violet' as Color of the Year in 2018 was based on its perceived symbolism of experimentation, non-conformity, and its ability to inspire individuals to push creative boundaries. Turning specific colours into specific symbolic, psychological, or metaphysical forces equals falling back into the world of chromatic essentialism and human nature, into the tyranny of form (Jay, 2018). 'For Benjamin, the emancipation of colour meant not only from objects and the faithful imitation of the perceived world, but also from rigid semiotic schemes that attributed natural qualities to distinct colours' (Jay, 2018, 26).

Rather, Benjamin finds traces and situations of an attunement to colour-as-process in works of art, in children's books and in children's unformed apprehensions, and later in the figure of the flaneur who perceives by surrendering him-/herself to the hues and intensities of urban commodity capitalism. Children, for instance, have not yet been educated into form, have not yet been formed into clear-cut distinctions 'of self and other, of substance and surface (. . .) and of subject and object' (Leslie, 2002, 269). And '[a]s every parent knows, children have to be taught to colour within the lines' (Jay, 2018, 23). In the beguiling prose miniatures that make up *A Berlin Childhood around 1900*, this is how Benjamin tries to remember, evoke and reflect such apprehension (2006, 110–111).

> In our garden there was an abandoned, ramshackle summerhouse. I loved it for its stained-glass windows. Whenever I wandered about inside it, passing from one coloured pane to the next, I was transformed; I took on the colours of the landscape that—now flaming and now dusty, now smouldering and now sumptuous—lay before me in the window. It was like what happened with my watercolours, when things would take me to their bosom as soon as I overcame them in a moist cloud. Something similar occurred with soap bubbles. I travelled in them throughout the room and mingled in the play of colours of the cupola, until it burst. While considering the sky, a piece of jewellery, or a book, I would lose myself in colours. Children are their prey at every turn.

Can organizational process research become prey to colour? What Benjamin offers is a notion of approaching and doing process that hinges on the organizational force of colour by replacing 'linguistic signification' as 'paradigm of experience' with 'chromatic differentiation' (Caygill, 1998, xiii). In fragments scattered across his work, enacting such chromatic differentiation took the form of writing from within concrete if often ephemeral scenes and situations, as attempts to write with, or perhaps in, colour. Positing colour as objects and organs of seeing therefore both prefigures and pushes to its limit the process-theoretical claim to reimagine 'the concreteness of the world' and to recognize 'the writer's involvement in it'; it is indeed 'entirely and utterly empirical' (Helin et al., 2014, 12). To ponder the chromatic attunement to the happening of the organized world, and how colour's sensuousness, relationality, and fleetingness both organizes and disorganizes, Benjamin (like other colour writers before and after him) preferred and performed a tender empiricism.

Tender Empiricism

In *Dialogue on the Rainbow*, Benjamin harks back to the Goethean notion of a 'primal image' (*Urbild*), as 'that which appears – that in which [the creator] is consumed (. . .)' (2011b, 216). Chromatic differentiation, in Benjamin, is something of a Goethean ur-phenomenon, 'within which one can have an intuition of multiplicity': 'the intrication of a reality whose iridescence opens up between multiple combinations of colours, according to a weave that constitutes an intra-worldly depth that is neither that of the subject (perspective) nor that of the object (extension)' (Alliez, 2016, 25 and 23). The *ur-* is not to be understood in a temporal sense, as if depicting a point of origin, but as a foundational phenomenon of experience: 'the smallest intelligible forms of our "blooming, buzzing, confusion"' (Jameson, 2020, 8, quoting William James).[4] Attempting to enter into this buzzing confusion requires what Goethe famously called tender empiricism, also translated as delicate empiricism: 'There is a delicate form of empiricism which enters into the closest union with its object and is therefore transformed into an actual theory' (von Goethe, 1998, §565). Becoming intimate with its 'object', method here is theory, and experiencing is thinking. Tender empiricism is encapsulated in, and fuelled by, Goethe's infatuation with the strange world of colour. For Goethe, to put it simply, colour is a matter of sensation and experience. And colour is utterly relational: a medium that entangles (and is irreducible to) perceiver and perceived and that in its 'physiological' forms is itself in incessant variation, in continuous movement between different hues, tones and intensities. '[E]ach colour, in its dependency upon other colours, must be considered as a veritable *relation of forces* (. . .)' (Alliez, 2016, 19; orig. emphasis), 'ever in movement', 'not to be arrested' (Goethe, 1840, 300).[5]

In methodological terms, the *Theory of Colours* and its practice of tender empiricism constitutes another ur-: 'the ur-scene of nomadic science' (Taussig, 2008, 6): 'Witness the perceiver becoming part of the perceived. Second point: the wonder. Third point: change, flow, and heterogeneity in a constant becoming. And fourth point: a nomadic following of the trace (. . .)'. In following colour's countless relational transformations, Goethe demonstrated how 'matter-force rather than matter-form seems to provide a more honest way of describing what is happening' (Taussig, 2008, 7). Based on a painstaking attention to chromatic experience, tracing matter-force foregrounded embodied intuitions and affects, being 'passionately

---

[4] To delve into the relation of Benjamin's modernist rewriting of the notion of experience through colour and Goethe's proto-modernist morphological thought, see Charles (2019) and in stupendous detail, exemplifying a tender archival empiricism, Brüggemann (2007).

[5] The *Theory of Colours* has been debunked numerous times by proper colour science. Yet its main problem precisely was that colour science had nothing to say about chromatic affects and intensities—after all, colour is never *experienced* 'as it physically is' (Albers, 2013, 1). So the *Theory of Colours* became the foundational text of a discourse of chromatics attuned to what colour does.

moved' by the empirical encounters, 'for the sake not of subjective fulfill-
ment but of a fuller record of [colour's] efficacies and effect' (Goldstein,
2017, 12; orig. emphasis). Tenderness here implies both an 'exact sensorial phantasy' (Goethe's term is perhaps better translated as 'exact sensorial
imagination'; Charles, 2019) and a cultivation of vulnerability as a practice
and ethics of inquiry. Goethe's experiments prefigure a radical processual
methodology: 'And such will be the meaning of the tenderness (. . .): the
method sets out to confront, and ultimately to cultivate, the observer's vulnerability to the object under view, recasting the scene of experiment as one
of bilateral metamorphosis that puts the subjects and objects of knowledge
into a spiral of "accommodation and reaction"' (Goldstein, 2017, 131).

As Amanda Jo Goldstein points out, in letting tenderness or delicacy
inform empirical method and embracing process, partiality, multiplicity,
and bodily involvement, all of this is close to what contemporary feminist
science studies, among other modes of thought, would come to call 'situated knowledge' (Haraway, 1988) and diffractive inquiry (Barad, 2014). In
fact, the notion of diffraction itself was coined in response to pre-Goethean
experiments with light and colour, when stripes of colour escaped or over-
flowed the play of light and shadow, confounding ideas of how light was
refracted and queering the dichotomy of lightness and darkness, calling
for reading different insights and different sensations through one another
(Barad, 2014). A similar Goethean sensibility can be found in affect-
theoretical experiments with an expanded empiricism, or an empiricism
of sensation, so as to apprehend the formless and unqualified, impersonal
and non-signifying forces and intensities that shape what bodies can do—
the force and intensity of 'movement-colour' for instance, first embraced by
Goethe, writes Deleuze (2005, 97; see Beyes and De Cock, 2017). Or consider recent non-representational methodologies and their attentiveness
and responsiveness to the affective, atmospheric and material agencies that
shape—both settle and unsettle—everyday life and organizing in which the
researcher is embedded (Beyes and Steyaert, 2012).

As presented here, then, colour summons an aesthetics of organizing
that entails what I suggest calling a chromatic empiricism. It is patiently
attentive to the multiple, moving, formless yet relational force of colour,
and to the ordering and disordering of situational knots of what can be
sensed, thought, and expressed. It avoids any semiotic or psychological
model that would attribute specific qualities to distinct colours. It rather assumes, and works with, colour's perplexing capacity to both provoke and
evade systematic inquiry: 'a more fundamental disarray (. . .) that baffles

the usual procedures of language' (Lichtenstein, 1993, 4) in general and of methodological prescriptions in particular. Paraphrasing the art historian Jaqueline Lichtenstein, moving from assumptions of a stable and representable relation between colour and systematic inquiry towards acknowledging and seeking to apprehend the organizational force of colour means risking 'methodological suicide'. Colour carries an ungovernable excess that evades method, understood as enacting the doxa of methodology and slotting what is presumed to be given, i.e. data, into recognizable, systematic and clearly articulated categories (St Pierre, 2018). This is precisely why colour embodies process and resists 'pressing an artificial *Stillleben* model upon the world and examin[ing] how we can make it fit' (Helin et al., 2014, 11; orig. emphasis). One reason why colour hardly finds its way into organizational analysis might simply be that it removes itself from ideas of applicable, replicable, and easily transferable methods, and thus from the *lingua franca* of getting things published.

Shades of a Chromatic Empiricism

Taking my cue from Goethe's notion and practice of tender empiricism and Benjamin's related sensitivity to colour experience, I can now begin to outline the contours of chromatic empiricism. This entails moving from Goethean (but also Benjaminean) registers of situatedness, and proceeding through experimental colour scenes and their embodied attunements to a perhaps more Benjaminean mode of estrangement and scholarly poetics, most notably the style of montage. Having placed colour at the heart of an aesthetics of process, even of an embodied mode of registering and writing particularly attuned to process, these notions concern the 'doing' of process research (also) in the study of organizing. As examples of chromatic differentiation, the following sections are accompanied by visual vignettes that Lydia Jørgensen (2019) constructed from photographic documentation of the emergence and movement of organizational atmospheres enacted in an architectural firm and a public organization. As a practice of 'visual fabulation' (p. 156), snapshots from organizational life were multiplied through both decolourization and excess colouring. In Jørgensen's study, these images are interspersed with textual vignettes of everyday organizational happenings, yet they do not represent or illustrate them. As empirical material in its own right, they invite the reader into becoming affected through chromatic differentiation, and into making sense of what she/he senses chromatically. This is not a process of representing what has been verbalized elsewhere, then, but of 'actual composition spun into representations' and states of sensory attention (Stewart, 2015, 24). I hope that these images here help colourize the abstracted textual sections, as exemplary compositions of colour's organizational force. 'Look! Look at colour! Become aware!', Taussig pleads (2009, 243; orig. emphasis).

Situation: In tracing what colour does, one is situated in the middle of chromatic situations. '[T]he middle is where things begin, and where they end. The midst is not then a site to be found, visited, and then left behind. Rather it is a mode' (Lorimer, 2015, 181). Chromatic empiricism dwells in this mode of the middle. It is embedded in situations of organizing that cannot be fully captured and which condition what Benjamin later, with exact conceptual imagination, would call the possibility not of knowledge but of a more processual and unstable *knowability* (*Erkennbarkeit*) (Weber, 2008, 168). In his seminal *Interaction of Colours,* Josef Albers insisted on a 'thinking in situations' (2013, 69) as educational concept for colour's knowability. This is the 'simple moral' of situated knowledges and partial perception espoused by Haraway (1988, 583) and prefigured by Goethe. It 'entails rejecting the disembodied, totalizing, and of course entirely imaginary stance of the Knower who stands apart from the Known in order to know it, and embracing the partiality, process, and bodily involvement of the perceiver (. . .)' (Gaskill, 2018, 246). A chromatic empiricism therefore perceives and performs the research process as moving through situations of organizing in which colour's organizational force is palpable. As with Benjamin's childhood memories, this will often mean specific settings where colour astounds and confounds; perhaps, a chromatic empiricism 'should *begin* with the too strange and the too much' (St. Pierre, 2018, 607; orig. emphasis) – see Jørgensen's montage called 'method' (Figure 7.1).

Scene: Goethe's experiments of entering into colour's relations of forces constitute scenes of chromatic differentiation, in which the distinction between a separate outer and inner space is discarded and 'seeing' becomes an embodied (tender, delicate) experience immersed in fluid and unbridled chromatic transformation:

> The hole [of the camera obscura] being then closed, let him[/her] look towards the darkest part of the room; a circular image will now be seen to float before him[/her]. The middle of this circle will appear bright, colourless, or somewhat yellow, but the border will at the same moment appear red. After a time this red, increasing towards the centre, covers the whole circle, and at last the bright

central point. No sooner, however, is the whole circle red than the edge begins to be blue, and the blue gradually encroaches inward on the red. When the whole is blue the edge becomes dark and colourless. This darker edge again slowly encroaches on the blue till the whole circle appears colourless.

(Goethe, 1840, 16–17)

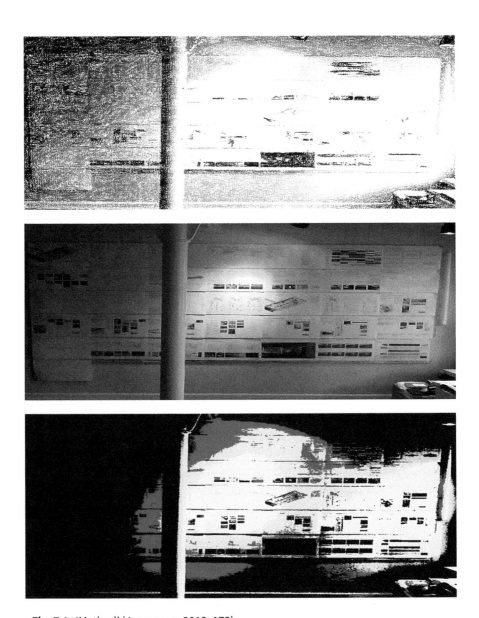

Fig. 7.1 'Method' (Jørgensen, 2019, 173).

It is a scene that calls for moving into chromatic situations and reconstructing them as scenes, moving away from principles of representation and distance that undergird, for instance, prevalent assumptions of how

Fig. 7.2 'Public green house' Jørgensen (2019, 219).

to construct case study research (Berlant, 2007). Scenes are looser and nimbler, singular occurrences often more ephemeral and transient (Rancière, 2013), like Jørgensen's 'public green house' depicted in Figure 7.2, or Benjamin's evocation of childhood colours, or the self-contained scenes of Brechtian epic theatre so important to him, or the colour flashes that came to mark urban life and early commodity culture in the Paris arcades (just as much, lest we forget, the colourful hell of the First World War).

Attunement: Goethe's exact sensorial imagination and Benjamin's children, who do not reflect but 'merely' experience, paradoxically denote a similar mode of attunement to what colour does. The perceiver is pulled into the perceived, inserted into the movement of colour, regaining a sense of wonder and amazement about colour's countless relational transformations. The anthropologist Kathleen Stewart calls such attunements 'worldings': 'intimate, compositional processes of dwelling' in mundane situations that are attentive to what moves, relates, speeds up and slows down, intensifies and decreases (2011, 445–446). This, too, is chromatic empiricism. Here is Stewart on the organizational force of redness in New England (2015, 24):

Redness saturated New England as an irreducible quality lodged in events in the arts and commerce, in religion, class, race, and migration. It spread across fields of vision hardened into kernel-scenes of red maples, sugaring houses, and red barns. It travelled, with the leaves of the maple tree in autumn, through picturesque calendars, a body of poetry, leaf tourism, and who knows what kinds of desires, fears, and dead ends. It took place as accidents, encounters, laws, horrors, exchanges, adventures, occasional appearances, dull routines, brightenings, chances, tools, milestones, and losses. It had events and so sites, actors, stakes, consequences, properties, competencies, modalities, attunements, and velocities (. . .). In the end, redness was far more than a symbolic element in a representational order and far more matter-of-fact as well. It was not a representation actualized but an actual composition spun into representations, objects, and states of sensory alert. It popped in the manner of an infrastructure repainted for its promise. It magnetized qualities and senses as it pulled objects into its orbit. It sat picturesquely evident in the field of Kerouac's speed-vision of an America *On the Road*. It sedimented into a pastoral clearing in the distance, a path to a horizon, a promise of encounter. It cast a spell over residents and tourists alike. It inspired a flood of photography, painting, literature, and postcards. It had become a germinal aesthetic, a tendril of practices and sensibilities gathered into an energetics of form. It had produced affinities, accidental admixtures, and refrains on which people and things travelled. It had worlded.

This kind of attunement might be called ethnographic (or historically ethnographic) in the way the researcher enters into the field and its situations and tries to write from within these (actual or historical) conditions, keeping methodological overdetermination at bay. Here, '[t]he ordinary is a moving target. Not first something to make sense of, but a set of sensations that incite' (Stewart, 2007, 93). Tracing the organizational effects and affects of colour thus reverberates with Silvia Gherardi's notion of 'affective ethnography' as first and foremost a style of research and its processual emphasis on 'affective attunement' as embodied experience towards all kinds of (human and non-human) matter (Gherardi, 2019) – something that Jørgensen's montage 'ways of working' seems to capture and make strange (Figure 7.3).

Estrangement: This kind of attentiveness is 'at once recognizably ethnographic and altogether estranged', to borrow a phrase that Lorimer uses to discuss non-representational approaches (2015, 186). What makes Goethe and Benjamin's empiricism strange, I think, is the insistence on colour's processuality and its excessive force as the ur-phenomenon of experience. Goethe's vigilant attentiveness to the shape-shifting intensities of colour is defamiliarizing in its radical mode of beholding, a gentleness almost violently posited against the violence of customary (scientific) method. Or consider Benjamin's attunement to the ephemerality of an experience of colours that *vorbeihuschen*, to use one of his favourite terms, that flit or fly past, and slip away, making possible *and* continuously deforming the organization of experience. What makes such attunements to colour unfamiliar, too, is the spirit of experiment in which they are conducted. Goethe literally performed decades of exploratory experiments by entering into the medium of colour and making his body vulnerable to its uncontrollable transformations. Benjamin experimented with the figure of the child as (Brechtian) 'estrangement effect by way of regression' (Jameson, 2020, 27). The child is itself an imaginary figure (albeit buttressed by studies of children's perception and development, and close observations of his own son) that allows intimations of a pure, unformed contemplation through colour (and according to Jameson offered Benjamin a way out of the forms

Fig. 7.3 'Ways of working' (Jørgensen, 2019, 198).

and confines of academic disciplines, and the commodification of ideas).[6] Finally, what is defamiliarizing is how this kind of attentiveness 'slow[s] down or even block[s] and divert[s] the way by which we so speedily, even instantaneously, transform sensory knowledge into knowledge' (Taussig, 2009, 188). This practice of slowing down, or slow motion (Beyes and Steyaert, 2012), stays with the roiling nuances of colour and thus unsettles the usual rhythms and intensities through which organizational analysis is performed, allowing us to apprehend processes of organizing differently, through chromatic differentiation. This defamiliarization might take the form of choosing different colours, of enacting chromatic differentiation, as in Jørgensen's visual fabulations that accompany these pages, opening one's eyes to the thrust and potential of colour in montage-like forms (see Figure 7.4).

Montage: Working with, and working through chromatic differentiation implies a mode of inquiry that branches out according to where colour, winged creature, flits, and where it is made to settle. This entails a discontinuous writing faithful to situations and scenes—itself enacting another defamiliarization, in this case of how reports are structured and presented. Goethe's patient tracing of colour's differential and generative principles through contrasts, mixing and opacity is simply arranged numerically so as to show more than tell (in the first two of three parts of the original *Farbenlehre*, that is, of which only the first one is fully translated into English; the third part on the history of knowing colour presents a discontinuous form of rendering different styles and literatures, performing colour in writing, so to speak). In its juxtaposition of scenes and findings, there are traces of a (modernist) method of montage, which Benjamin a century later would not only encounter as avant-garde art practice, in the experience of urban life and in the then new technology of film, but also glean from children's books and their wild arrangements of colours and things, a way of trying to reflect and mimic what colour does. For both, this is a rescue act for experiences unacknowledged, or experiences under threat. As such, implicated in following and apprehending chromatic transformation (and thus in a sense going beyond Goethe) is registering the ensuing interruptions and shifts in organizational processes.

The properties of the montage are thus amenable to a chromatic empiricism that seeks to slow down and tarry rather than pin things down,

---

[6] In Benjamin's writings, the children are archetypal figures, 'whose very relationship with their toys betrays not enjoyment or consumption, but rather the delight in production as such' (Jameson, 2020, 42).

Fig. 7.4 'Floor work' (Jørgensen, 2019, 182).

as it tingles with the shiftiness and inconclusiveness of colour that os-
cillates between order and disorder, managerial tool and unmanageable
force. The notion of montage therefore points to a way of proceeding that
Benjamin raised to a programme of critical inquiry into organized life.
It prioritizes simultaneity, discontinuity, and contradiction over chronol-
ogy, continuity, and frictionless coherence, difference over identity, and

juxtapositions of details, episodes, and scenes over system or linear narra-
tives (Weigel, 2015). For instance, the use of montage allows juxtaposing
different research methods that inhabit different time-spaces, so that one
can address colour's organizational force in (some of) its multiplicity—a
more open way of proceeding that has recently been updated through the
notion of research assemblage (Fox and Alldred, 2021). Consider one more
time Jørgensen's visual vignettes (see Figure 7.5, 'materiality'): Informed
by a montage aesthetics in their own right, they are arranged next to textual vignettes of everyday organizational happenings that are drawn from
observations, hanging out, shadowing, informal talks, and research interviews. But the notion of montage is not 'merely empirical'. It fuses material
gleaned from research tools with theory and conceptual reflections; with
findings from extant studies; with habitual dispositions of disciplinary research cultures and their hierarchies of who is allowed or encouraged to
notice differently; with frameworks for and textual organizations of research output (such as a book contribution or the more rigid and colourless
forms of journal writing); and with the affordances of technological media
of writing.

Poetics: Montage is, of course, an artistic and literary practice, translated by writers such as Kathleen Stewart into the study of the social but
otherwise rarely encountered in the world of scholarship. Yet a chromatics of organizing attuned to colour as process entails a reconfiguration
of the modes of presenting scholarship towards a style that is ensnared
in colour constellations. It attempts writing from within them, enacting
in words (and images) how colour flits from one organizational 'form' to
the next. 'Compositional writing', Stewart has written with regard to the
colour red 'has to stay nimble' to keep up with redness's movement through
manifold registers, connections and differences (2015, 21). In the midst of
colour happening (organizing, disorganizing), such writing 'fastens onto
the tendons of a scene or the interruption of a rhythm' (Stewart, 2018,
187). Its words blur with things and forces more than they seek to represent them, 'as if everything becomes prismatic, angled, composed of shards
that can harden into nodes of condensation or shift modes or seasons
without warning' (p. 187). Such writing experiments with montage-like
arrangements, made up of juxtaposition, simultaneous contradiction and
speculative construction, as it seeks to capture chromatic differentiation
and its unacknowledged experiences.

A chromatic empiricism therefore resembles a 'poetic empiricism capable of registering and representing the transfigurative activity [of colour]

Fig. 7.5 'Materiality' (Jørgensen, 2019, 180).

against the grain of an intellectual culture Goethe diagnosed as "shy of the real"' (Goldstein, 2017, 75). It 'gathers together all that is otherwise inarticulate and powerful in the bouquet of the imagery and gamut of feelings'

(Taussig, 2009, 155). The poetic here is not without its irony (Beyes and Holt, 2020). It acknowledges that any scholarly-poetic claim to state what colour does remains just that, a claim, itself made rhetorically, and partially and prone to situational conditions. The poet-scholar relies on attentiveness, and rhetorical force, and with this details the experience of being in the company of what is beyond (or before) language and to some degree evades control and prediction. Yet at the same time, 'if the sensory basis of empirical knowledge is poetic down to its very nerves and fibers, the epistemic status of poetic language changes: the tropes, figures, images, and metaphors formerly thought to adorn or obscure the simple evidence of sense may instead index fidelity to it— may constitute the best possible linguistic register' (Goldstein, 2017, 9) to trace and apprehend colour understood as organizational force and polymorphous magical substance.

Conclusion: Novelty, Speculation, Tyranny

Situation, scene, attunement, estrangement, montage, poetics: these are shades of a chromatic empiricism. Given the paucity of chromatic engagements in the study of organization, they constitute sensitizations to what colour does, potentially to be engaged—and further developed and rewritten—by empirical inquiries into colour as organizational force. These sensitizations are surely in tune with more radical process thought. What emerges in a chromatics of organizing is organization understood— or better, apprehended—as 'endlessly emergent, porous, improvisatory, associational and circumstantial' (Lorimer, 2015, 180). For colour is a prime processual—volatile, fleeting, and thoroughly relational—medium and immanent force of organizational becoming. Before and beyond language and communicative forms of sensemaking, colour is at work shaping and unsettling sense perception. It animates matter and befalls human bodies. Is there any other phenomenon that so comprehensively forces us to notice differently? A chromatics of organizing therefore pushes the apprehension and the writing of process in organizing further towards its embodied, affective, aesthetic, and speculative configurations.

Much of this is not new (or in diffractive terms, '[t]here is nothing that is new; there is nothing that is not new'; Barad, 2014, 168). On a minor note, this chapter sought to show that the usual claims of novelty—as in new methodologies of process research, or 'post qualitative inquiry' (St. Pierre, 2018)—can blind us to the persistency of old concerns, for instance with regard to what we today might call situated knowledge, expanded empiricism, diffractive inquiry, or non-representational writing. The colour work of Goethe and Benjamin, among others, strikingly counters the presentism also prevalent in organizational research, a forgetfulness of recurring themes and their histories, such as on the chromatics of process.

Of course, the dominant responses to the task of noticing differently is either not noticing at all, or inscribing colour into organizational logics of surface appearance. And what a powerful technology of organization it is: subject to all sorts of managerial imperatives and the everyday ordering work enacted through charts, diagrams, power-point presentations (Pias, 2020), symbolic categories and codes. Yet this ordering work is predicated on colour's perennial and processual unruliness, and on colour experience's resistance to become a still life of reliable communication and control. Colour therefore invites an immanent *and* speculative critique attentive to mundane and ephemeral situations and its neglected details, which harbour 'the possibility (. . .) of a reorganisation of experience through colour' (Caygill, 1998, 152).

As a way of ending (which is in the middle), here are Martin Jay's reflections on how colour can emancipate from the tyrannies of thought and method, transposed from art history to the study of organization. First, the 'tyranny of the drawn line or distinct form, the primacy of spatial order and relational intelligibility' is dislodged by the 'messiness, instability, luminosity, and vibrancy of hue and tone' (2018, 17). A chromatics of organizing foregrounds colour's processual force, and a chromatic empiricism is attuned to how colour feeds on and is unsettled by the 'speculative excess of colour over the forms of experience in which it finds itself' (Caygill, 1998, 150). Can organizational process studies learn to think colour before form? Second, 'the tyranny of mimetic reproduction', and the imperative to represent material ordering, is confronted with the question of unrepresentability, radical processuality and the limits of text-based communication. Rather than lecturing on colour as organizational force, of which this chapter is clearly guilty, can organizational process studies find inspiration in the more-than-representational montages of art, poetry and the in-between forms of colour writing such as Stewart's, so as to learn to present and perform colour scenes? Third, a chromatics of organizing unsettles the institutional tyranny of 'official academies with their prescribed rules' of what we might call research design, methodology and research presentation, encapsulating the sway of design over colour. 'The academy is the surest way of destroying the power of the child', Kandinsky wrote with regard to art academies (here quoted after Jay, 2018, 28, fn 12). It is, as things stand, the surest way of avoiding or neglecting the organizational force of colour. Perhaps, a chromatic empiricism will not and cannot amount to a methodology in that, beyond abstracted notions like scene, attunement, and estrangement, it cannot be formalized. Yet we relegate colour to invisible spectre, mere appearance or profane ordering device at our own peril.

Acknowledgments

This chapter owes a lot to Line Revsbæk and Barbara Simpson's thoughtful and generous reading and their suggestions. And I'm very grateful to Lydia Jørgensen for allowing me to borrow and reprint some of her chromatic differentiations.

References

Albers, J. (2013). *Interaction of Colour* (50th Anniversary Edition). New Haven: Yale University Press.

Alliez, É. (2016). *The Brain-Eye: New Histories of Modern Painting*, transl. R. Mackay. London: Rowman and Littlefield.

Barad, K. (2014). Diffracting Diffraction: Cutting Together-Apart. *Parallax, 20*(3), 168–187.

Batchelor, D. (2000). *Chromophobia*. London: Reaktion Books.

Benjamin, W. (2006). *A Berlin Childhood around 1900*, transl. H. Eiland. Cambridge (MA): Belknap Press.

Benjamin, W. (2011a). A Child's View of Colour. In: *Walter Benjamin: Early Writings, 1910-1917* (pp. 211–213). Cambridge (MA): Belknap Press.

Benjamin, W. (2011b). The Rainbow: A Conversation about Imagination. In: *Walter Benjamin: Early Writings, 1910-1917* (pp. 214–223). Cambridge (MA): Belknap Press.

Berlant, L. (2007). On the Case. *Critical Inquiry, 33*(4), 663–672.

Berlant, L., & Stewart, K. (2019). *The Hundreds*. Durham: Duke University Press.

Beyes, T. (2017). Colour and Organization Studies. *Organization Studies 38*(10). 1467–1482.

Beyes, T., & De Cock, C. (2017). Adorno's Grey, Taussig's Blue: Colour, Organization and Critical Affect. *Organization 24*(1), 59–78.

Beyes, T., & Holt, R. (2020). The Topographical Imagination: Space and Organization Theory. *Organization Theory*. https://doi.org/10.1177/2631787720913880

Beyes, T., & Steyaert, C. (2012). Spacing Organization: Non-Representational Theory and Performing Organizational Space. *Organization, 19*(1), 45–61.

Blaszczyk, R. L. (2012). *The Colour Revolution*. Cambridge (MA): MIT Press.

Brüggemann, H. (2007). *Walter Benjamin über Spiel, Farbe und Phantasie*. Würzburg: Königshausen & Neumann.

Caygill, H. (1998). *Walter Benjamin: The Colour of Experience*. London: Routledge.

Charles, M. (2019). *Modernism between Benjamin and Goethe*. London: Bloomsbury.

Connellan, K. (2013). The Psychic Life of White: Power and Space. *Organization Studies*, 34(10), 1529–1549.

Cooper, R. (1998). Interview with Robert Cooper. In R. Chia (Ed.), *Organized Worlds: Explorations in Technology and Organization with Robert Cooper* (pp. 121-165). London: Routledge.

Cubitt, S. (2014). *The Practice of Light: A Genealogy of Visual Technologies from Prints to Pixels*. Cambridge (MA): MIT Press.

Deleuze, G. (2005). *Francis Bacon: The Logic of Sensation*, transl. D. W. Smith. London: Continuum.

Fox, N. J., & Alldred, P. (2021). Applied Research, Diffractive Methodology, and the Research-Assemblage: Challenges and Opportunities. *Sociological Research Online*, https://doi.org/10.1177/13607804211029978 [accessed 1 August 2021].

Gaskill, N. (2018). *Chromographia: American Literature and the Modernization of Colour*. Minneapolis: University of Minnesota Press.

Gherardi, S. (2019). Theorizing Affective Ethnography for Organization Studies. *Organization, 26*(6), 741–760.

Gilroy, P. (2005). *Postcolonial Melancholia*. New York: Columbia University Press.

Goldstein, A. J. (2017). *Sweet Science: Romantic Materialism and the New Logics of Life*. Chicago: University of Chicago Press.

Haraway, D. (1988). Situated Knowledges: The Science Question in Feminism and the Privilege of Partial Perspective. *Feminist Studies, 14*(3), 575–599.

Helin, J., Hernes, T., Hjorth, D. & Holt, R. (2014). Process Is How Process Does. In J. Helin et al. (eds), *The Oxford Handbook of Process Philosophy and Organization Studies* (pp. 1–16). Oxford: Oxford University Press.

Holt, R., & Cornelissen, J. (2014). Sensemaking Revisited. *Management Learning*, 45(5), 525–539.

Jameson, F. (2020). *The Benjamin Files*. London: Verso.

Jay, M. (2018). Chromophilia: Der Blaue Reiter, Walter Benjamin, and the Emancipation of Color. *Positions: Asia Critique 26*(1), 13–33.

Jørgensen, L. (2019). *Moving Organizational Atmospheres.* Phd thesis, Frederiksberg: Copenhagen Business School. URL: https://research.cbs.dk/en/publications/moving-organizational-atmospheres [Accessed 23 September 2021].

Leslie, E. (2002). *Hollywood Flatlands: Animation, Critical Theory and the Avant-Garde.* London: Verso.

Lichtenstein, J. (1993). *The Eloquence of Colour: Rhetoric and Painting in the French Classical Age*, transl. E. McVarish. Berkeley: University of California Press.

Lorimer, H. (2015). Afterword: Non-representational Theory and Me Too. In P.Vannini (ed.), *Non-Representational Methodologies: Re-Envisioning Research* (pp. 177–187). London: Routledge.

Menke, C. (2013). *Force: A Fundamental Concept of Aesthetic Anthropology.* New York: Fordham University Press.

Nelson, M. (2009) *Bluets.* Seattle: Wave Books.

Pias, C. (2020). Overhead Projector. In T. Beyes, R. Holt and C. Pias (eds), *The Oxford Handbook of Media, Technology and Organization Studies* (pp. 286–300). Oxford: Oxford University Press.

Rancière, J. (2013). *Aisthesis: Scenes from the Aesthetic Regime of Art*, transl. Z. Paul. London: Verso.

Riley, C.A.II (1995). *Color Codes: Modern Theories of Color in Philosophy, Painting and Architecture, Literature, Music, and Psychology.* Hanover (US): University Press of New England.

Rossi, M. (2019). *The Republic of Color: Science, Perception, and the Making of Modern America.* Chicago: University of Chicago Press.

St. Pierre, E. A. (2018). Writing Post Qualitative Inquiry. *Qualitative Inquiry, 24*(9), 603–608.

Stewart, K. (2007). *Ordinary Affects.* Durham: Duke University Press.

Stewart, K. (2011). Atmospheric Attunements. *Environment and Planning D: Society and Space 29*(3), 445–453.

Stewart, K. (2015). New England Red. In P. Vannini (ed.), *Non-Representational Methodologies: Re-Envisioning Research* (pp. 19–33). London: Routledge.

Stewart, K. (2018). Writing, Life. *PMLA/Publications of the Modern Language Association of America 133*(1), 186–189.

Taussig, M. (2008). Redeeming Indigo. *Theory, Culture & Society 25*(3), 1–15.

Taussig, M. (2009). *What Colour is the Sacred?* Chicago: University of Chicago Press.

van Leeuwen, T. (2010). *The Language of Colour.* London: Routledge.

von Goethe, J. W. (1840). *Theory of Colours*, transl. C. L. Eastlake. London: John Murray.

von Goethe, J. W. (1998). *Maxims and Reflections*, transl. E. Stopp [e-pub]. London: Penguin.

Weber, S. (2008). *Benjamin's -abilities*. Cambridge (MA): Harvard University Press.

Weigel, S. (2015). The Flash of Knowledge and the Temporality of Images: Walter Benjamin's Image-Based Epistemology and Its Preconditions in Visual Arts and Media History. *Critical Inquiry*, 41(2), 344–366.

8

The Ethnographer as Conceptual Persona

On the Many Shopping Centres

Sideeq Mohammed

Prologue

As you get off the bus, the warm spring breeze lightly inflected with the smell of diesel hits your face. You walk past ornate flower baskets and illuminated advertisements for forthcoming events and get on an escalator that takes you into a tunnel like area with faux-marble floors and a high arch ceiling. The doors at the end seem to beckon to you.

You enter the shopping centre. The bright April sun permeates through the glass ceiling. The ornamental palm trees provide little shade. Ostentatious gold-painted plaster work adorns the walls. Roses are embossed on the decorative moulding and are frosted into the glass of the polished banisters glinting in the sun. The attractive displays tempt your eyes, and you notice the array of pastel tops that are currently in fashion. The air is cool and full of a blooming buzz. You are enticed by the smell of popcorn. You pass through a gaggle of your fellow shoppers and catch snippets of conversation about football, *The Voice* being filmed nearby, Hannah's surgery, a neighbour's new extension, or a co-worker who retired early. The mall stretches out before you in a slow curving arc, a vertical horizon which at that moment seems infinite, endless both in time and space. The precipitation of all of the conversation, music snippets, whirring machines, and the percussion of feet on the chocolate-coloured tile, is a low rumbling in B-flat.

Yet at the same time as you notice all of this, you also cannot notice it. Like many actors who find themselves enmeshed in the plays of contemporary capitalism in its various enactments under the bright lights of the shopping centre, you live at speed. A dromomaniacal agent, capable only

Sideeq Mohammed, *The Ethnographer as Conceptual Persona*. In: *Doing Process Research in Organizations, Noticing Differently*. Edited by Barbara Simpson and Line Revsbæk, Oxford University Press.
© Oxford University Press (2022). DOI: 10.1093/oso/9780192849632.003.0008

of rushing between events. You are in a hurry to pick up your dry-cleaning, purchase a present for your mother, grab lunch at the food-court, renew the prescription on your glasses, or whatever errand brought you to the shopping centre today. Despite its rich cross-sectional tapestry, a living mosaic of interconnected sociality, the shopping centre is merely the background, part of the *mise-en-scène* of the drama of your life. It is both an exorbitant panoply of sensory stimulation that requires you to be *affected* in response, and a white noise which cannot be noticed as you hurry towards some goal of whose exact nature you will never be sure.

Conceptual Personae: The People of the Shopping Centre

To whom or what does the second person 'you' in the preceding account refer?

In their final co-authored work, philosophers Gilles Deleuze and Felix Guattari (1994, 8) ask us to consider the question, 'what is philosophy?'. Through extended rumination and exegesis, they conclude that philosophy is the 'continuous creation of concepts'. Throughout the text, they describe the role and properties of the concept. Concepts are tools for thought, apparatuses by which we might apprehend the world. In trying to allude to a concept's nature and different functions, they describe it as a 'heterogenesis', 'a refrain', 'an incorporeal', 'an absolute surface', 'inseparable variations', 'a condensation', 'a centre of vibration', and 'an array of joints and bridges'. These colourful descriptions prove to be of secondary importance to what truly makes Deleuze and Guattari's concept of a concept a novel one. For them, a concept has a *history*, a series of problems to which it was connected and out of which it is developed as a response, but it also has a *becoming*, a trajectory that is formed out of its relation to different concepts, encounters, connectives, and disjunctures, within a milieu. Concepts are thus never fixed. They are always in process, always becoming, always productive, always 'doing' something, and each time that they occur, in life or in text, they take on a new meaning, forging new associations, and developing themselves anew (Deleuze and Guattari, 1994).

This manner of thinking about concepts has already been of much interest to organizational scholars (Styhre, 2002; Linstead and Thanem, 2007). The question that perhaps remains to be answered is one that considers what the conditions for the emergence of concepts are. Deleuze and Guattari (1994, 11) suggest that the concept is not given, it is created; it is to be created. It is not formed but posits itself in itself – it is a self-positing. Creation and self-positing mutually imply each other.

The notion of 'creation' here is one that eclipses and effaces the subject or author who we would ordinarily assume to be involved in the creative act. Much like Barthes and Foucault, Deleuze and Guattari suggest that the concept does not emerge *because* of an author, rather, the author is part of a milieu in which particular forms of conceptualization, and the articulation thereof, become possible. Smith (2012) explains this using the example of eponymous diseases, like Alzheimer's, which will have existed long before the scientist after which it is named was able to study and document it, isolating its qualities within the milieu and creating a concept with which to understand them. The proper name of the author is little more than a mask, an obfuscation mechanism, or placeholder that we use to gesture at the 'you' or 'I' who we typically assume is involved in the concept's creation. To suggest that a concept is capable of positing itself, that it has a 'virtual' life and exists as a potentiality which is only actualized through a particular medium, poses a profound challenge to our commonly held notions of agency, subjectivity, and our assumptions of the autonomy and insight of the researcher.

Yet, for Deleuze and Guattari (1994, 5), the concept also does not emerge independent of a creator, 'they must be invented, fabricated, or rather created and would be nothing without their creator's signature'. The ontogenetic process of a concept's emergence requires a vector. A medium. Someone or something to or through which they become available. Thus, while to say that a concept posits itself is to acknowledge that there is more to its emergence than just an author, it is also to acknowledge that for concepts to be created, to be brought into the world, they need a friend. For Deleuze and Guattari, this friend is the conceptual persona. The work of philosophy involves constantly bringing these conceptual personae to life because concepts need conceptual personae to play a part in their definition, description, and development.

Deleuze and Guattari (1994, 64) summarize this tension as follows:

The conceptual persona is not the philosopher's representative but, rather, the reverse: the philosopher is only the envelope of his principal conceptual persona and of all the other personae who are the intercessors.

The conceptual persona helps to actualize the concept. They are able to help articulate and ambulate it as the vocalization of a collective assemblage of enunciation. These persona arrive 'from elsewhere as if they had gone through a catastrophe' (Deleuze and Guattari, 1994, 5), a chaotic dispersal of the subject, or a realization of that 'harshest exercise in depersonalization' (Deleuze, 1995, 6), via which one is able to open oneself up to the multiplicities of voice present within a milieu. Throughout *What is Philosophy?* Deleuze and Guattari highlight examples of conceptual personae in the history of philosophy and develop their theorization of the function of these friends of the concept like Neitzsche's Zarathustra and Plato's Socrates, figures that emerge who are able to speak and engage in the work of producing concepts. Conceptual personae confront us with the mechanism or process of philosophy. The suggested role of the conceptual persona 'is to show thought's territories, its absolute deterritorializations and reterritorializations' (Deleuze and Guattari, 1994, 69). They are how the philosopher is able to say 'I am no longer myself but thought's aptitude for finding itself and spreading across a plane that passes through me at several places' (Deleuze and Guattari, 1994, 64) and in so doing acknowledge the plurality of personae which might inhabit or pass through them in the writing of a text. This critique of the coherency of the subject is a theme throughout Deleuze's work that extends well beyond his collaborations with Guattari (see Deleuze, 1991). For example, in *Difference and Repetition*, he comments that:

> Underneath the self which acts are little selves which contemplate and which render possible both the action and the active subject. We speak of our "self" only in virtue of these thousands of little witnesses which contemplate within us: it is always a third party who says "me".
>
> (Deleuze, 2001, 75)

A conceptual persona is also always already plural, always an aggregation of multiple vocalizations, and always subject to production and reproduction by different readers and antagonists who multiply them. Each time a text is read, and a concept is drawn out of it, it is produced anew, and different versions of the conceptual persona emerge in order to facilitate this production. To acknowledge their presence in this way is to acknowledge the 'dramaturgy' of philosophy (Lambert, 2019), and its continuous formation and interplay with different con-texts.

In a certain way, however, to think about the many conceptual personae who may dwell in a field and find their vocalization through the movements and writings of the ethnographer is nothing new. Indeed, as James Clifford (1986, 7) famously noted, ethnographic texts 'are systems, or economies, of truth. Power and history work through them, in ways their authors cannot fully control', signalling the emergence of a new tradition of ethnographic work that is interested, not only in more reflexive and circumspect practices of writing of ethnographic work (see Cunliffe, 2003), but also in exploring the new forms of theorization and conceptualization that might come from it (Da Col and Graeber, 2011). Such work deviates from the traditional Malinowskian image of the ethnographer as arbiter of truth and chronicler of reality. In this tradition, let us now try to imagine that ethnography is an exercise in practical philosophy. Many already do, and those associated with the ontological turn (Holbraad and Pedersen, 2017; Viveiros de Castro, 2014) or the move towards new empiricisms (Gane, 2009; St Pierre, Jackson, and Mazzei, 2016) and post-qualitative research (St Pierre, 2019; Gherardi, 2019), perhaps already think of fieldwork as a potential site for the emergence of new concepts, new modes of conceptualizing experience, and of course, new conceptual personae, the 'people' who become of and through the field. Organizational ethnographers are increasingly aware that, if we hope to tell meaningful stories of the field, 'we need to avoid ready-made concepts and explanations which act to short-cut explanation' (O'Doherty and Neyland, 2019, 461) and seek out modes of conceptualizing our experiences which are immanent to the mores, languages, and forms of sense of the field (see O'Doherty, 2017). Our accounts need to highlight the ways in which fieldsites 'make sense' on their own terms. As such, let us ask an obscene question again.

You enter the shopping centre. Who or what is this 'you' and who or what names it as such? Is it merely an ethnographer? Could it be a conceptual persona which brings into being the very concept of the shopping centre? Could more than one such concept emerge? Would such conceptualizations of shopping centres have anything in common (e.g. their status as key sites of the performance of 'capitalism')? Are such commonalities related to the emergence of the 'you'? Whatever we might call this 'you' is surely becoming something other as it is affected by the shopping centre, it becomes a vehicle for someone or something else, another party in the shopping centre, which may want to speak. 'A particular conceptual persona, who perhaps did not exist before us, thinks in us' (Deleuze and Guattari, 1994, 69). Concept and conceptual persona might in this case envelop each other, developing a trajectory out of their entangled histories, one which is mutually constitutive of something new, a 'you' and a 'shopping centre' emerge together. But how could we render ourselves available to this move of double articulation whereby the philosopher and conceptual persona envelop one another, mutually constituting each other in a process of double subjectivation, in order to make this a part of an account of the field? What madnesses would we have to cultivate within ourselves in order to better attend to the multiple realities of the field which are unique to our interlocutors without subsuming them all under the gaze of the ethnographer, or more accurately, how can we sufficiently dissociate ourselves from ourselves in order to render the coherency and author(ity) of the ethnographer as rational subject open to doubt.

Any gesture in this direction would involve a tracing of becomings (Deleuze and Guattari, 2005), committing oneself to remaining open and available to the forms of sense that are germane to a field, and becoming a transversal point for the emergence of the concepts and ways of knowing that these might generate. It would involve moving beyond reflexivity and its accordant attention to the embodied and affectual relations in the field, and into the uncharted territory of the self-perceptive spiral, trying to see oneself as seeing and seen by a shopping centre that is also becoming as it sees and is seen. It would involve divorcing ourselves from 'the rational' and indulging panpsychist considerations, asking what the shopping centre might desire, and whether such desiring might be intelligible or describable within language. It would involve seeing the thick-description of the Prologue, not as *an* account of *the* shopping centre, but as *the* account of *a* shopping centre, one which became available by remembering the space and becoming imbricated within the different 'conceptual entanglements' (Mohammed, 2019) that such memory work makes possible, and consequently one witnesses the blurring of the lines between subject and object, ethnographer and field, reality and fiction (cf Watson, 2011). Once we can say that many shopping centres are possible and that they come about because of different conceptual personae involved in the producing of new concepts, we can begin to let go of the habit of our proper names, of the belief in the ethnographer as subject, and try to sense the space, times, and sensory discord of the shopping centre. Staying with these becomings, we might notice that something else begins to speak.

The Disembodied

You enter the shopping centre. The warm yellow of the fluorescent lights glistens off the sign that directs you to the anchor store at the other end of the mall, as well as other sites and locations within the shopping centre like a prayer room or a food court dubbed 'The Orient'. The signs that you see mark the shopping centre out as an example of what Augé (1992) calls a non-place, serving prescriptive and descriptive functions that tell you about the space and how to comport yourself within it.

The rancorous cacophony of sights, sounds, and smells waylays you with bombast and aggressive insistence. Everything demands to be seen, heard, smelled, tasted, touched, sensed, moved, interacted with, and at the same time, there is an ineffable sense of pervasive control that seems to remind you that the many sensoria of the shopping centre exist for someone other than you, that you are not 'meant to' notice any of it. Scents of perfume, fast food, and the curious quality of filtered air passing through an air-conditioner playfully flirt with your nostrils but never overwhelm or do more than entice you; the measured, calculated, and ventilated blandness of an 'urban smellscape' (Henshaw, 2013) that seeks to avoid offence. The songs that you hear being played are part of a meticulously curated list of muzak that aims to do little more than colour the retail atmosphere, gently floating along the malls (Anderson, 2015; DeNora, 2004). Such an aesthetic might recall some 'hyperreal' (Baudrillard, 1994) image of an American shopping mall in the 1980's, one that could be said to have that unique aesthetic that has come to be synonymous with Vaporwave's derivative, 'mallsoft'. It occurs to you that a shopping centre is a hypercontrolled and mediated nexus of a highly plural concordance of disciplinary regimes. Yet at the same time the spaces of shopping centres are involved in prolonged flirtations with boundary extension and obfuscation, paradox and pastiche. In their mimicry of its affects they capitalize upon a nostalgia for the old town square and present themselves as public spaces, yet they are privately owned (Goss, 1993). Shopping centres seem to be open to all members of the public and yet their design often seeks to invite the patronage of a particular middle-class community, while outliers, like the homeless, are overtly policed out (Thanem, 2012). Your body begins to tremble with the weight of the push and pull of various paradoxical practices, or maybe this is simply a migraine brought on by the sheer plurality of sights, smells and sounds. You sit on a bench and dissociate under the benign blanket of the dull murmurs of conversation and regular-ness that make up the shopping centre's atmospherics.

You begin to feel a perverse and growing sense of paranoia, one that is enveloped by a certain systematic uncertainty around the question of where 'you' end and where the shopping centre begins. So much of the sound of the crowd, the neutral and inoffensive smells of the air, and its fast food are now within your body—the shopping centre gave you the clothes that you wear and the glasses with which you see—how could you say that it is not a part of you? Your vision blurs and the outline of people, tables, displays, statues, and the many shapes of the malls grow fuzzy and become difficult to discern. 'A body is defined only by a longitude and a latitude' (Deleuze and Guattari, 2005, 260)—by the lines of material, affect, and velocity, that crisscross and intersect on a plane.

A concept emerges: A line. 'Whether we are individuals or groups, we are made up of lines' (Deleuze and Parnet, 2007, 124). Lines constitute words, allow the notation of music, map airflow, create boundaries, and designate trajectories of people and things that move through the shopping centre. You begin to obsess over lines and their lives. 'To lead a life is to lay down a line' (Ingold, 2015, 118). A line may constitute a vector of escape, a line of flight, from a particular state of affairs as well as the gesture which cuts off such escapes (Deleuze and Guattari, 2005). The interweaving, intersection, and knotting of lines is what defines and demarcates bodies. It is lines that separate and distinguish them, lines that constitute bodies as discrete entities. Lines seem to you to be the boundaries that define an organization. The skin is such a line, but much like the walls of the shopping centre it is porous, undulating, folding, and ultimately permeable. That is to say, lines have a solidity that can only be maintained in the moment of their construction. Your body's lines blur upon examination. You notice a line of people formed outside the Apple store. It will not open for another fifteen minutes, but they have formed an orderly queue using the lines on the tile as a guide system. The lines of the tile seem to you to form an infinite grid or chessboard on which many moves of great or little importance are made, intercut occasionally by a stain or a shadow from an overarching dust-covered palm tree. The lines of the security grating form staves that flow into each other onto which your mind plots the music that the shopping centre is playing for you. Gold undulating lines are embossed upon the concrete to accentuate the distinction between the first and second floors. A line of dialogue comes over the tannoy and interrupts your thoughts:

'If you lose members of your party please meet at the customer services desk in the main dome. Thank you.'

The Insomniac

You enter the shopping centre. A dull ache in the temples and a foggy sense of confused uncertainty forms an indefinite malaise or torpor that is less akin to lethargy and more akin to vertigo. You have not slept in several days and have been struggling intermittently with insomnia for some time before that. You feel unmoored, like a ship floating in the storm, or a customer wandering through the shopping centre unsure of why they are there and where they might want to go. Over time you adjust to the fatigue and the haze. It becomes naturalized, something that you learn to live with, even as you begin to suspect that it is the shopping centre which does not want you to sleep. What few moments of sleep you manage to have are filled with dreams of walking the malls, parading in a loop that never ends. So, you begin to count. It is never clear to you why. You can only say that you are gripped by the paralyzing fear that you might be losing time. Because it disrupts the body's internal rhythms, insomnia makes the passage of time feel different and since the shopping centre has no visible clocks you are never sure what time it is. The shopping centre obsesses over your time *and* wants you to ignore it. It wants to think about wage hours, delivery slots, and deadlines, while you are taken in to a flight of fantasy wherein you lose track of yourself and indulge hedonistic plays. It wants to induce the 'Gruen effect' or the 'dreamlike state in which consumers lose track of time and place' (Csaba and Askegaard, 1999, 34). Over time you begin to obsess over patterns and routines. What time the middle-aged Asian cleaner passes in front of Selfridges with their cart. What time of day the crowds in the food court become most dense. What time the lights turn on as the sun sets. What time throngs of people exit the movie theatre. You start to see and hear patterns constantly. A metronomic click. 4/4 at 60 beats per minute. Insomnia has made of you a time machine. You elaborate this into cycles of four, 15 bars per minute, 900 per hour, and thus the simple clicking of a metronome becomes a structure, a crutch for your insomnia-addled mind to keep track of time.

In a haze, you notice a group of dancers who have congregated on the shopping centre's food-court. The usual assortment of wooden chairs and tables have been moved to the side and the area has been roped off to give the dancers room to manoeuvre. A band is playing a song and the water feature at the centre of the food-court seems to reverberate with their sound. You do not recognize the piece, but you can make out the rhythm, 3/4, a waltz. At least it sounds that way to you, echoing off the high ceiling and intermingling with the sounds of the arcade, the clatter of cutlery, people moving around, children laughing, and general conversation. You become enthralled by the movement of the dancers and their feet cresting across the brown tile of the floor.

A concept emerges: A rubato waltz. A rhythm that varies outside, in-between, and through the different times and temporalities that might be true in a shopping centre. There seems to you to be an aesthetic to the experience of time in the shopping centre. One that can scarcely be believed, because many of us are still wedded to images of time that rely on the maintenance of binary oppositions like between our lived experience of time and clock time (Legge, 2009), or because we often prefer to think of time via metaphors (Hassard, 2001), or in terms of 'classified variants and unlocated theorization' (Holt and Johnsen, 2019, 1569), but the aesthetics of time are often bluntly intuited. Alan Lightman (1993) managed to find a language to speak about it when writing *Einstein's Dreams*, exploring the ways in which time might come to feel and move differently in different spaces. Time might be sticky, and it might move slower in some places than others. In some worlds, time might be accelerated and a person's entire life might be truncated into a day and in other worlds, time exists as an abstract quality, like a kind of luminescence. 'Time is not an a priori form; rather, the refrain is the a priori form of time, which in each case fabricates different times' (Deleuze and Guattari, 2005, 349), new times are always being created, the question is simply whether you are able to sense and understand them.

A shopping centre of time presents itself to you as an agglomeration of sensation so absurd in its manifold complexity that you could never call it anything but a waltz. The aesthetics of time in the shopping centre is the Dvorak that you can swear you hear in the air. The waltz of the shopping centre dances on in the sound of footsteps clicking on the faux-marble floors. 1, 2, 3. 1, 2, 3. The simple 4/4 of the pop/dance music emanating from the stores melding into a curious crescendo that merges with the buzzing of a thousand voices. It takes the fountain made of six stone dolphins a minute and a half to cycle through its pre-programmed rotation, culminating in three perfunctory bursts that stretch into the ornate dome above. Something like 'organization' is momentarily adumbrated in the fraction of an instant between when the water shoots into the air and when it comes crashing back into the basin below (O'Doherty, 2017). A lightning flash that perhaps reflects off the coins that many people throw as they make wishes, which the shopping centre collects and donates to charities, lets you finally see the connections between a global banking sector still recovering from crisis, the precarity and instability of the mores of contemporary work, and a shopping centre at the epicentre of it all. A 'timeful simultaneity of interpenetrating pasts and futures' (Simpson, Tracey, and Weston, 2020, 83). Or at least you think you see it, you have not had a good night's sleep in a long time, and can no longer be sure of what you are seeing anymore.

The Paramnesiac

You enter the shopping centre. You are fairly certain that you are in a dream but wonder vaguely whose dream you are in, followed immediately by a questioning of whether people who are dreaming wonder about that kind of thing. There is a blurry quality to those things that you notice, as though they are far away, or occurring in some far-removed time and place. The people in the crowd seem to move dragging tails of light behind them, as though you were looking at them through astigmatic eyes at night. The rain pours onto the glass ceiling. A man carrying a newly purchased stereo on his shoulder walks by. Everything insists upon being remembered and yet it also seems to be impossible to hold on to.

A boy waving a plastic sword and wearing a dinosaur backpack runs past you. You will see him many times after this moment with your sleeping and waking eyes and indeed, you are not sure that this is the first time that you have seen him race by. He is a blur. He reaches into the fountain to try to retrieve coins with a face full of laughter. The feeling of *déjà vu* is overpowering. You feel lost in a memory, one that you are not sure is yours, one which may belong to a different past, a dream that the shopping centre has animated. Indeed, shopping centres have always been designed as a 'stimulus to intoxication and dream' (Benjamin, 1999, 216). The indiscriminate juxtaposition of signs (Baudrillard, 1998) that seems to you to characterize shopping centres makes it difficult to tell what is 'real', and what is corresponding to that peculiar dream logic where things flow together without clear rationale or reasoning, blurring into an undulating parade of remembering that becomes difficult for you to disentangle in your mind; a new form of paramnesia. For Henri Bergson, *déjà vu* or false recognition, is a memory of the present. He speaks about it as a kind of 'depersonalization', what occurs when you slip into the indulgence of that singular feeling of *déjà vu*, and become a stranger to yourself, a spectator of your own life, certain that you are remembering the present and are able to predict the future because you have lived it before, perhaps in another past-present-future. You feel like this as you see fragments of images in rapid succession: a straw passing between pursed lips, a glint of light from an empty store, a cleaning cart, a discarded receipt, a cigarette butt, a flower in the wind, a 'Caution: Wet Floor' sign—each one seems to be in your memory for the first time, while also being present to you a multitude of times before and after that.

You lock eyes with a ceramic elephant that has appeared on the malls. You are sure that you remember seeing it before, but the nuanced undulation of lines that pattern its surfaces is so unique that you are certain that you would have remembered seeing it before. You hear the quiet movement and unmistakable music of the carousel. It seems to have sprung up overnight surrounded by flyers and heraldry. There will no doubt be moments when, to you, its motion will have been revolutionary. Indeed, there will be moments when to you it seemed to be an 'I', a thing such as yourself which is bound in a simple, linear track of prehension, revolving in a world that was standing still, one whose experience, much like yours, was incommunicable within the bounds of language. Yet perhaps it was always there. Even in the moments before the land had been purchased from a shipping company, before the ground was flattened, compacted, and tiled, perhaps the carousel was in its place and standing still. All of the tumultuous and multitudinous changes made within the shopping centre, seem to you to be a torrent, one that has occurred while the carousel has been standing still. Moving in place, moving in another time, a revolving spectacle, a rotating amusement, a new metaphor for organization itself (see Morgan, 1997).

A concept emerges: a palimpsest. A memory device comprised of a thin film and a wax surface onto which anything can be written. For Freud (1961), it was the model of the unconscious mind, things written but buried from view, because if the film is lifted off of the wax everything seems to be forgotten but beneath, traces of what was written remain. You become obsessed with looking for these traces, fragments of a remembering, that might ground you to a shopping centre that is more real than the dream that you sometimes wonder if you are stuck in. A sign on a bench commemorating the life of a long dead worker. A crack in the tile. An area where the paint is better preserved than the wall around it because something was in the way. A tradition that no one can remember the origin of. An aesthetic which itself seems to call back to some impossible to remember nostalgia for a Greco-Roman grandiosity; which is to say that the bodily experience of a shopping centre is best compared to a feeling of nostalgia for a place and time that never will have been, a hauntology (Fisher, 2014). You see the spaces of the shopping centre as a palimpsest. You watch as it is written-over by the seasons. Christmas fares and decorations give way to spring fashions which are replaced by beach themes and a sand pit for children which only ever portends the crunch of the leaves underfoot in the autumn. Each time what was is erased and returned to a blank surface with the traces of what once was remaining in subtle lines of mould and spaces on the floor that are more worn by foot traffic. Yet even as things are prodigiously cleaned and restored each day, there is always *a remembering*. However, lost between a dream and the real, you are not sure precisely who is remembering and why. Yet all the while you are aware that these traces and rememberings are not what lingers from what was forgotten, but rather, what disguises that past and present, virtual and actual (Deleuze, 1997), are contemporaneous and ultimately indistinguishable.

On Noticing

In his essential book, *Postmodernism, or, the Cultural Logic of Late Capitalism*, Fredric Jameson (1991) comments on an encounter with The Westin Bonaventure Hotel. He catalogues that in its organization, the space is constructed in a way that one may easily become lost and unable to locate oneself, passing seamlessly from retail space to hotel to open plan eating with little sign or direction. In a certain reading, Jameson saw the space itself as inhospitable, affecting a psychic malaise on those who walked through it by breeding confusion and disorientation. Jameson would conclude that 'we are here in the presence of something like a mutation in built space itself. [. . .] We do not yet possess the perceptual equipment to match this new hyperspace' (Jameson, 1991, 38) or indeed, the cultural logic of capitalism which produces such a space.

Similarly, studying a shopping centre in a serious way is an experience that conjures madnesses of many kinds. The space is so plural, paradoxical, blustering, elegant, gaudy, garish, subtle, refined, sacred, and profane, as to be unknowable. We do not yet possess the intellectual and perceptual tools that would be necessary in order for us to study it effectively. One can only speculate that this has nothing to do with the shopping centre's design and purpose at all, but rather it is simply where the schizophrenic processes of capitalism, which Deleuze and Guattari (2000) describe, present themselves most saliently to be apprehended by human sensoria. If capitalism is the 'terrifying nightmare' that they depict, haunting all previous forms of social formation because it liberates flows of desire, then of course it is impossible for us to understand or fully apprehend it as it appears to us in the shopping centre. Something will always escape and go by unnoticed; these hyperspaces are simply too much to conceptualize.

But there is more at stake than this. Any serious analysis of the shopping centre must necessarily become an analysis of the psychic affects that it produces. Hedonistic flights, dissociation, melancholia, anxiety, paranoia, insomnia, paramnesia, ambiguous nostalgia, and a disaffected torpor that by its very nature is difficult to accurately describe, cannot be understood as individual pathologies but rather, in the tradition of the anti-psychiatry movement, must be understood as the responses of a collective unconscious to the space itself, and perhaps by extension, to the mores of capitalism which it both reflects and reproduces (Fisher, 2009). More recent analyses of the affects of capitalism highlight the acute feeling of helplessness that it engenders, juxtaposed against the boundless optimism and promise of freedom that it has always offered, and suggest simply that 'it might be best to abandon the concept entirely' (Latour, 2014). In this regard, we ask whether such broad and general concepts as 'capitalism', which take on an almost transcendental quality, can be relevant to us in understanding something like a shopping centre. On the one hand, a turn towards immanent analyses that highlight the production of concepts within a field is cause for celebration among organizational ethnographers who are increasingly involved in this kind of work (see O'Doherty and Neyland, 2019), and yet on the other hand in order to do this kind of work in the shopping centre, we must continuously labour to *not notice* the schizophrenizing processes of capitalism, endlessly deterritorializing, endlessly axiomatizing, and always taking place in every transaction, every interaction, and every process which informs the shopping centre's everyday lives. This tension is difficult to resolve because 'the ethnographer' can be conceived in the same manner.

The acute ecstasies and disaffection of life in the shopping centre produces conceptual personae, its spaces becoming home to these other people, the concept's friends, who enable new forms of thought and thinking to emerge. Whether these are *capitalized* subjects or not is irrelevant, as the double-tension remains the same. A 'you' inhabiting the space will, over the course of a year, become cognizant of the existence of many others and their becomings. At the same time, these must be denied as the ethnographer is called upon to represent themselves as a coherent, self-aware, and reflexive subject. Indeed, increasingly there are calls for ethnography to produce replicable or generalizable findings (see Lubet, 2018) as though this were ever possible without an elaborate performance that denies the plurality and multiplicity of others who will always have spoken to and through the ethnographer. In acknowledging that ethnography could only continue to meaningfully develop in a post-positivistic, post-qualitative academy, we would have to reckon with the heterotopias which the rational figure of 'the ethnographer' obfuscates and recognize that the ethnographer is being constituted by us as readers in the parsing of an ethnographic text. We would also have to reflect collectively on what powers and potencies we imbue this literary figure who wanders the shopping centre, the airport, the offices of Wall Street, the operating theatres of doctors at war, and so on, and thus come to terms with what voices and forms of sense we are excluding as this persona performs. Indeed, the ethnographer was always a conceptual persona. One who learns, who studies, who makes fieldnotes, who tries to be reflexive, who tries to adhere to the standards of research ethics, who writes up findings to report to the academy with an awareness of the colonial histories of their tradition, and so on. Such a persona is always only involved in the production of certain kinds of fields. In this way it is an intellectual distancing device, an intentional blindness, a turning away, used to fend off the sensorial excesses of the shopping centre. What other conceptual personae become *unavailable* because of the ethnographer and its fabulation? What other shopping centres might exist without the ethnographer or if one were able to do ethnography in a way which acknowledged the production of conceptual personae and their mutual envelopment in and by the field?

It only makes sense to us to say that paranoia and dissociation, insomnia, and *déjà vu* and paramnesia, were *produced* by the shopping centre in the ethnographer. In this way, the ethnographic subject became undone and unmade by the shopping centre and as someone or something else began to speak of its collective dreamings, new personae emerged. They were affected by their experiences and enjoined to become other by the tumults and vicissitudes of the spaces and times of the shopping centre, a process that involves a fracturing out, a splintering, a proliferation of subjects *qua* conceptual personae, each one with its own way of noticing.

Each one producing new concepts by which it can make sense of the shopping centre. Consequently, each one produces a new shopping centre. A shopping centre of lines and their intersection. A shopping centre of abstract rhythms and a unique temporal aesthetic. A shopping centre that flirts with the boundaries between dream and reality, prompting memories of the present. Each one of these shopping centres is unique. They become differentially available. No return to one of these shopping centres would ever have been possible because the conceptualized 'you' *qua* ethnographer and the concept of the shopping centre that it produced will always have been becoming other through their mutual envelopment. Again, there is a double-move here that this chapter has sought to illustrate: the 'you' becomes a vehicle for the actualization of different personae which are at work in the field and is thus a part of the novel production of concepts. At the same time, the different shopping centres which become available through these concepts produce different conceptual personae in order to apprehend them. It is by this ouroboric set of relations that the concept is able to posit itself, that the shopping centre is empowered to auto-conceptualization and we might be able to sketch an answer to a question at the limits of our current analytical capacities: 'How does a shopping centre think and what are the concepts it uses in order to do so?' We should always be seeking the limits of thought, for it is there that we might be able to say something new or meaningful about the organizations that we seek to study; a shopping centre pushes us always towards such a limit, where other shopping centres become available to be thought and 'organization' itself becomes possible to conceptualize in the tracing of boundaries (see Burrell and Parker, 2016).

How do we begin to notice all of these shopping centres and open up to the conceptual personae that help us to conceptualize them? Increasingly, voices across the academy are arguing that our methods need to actually reflect the theorists upon whom we seek to draw (St Pierre, 2021; Jackson and Mazzei, 2012), but here we can offer no methodological prescriptions. Following Deleuze and Guattari (2005), we maintained a commitment towards *experimentation,* but there was no technique, no principles, and no rules that governed this. Instead, we simply tried to remain open to the shopping centre's dynamics, to what conceptual personae were living there and experimented with different concepts that seem to us to be resonant or useful to understand what we felt that they wanted to say. Doing this, inviting a kind of possession, was a risk, one that might just as well have taken us to a point where we can say confidently that 'we are no longer ourselves [...] we have been aided, inspired, multiplied' (Deleuze and Guattari, 2005, 3), as it might have plunged us into a black hole of madness and instability. Yet it felt at times as if madness was what the paradoxicality of the shopping centre demanded, what it desired, almost as though it wanted to realize the dreams of 'a time of day, of a region, a climate, a river or a wind, of an event' and all of those things other than the human which might be individuated (Deleuze, 1995, 26) and so try to speak. In this context, to hold on to the image of *a* singular ethnographer is thus to deny the experiences and associations of the field, writing over our anxieties about our own authority and academic responsibility, and consequently denying the different shopping centres that became available.

The disembodied, the insomniac, and the paramnesiac are all bound to the shopping centres that they produce and are produced by. Their existence and ways of noticing are wholly immanent to the shopping centre and cannot be transferred or applied elsewhere. Where ordinarily we would assume that 'the ethnographer' moves transcendentally between the spaces and times of the shopping centre, carrying with them their subjectivities and ways of knowing, here we can see them being replaced by these conceptual personae. It is in the treacherous slippages between immanence and transcendence that shopping centres emerge, replete with distant murmurs of conversation, children crying, miscellany being dropped, crumpling paper bags, phones ringing, and the tell-tale squeak of the soles of rubber shoes on the tile. Yet these are all images that are a part of *a* shopping centre, one that is involved in the becoming of a particular conceptual persona and the emergence of particular concepts. What other personae and what other concepts might emerge in other times and other places, finding their voices through other vectors? Much more importantly, what other shopping centres might there be? It is perhaps only the transmutation of the ethnographer into some other persona, which we have tried to trace in this paper, that can lead to their conceptualization. Whatever the answer, you must enter a shopping centre in order to find out.

References

Anderson, Paul Allen. (2015). Neo-Muzak and the Business of Mood. *Critical Inquiry*, 41 (4): 811–840. https://doi.org/10.1086/681787.

Augé, Marc. (1992). *Non-Places: Introduction to an Anthropology of Supermodernity*. London: Verso.

Baudrillard, Jean. (1994). *Simulacra and Simulation*. Ann Arbor: The University of Michigan Press.

Baudrillard, Jean. (1998). *The Consumer Society: Myths and Structures*. London: SAGE Publications.

Benjamin, Walter. (1999). *The Arcades Project*. London: Harvard University Press.

Burrell, Gibson, and Martin Parker, eds. (2016). *For Robert Cooper*. Abingdon: Routledge.

Clifford, James. (1986). Introduction: Partial Truths. In James Cliffordand George Marcus(eds), *Writing Culture: The Poetics and Politics of Ethnography*, 1–26. London: University of California Press.

Csaba, Fabian, and Søren Askegaard. (1999). Malls and the Orchestration of the Shopping Experience in a Historical Perspective. *Advances in Consumer Research*, 26 (1): 34–40.

Cunliffe, Ann L. (2003). Reflexive Inquiry in Organizational Research: Questions and Possibilities. *Human Relations*, 56 (8): 983–1003. https://doi.org/10.1177/00187267030568004.

Da Col, Giovanni, and David Graeber. (2011). Foreword: The Return of Ethnographic Theory. *HAU: Journal of Ethnographic Theory*, 1 (1): vi–xxxv. https://doi.org/10.14318/hau1.1.001.

Deleuze, Gilles. (1991). A Philosophical Concept... In Eduardo Cadava, Peter Connor, and Jean-Luc Nancy(eds), *Who Comes After The Subject?*, 94–95. London: Routledge.

Deleuze, Gilles. (1995). *Negotiations*. New York: Columbia University Press.

Deleuze, Gilles. (1997). *Cinema II: The Time-Image*. Minneapolis: University of Minnesota Press.

Deleuze, Gilles, and Félix Guattari. (2000). *Anti-Oedipus: Capitalism and Schizophrenia*. Minneapolis: University of Minnesota Press.

Deleuze, Gilles. (2001). *Difference and Repetition*. London: Continuum.

Deleuze, Gilles, and Félix Guattari. (2005). *A Thousand Plateaus: Capitalism and Schizophrenia*. London: University of Minnesota Press.

Deleuze, Gilles, and Félix Guattari. (1994). *What Is Philosophy?* London: Verso.

Deleuze, Gilles, and Claire Parnet. (2007). *Dialogues II*. New York: Columbia University Press.

DeNora, Tia. (2004). *Music in Everyday Life*. Cambridge: Cambridge University Press.

Fisher, Mark. (2009). *Capitalist Realism: Is There No Alternative?* Alresford: Zero Books.

Fisher, Mark. (2014). *Ghosts of My Life: Writings on Depression, Hauntology and Lost Futures*. Alresford: Zero Books.

Freud, Sigmund. (1961). A Note upon the 'Mystic Writing-Pad'. In *The Standard Edition of the Complete Psychological Works of Sigmund Freud*, 227–232. London: The Hogarth Press.

Gane, Nicholas. (2009). Concepts and the 'New' Empiricism. *European Journal of Social Theory*, 12 (1): 83‒97. https://doi.org/10.1177/1368431008099645.

Gherardi, Silvia. (2019). Theorizing Affective Ethnography for Organization Studies. *Organization*, 26 (6): 741–760. https://doi.org/10.1177/1350508418805285.

Goss, Jon. (1993). The 'Magic of the Mall': An Analysis of Form, Function, and Meaning in the Contemporary Retail Built Environment. *Annals of The Association of American Geographers*, 83 (1): 18–47. https://doi.org/10.2307/2569414.

Hassard, John. (2001). Commodification, Construction and Compression: A Review of Time Metaphors in Organizational Analysis. *International Journal of Management Reviews*, 3 (2): 131. https://doi.org/10.1111/1468-2370.00059.

Henshaw, Victoria. (2013). *Urban Smellscapes: Understanding and Designing City Smell Environments*. https://doi.org/10.4324/9780203072776.

Holbraad, Martin, and Morten Axel Pedersen. (2017). *The Ontological Turn: An Anthropological Exposition*. Cambridge: Cambridge University Press.

Holt, Robin, and Rasmus Johnsen. (2019). Time and Organization Studies. *Organization Studies*, 40 (10): 1557–1572. https://doi.org/10.1177/0170840619844292.

Ingold, Tim. (2015). *The Life of Lines*. London and New York: Routledge.

Jackson, Alecia Y., and Lisa Mazzei. (2012). *Thinking with Theory in Qualitative Research: Viewing Data across Multiple Perspectives*. Oxon: Routledge.

Jameson, Fredric. (1991). *Postmodernism, or, the Cultural Logic of Late Capitalism*. London: Verso.

Lambert, Gregg. (2019). Who Are Deleuze's Conceptual Personae? In Dorothea Olkowskiand Eftichis Pirovolakis (eds), *Deleuze and Guattari's Philosophy of Freedom: Freedom's Refrains*, 68–78. London: Routledge.

Latour, Bruno. (2014). On Some of the Affects of Capitalism. *Royal Academy, Copenhagen*, 1–13.

Legge, Karen. (2009). Time. In Philip Hancockand Andre Spicer (eds), *Understanding Corporate Life*, 79–95. London: Sage.

Lightman, Alan. (1993). *Einstein's Dreams*. London: Corsair.

Linstead, Stephen, and Torkild Thanem. (2007). Multiplicity, Virtuality and Organization: The Contribution of Gilles Deleuze. *Organization Studies*, 28 (10): 1483–1501. https://doi.org/10.1177/0170840607075675.

Lubet, Steven. (2018). *Interrogating Ethnography: Why Evidence Matters*. New York: Oxford University Press.

Mohammed, Sideeq. (2019). Unthinking Images of Time in Organizations: 'The Shopping Centre Keeps Time with a Rubato Waltz'. *Organization*, 26 (2): 199–216. https://doi.org/10.1177/1350508418808241.

Morgan, Gareth. (1997). *Images of Organization*. London: Sage.

O'Doherty, Damian. (2017). *Reconstructing Organization: The Loungification of Society*. London: Palgrave.

O'Doherty, Damian, and Daniel Neyland. (2019). The Developments in Ethnographic Studies of Organising: Towards Objects of Ignorance and Objects of Concern. *Organization*, 26(4), 449–469. https://doi.org/10.1177/1350508419836965.

Pierre, Elizabeth Adams St. (2019). Post Qualitative Inquiry in an Ontology of Immanence. *Qualitative Inquiry*, 25 (1): 3–16. https://doi.org/10.1177/1077800418772634.

Pierre, Elizabeth Adams St. (2021). Post Qualitative Inquiry, the Refusal of Method, and the Risk of the New. *Qualitative Inquiry*, 27 (1): 3–9. https://doi.org/10.1177/1077800419863005.

Pierre, Elizabeth Adams St, Alecia Y. Jackson, and Lisa A. Mazzei. (2016). New Empiricisms and New Materialisms: Conditions for New Inquiry. *Cultural Studies – Critical Methodologies*, 16 (2): 99–110. https://doi.org/10.1177/1532708616638694.

Simpson, Barbara, Rory Tracey, and Alia Weston. (2020). The Timefulness of Creativity in an Accelerating World. In Juliane Reinecke, Roy Suddaby, Ann Langley, and Haridimos Tsoukas(eds), *Time, Temporality, and History in Process Organization Studies*, 69–88. Oxford: Oxford University Press.

Smith, Daniel W.(2012). *Essays on Deleuze*. Edinburgh: Edinburgh University Press.

Styhre, Alexander. (2002). Thinking with AND: Management Concepts and Multiplicities. *Organization*, 9 (3), 459–475. https://doi.org/10.1177/135050840293012.

Thanem, Torkild. (2012). All Talk and No Movement? Homeless Coping and Resistance to Urban Planning. *Organization*, 19, 441–460. https://doi.org/10.1177/1350508411414228.

Viveiros de Castro, Eduardo. (2014). *Cannibal Metaphysics: For a Post-Structural Anthropology*. Minneapolis: Univocal.

Watson, Tony J.(2011). Ethnography, Reality, and Truth: The Vital Need for Studies of 'How Things Work' in Organizations and Management. *Journal of Management Studies*, 48 (1): 202–217. https://doi.org/10.1111/j.1467-6486.2010.00979.x.

9

Eight Ways to Notice Mindfully in Process Organization Studies[1]

Boris H. J. M. Brummans

Cultivating awareness of the impermanent, interdependent nature of phenomena, Buddhist philosophy suggests, makes you mindful of the tendency to sense and make sense of what's going on by clinging to a fixed idea of self in relation to others. By viewing themselves and others as independent selves or territories that need to be maintained, defended, and expanded, individual people as well as larger social collectives such as organizations try to impose conceptual distinctions on a world that's always changing and in which nothing is permanent because it's composed of countless interdependencies. Buddhism claims that this individual and collective 'self/ego-clinging' leads to suffering by creating negative emotions like anger, sadness, or jealousy. The drawing of distinctions is thus believed to be the cause of human suffering, since it cuts you off from the constant flux of *dependent origination* (Gyatso, 2015) within which the world's becoming unfolds. Practising Buddhist mindfulness entails cultivating awareness of this ego-clinging, not only in meditation but throughout everyday life; and not only on an individual level but also on collective (organizational, societal) ones. It in turn helps people and collectives become skilled at discerning what thoughts, concepts, ideas, feelings, and actions advance suffering and which ones advance happiness, which allows them to enact life with wisdom and compassion (see Brummans, 2012, 2014, 2017; Brummans, Hwang, & Cheong, 2013, 2020; see also Purser & Milillo, 2015; Weick & Putnam, 2006).

[1] Kind thanks to Natalie Doonan, Ana Ramos, and Camille Vézy for conversations that always inspire new ways of noticing, to Barbara Simpson and Line Revsbæk for valuable editorial comments and suggestions, and last but not least, to Connie Hwang and Julio Martínez for creating the b e a u t i f u l images. This chapter is dedicated to my dear Dharma friend and mentor, Henry Vyner.

Boris H. J. M. Brummans, *Eight Ways to Notice Mindfully in Process Organization Studies* In: *Doing Process Research in Organizations, Noticing Differently.* Edited by Barbara Simpson and Line Revsbæk, Oxford University Press.
© Oxford University Press (2022). DOI: 10.1093/oso/9780192849632.003.0009

There are intriguing parallels between Buddhism and process philosophy (see Faber, 2020; Fan, 2022). Like Buddhism, process philosophy invites new ways of sensing, experiencing life's openness. The writings of William James and Alfred N. Whitehead, as well as of contemporary process philosophers who draw from James and Whitehead, such as Erin Manning, Brian Massumi, and Ana Ramos, reveal how life teems with vitality and creativity, and how what has come before informs the actualization of life's infinite potentialities. It's important, these philosophers note, similar to Buddhist philosophers, to be attuned to the way a particular micro-moment makes a 'qualitative difference' (Massumi, 2011, 92) that is 'felt' (p. 3); and to how series of micro-moments that make felt-differences constitute the singular *events* (Massumi, 2011; Ramos, 2019, 2020) through which people and social collectives are formed and transformed in/as fields of relation (Massumi, 2015, 200; see Brummans & Vézy, 2022; see also Cooper, 2005). From this process philosophy perspective, it becomes more insightful to trace these fields of relation in their ongoing formation as well as transformation (their dependent origination, as Buddhists would say), rather than to analyse inter-actions *between* already-formed, already-constituted entities, be they human or other-than-human, individual or collective (see Brummans & Vézy, 2022). Thus, similar to Buddhism, process philosophy aims to cultivate awareness of the eventful nature of experience; how events are made of felt micro-moments—'actual occasions' in Whitehead's (1978) vocabulary (see also Ramos, 2019). This view doesn't imply that individual or collective entities cease to exist. It rather implies that entities don't exist outside events (see also Cobb, 2007; Hussenot & Missonier, 2016); they're *immanent to* them (Massumi, 2011; Ramos, 2019).

This chapter aims to highlight how the parallels between Buddhism and process philosophy may inform process organization studies. Drawing on these parallels, it shows, through the interplay of textual form and content, eight mutually-supporting ways process organization scholars may cultivate mindfulness of the eventful, non-dual nature of phenomena in their work, so they can hone their ability to notice mindfully. The accompanying commentaries, in turn, provide explanation and show how each way plays out in the practice of research. Hence, these ways offer fleeting insights and small—grassroots, or maybe bamboo shoots—actions that enable you to *become-with* the processes of organizational becoming (Chia, 1995) you're intending to study and understand. By acting as Buddhist 'pith instructions' (e.g., see Khyentse, 2015), their aim is to demonstrate different manners of attuning to the multiple and singular (Manning, 2013), actual and potential (Massumi, 2011), as well as latent and manifest (Cooper, 2005) in process organization research.

TO
DROP

your-self

as principal tool
of organizational inquiry

1

The idea that the researcher is the 'primary [human] data-gathering instrument' (Lincoln & Guba, 1985, 39) has become a tenet of qualitative inquiry. In process organization studies, it's more useful to view yourself as a *vector* that affects and is affected by the unfolding organizational field of relation you're trying to study (see Brummans & Vézy, 2022). Extending Karl Weick's (1996) 'drop your tools' allegory, process organizational research asks that you drop yourself—that is, *your self*—as primary data-gathering instrument. Being mindful of the events through which social collectives are brought forth, rather than subject–object relations, creates a basis for acting wisely—'fully in contact with the realties and needs of the situation and unencumbered by the strategies of the self-centered ego or by preconceptions or methods', as Eleanor Rosch (2008, 153) put it, echoing Karl Weick and Ted Putnam's idea of Eastern wisdom (see Weick & Putnam, 2006). The importance of dropping your-self—or *letting your-self be dropped*—in organizational research became clear to me when the Buddhist monastery in the Indian Himalayas where I was conducting ethnographic fieldwork was struck by a mudslide. As I wrote afterwards, '[t]he unexpected chain of events enveloped both the people I was studying and me, creating a field that was new to all of us' (Brummans, 2012, 444). This field allowed me to gain insights into the monks' ways of life that I wouldn't have gained if I had clung on to my-self as principal tool of organizational inquiry (see also Brummans, 2014). These insights, that is, were yielded *by the unfolding field of relation*, not by me as an independent entity or agent.

TO VIEW

an organizational field of relation

AS MANY PATHS

that lay themselves down
in walking

2

In the 1980s, Francisco Varela began questioning traditional opposites in biology, such as objectivism vs. subjectivism, mind vs. body, or perception vs. action. As an alternative, he suggested a Buddhist-inspired middle-way view, according to which 'knowledge and its world are as inseparable as the inseparability between perception and action' (Varela, 1987, 62). 'In this middle-way view', Varela noted, 'what we do is what we know, and ours is but one of many possible worlds. It is not a mirroring of the world, but a *laying down* of a world, with no warfare between self and other' (p. 62, emphasis in original). This view became the basis for Varela, Thompson, and Rosch's (1991) book, *The Embodied Mind*, which showed how cognitive science and Buddhism together can provide insight into human experience (around this time, Varela and the fourteenth Dalai Lama, Tenzin Gyatso, co-founded the Mind & Life Institute for promoting dialogue between science and Buddhism). Interestingly, this book introduced the idea of *enaction* (how perception contributes to the world's enactment), paralleling Weick's (1979) notion of *organizational enactment*. In line with these ideas, and in line with commentary 1, I've come to see an organizational field of relation as many paths that lay themselves down in the process of fieldwork, deskwork, and textwork (Yanow, 2000). Nowadays, the organizational 'secrets' I'm trying to understand are 'not as important as the paths that [lead] me to [them]' (Borges, 1998, 335); the secrets *are* paths—and the paths the secrets. Hence, what I've learned in the course of my research on Buddhist organizations in India as well as Taiwan is that process organization research requires you 'to work with whatever happens in the field and to let things happen instead of trying to force or impose predetermined meanings on situations' (Brummans, 2014, 442). In this case, '[p]racticing mindfulness requires being open to the eventfulness of situations because everyday life's changing, interdependent nature prevents predetermination' (p. 442).

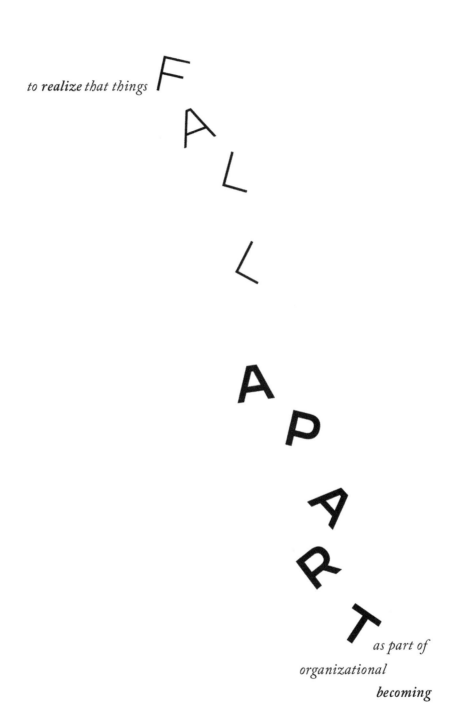

to realize that things F A L L A P A R T *as part of organizational becoming*

3

In *When Things Fall Apart*, Pema Chödrön (2000) reflects on the importance of moving *toward* suffering, rather than away from it, and '[relaxing into] the essential groundlessness of our [entire] situation' (p. ix). Attuning to suffering may seem counter-intuitive, but it's the only way to rid yourself of it, according to Buddhists. Suffering, Buddhists believe, is caused by sentient beings' thirst or craving for objects of sense desire, existence, and non-existence (see Gethin, 1998, 59). This thirst is what keeps sentient beings locked into the karmic cycles of birth, death, and rebirth (*samsara*), because 'in a world where everything is always changing, in a world of shifting and unstable conditions, craving of whatever kind will never be able to hold on to the things it craves' (Gethin, 1998, 70). Thus, attuning to suffering, becoming aware of it and of its cause, are the first steps toward freeing yourself from it. Life helps you all the time in this regard, for things do fall apart constantly. So you rarely get what you want—and if you do, you find it's not what you wanted in the first place, or it's gone before you know it. 'Life is a good teacher and a good friend', Chödrön (2000) writes. 'Things are always in transition, if we could only realize it' (p. 10). Because understanding the transitory nature of organizations is one of the main goals in process organization research, it's important to examine how micro-moments come into being and 'fall apart', one moment becoming actualized through *prehending* (Whitehead, 1978) the previous one and tending toward a new moment, again full of potential (see Massumi, 2011). For example, such an 'events-based approach' (Hussenot & Missonier, 2016) can illuminate the ways organizing and *dis*organizing go hand-in-hand in organizational becoming (see Vásquez & Kuhn, 2019; see also Brummans & Vézy, 2022). However, in line with Chödrön's writings, my work with Buddhist monks and nuns in India, as well as with volunteers from a Buddhist NGO in Taiwan, has shown me that it's also important to examine how ignoring the creative, momentary becoming of life and clinging to permanence causes individual, organizational, and social suffering (see Brummans, 2014). Hence, there's ample opportunity for process organization research to deepen insight into how forms of attachment affect and are affected by the becoming of organizations (see also Purser & Milillo, 2015; Weick & Putnam, 2006).

FORM = EMPTINESS = (ORGANIZATIONAL) FORM =

to contemplate:

4

'Form is emptiness, emptiness is form' reads the Heart Sutra (Gyatso, 2002/2015, 114), a canon in Mahāyāna Buddhism. Countless Buddhists have contemplated these words and the *sutra* in which they appear. Its meanings become increasingly elusive the more you meditate on them, and perhaps that's their aim: to halt your incessant sensemaking and your clinging to sense. If the forms with which you engage and identify in everyday life, including your body and material possessions, emerge and subside due to dependent origination, nothing exists independently, intrinsically— which doesn't mean that nothing exists (see Gyatso, 2002/2015, 117). So clinging to these 'empty' forms is detrimental, according to the Heart Sutra and the Buddhist *dharma* more generally, for it only leads to suffering (see commentary 3). However, trying to cling to the emptiness from which these forms emerge and into which they subside is just as detrimental, because it leads to yet another 'extremist' view and corresponding rigidified actions. As Thupten Jinpa explains in the documentary, *Journey of the Heart* (Verma, 2013), '[I]t's like . . . using emptiness as a medicine to cure our grasping at form, but then using *another* medicine to cure the potential of grasping at emptiness itself, so that the medicine does not turn into a poison.' 'And so that's why there's this constant. . .kind of play', Jinpa notes, 'between form and emptiness, and emptiness and form.' Although drawing on different sources, Robert Cooper (2005) shows how important it is to contemplate words like these when thinking about and investigating social collectives from a processual, relational perspective. Forms such as organizations and their human as well as other-than-human constituents, Cooper suggests, manifest from the formless 'ground' of *latency*. Yet latency itself can only manifest in forms—*re-late* through the expression of forms. Thus, the interplay between the manifest and latent is like the play between form and emptiness, or between the actual and potential in Whitehead's process philosophy (see Massumi, 2011, 1–2). Latency (or emptiness, potentiality), Cooper (2005) states, 'presents itself always as a missing power that is concealed by what re-presents it. And yet its missingness is immanent in all human expression as an invisible wholeness which. . . can never be fully conceived' (p. 1697). These insights are valuable for process organization studies, for they remind you to be aware of traps of clinging to any extremities, including the very notion of 'process' itself.

to be undiscouraged
by moments of

S

I

L

E

N

C

E

in organizational research

5

Silence is a fundamental aspect of most Eastern contemplative traditions. For instance, the Indian Buddhist master Tilopa is said to have stated that 'muteness is the ineffability of experience' (see Guenther, 1963/1999, 10 41). For many Buddhists, silence thus becomes a way into the ineffability of experience, into the non-conceptual ('empty') ground of dependent origination that's the source of all forms of life (see commentary 4; see also Wallace, 2011). They therefore often prefer to meditate on insights or experiences, rather than to speak about them, assuming that verbalization, conceptualization, and intellectualization will promote ego-clinging. In organization studies, silence has typically been viewed as 'exclusionary, oppressive, needing to be overcome, and as a strategy to resist oppression' (Bigo, 2018, 121), not as a generative force. Silence is key to understanding processes of organizational becoming, though, as Vinca Bigo (2018) points out: 'Silences forge an emptiness, and so a space for the possible emergence of something new, beyond existing beliefs, norms and practices. Certain silences facilitate creativity, including creativity of an ethical sort' (p. 121). Based on the research I've conducted on Buddhist organizations, the experience of teaching in Japan, and the ongoing personal practice of Buddhism, I've come to see silence in ways that parallel Bigo's views, as well as Cooper's (2005) views on latency (see commentary 4). Silence is not merely the 'absence of sound or noise' (Merriam-Webster), but that without which sound isn't possible, that which creates the *potential for* sound, as well as contemplation, introspection, creativity, becoming (see Brummans, 2012). Like the young Portuguese Jesuit priest in Shūsaku Endō's (1969/2015) novel, I've come to believe that silence isn't something to be discouraged by or feared; it's a vital force that needs to be attuned to, tuned into, and investigated, both in organizational research and in life as such.

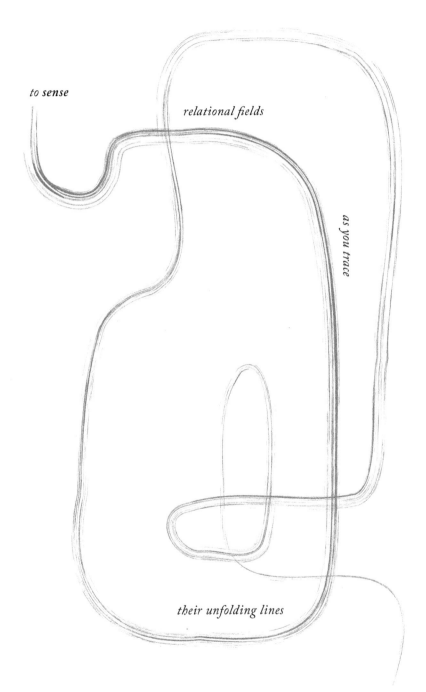

to sense

relational fields

as you trace

their unfolding lines

of becoming

6

More than twenty-five years ago, Robert Chia (1995) introduced the ontology of becoming to organization studies by drawing on postmodern thought as well as Eastern contemplative traditions, including Zen Buddhism, thus laying the foundation for what is now known as process organization studies. As described in the previous commentaries, conducting process organization research in mindful ways asks you to '[fold] into, or with, the concrete situations that bring forth [organizational becoming]' (Brummans, 2014, 444). One technique for becoming-with organizational becoming, attuning to it, and being mindful of your participation in it is mapping or tracing how the linguistic and extralinguistic expression of events makes felt qualitative differences in the formation and transformation of an organizational field of relation (see also the introduction to this chapter). This technique is inspired by Fernand Deligny's beautiful mappings of the movements of autistic persons living in a social collective in the Cévennes mountains in southern France (for illustrations, see Deligny, 2015, 230–249). Drawing 'wander lines' (Deligny, 2015, 54) enables you to trace *affective movements* (Harris & Holman Jones, 2021). These lines may be varied in shape, color, and thickness, as in Deligny mappings, to signify variations in speed, intensity, and so on across space and time. *In the creative act of drawing*, this technique creates vectors of becoming that show how a social collective unfolds dynamically as a relational field. They show how the collective's becoming—as well as the becoming of its human and other-than-human constituents—are immanent to the unfolding events, which come into being through the extra/linguistic expression of moment-to-moment felt qualitative differences. This technique is useful, for example, for tracing the dis/organizing effects of series of events that are brought into being by specific moments, such as the moments giving rise to the foundation of the monastic total institution in India where I conducted fieldwork, or the moments giving rise to a boy's escape from a youth detention center in France, as can be seen in the famous ending of François Truffaut's 1959 French New Wave film, Les Quatre Cents Coups— the film depicts the semiautobiographical story of Antoine Doinel, a boy who, neglected by family and school, ends up on the streets of Paris and subsequently in a youth detention center, from which he tries to escape (for more details on this technique and these empirical illustrations, see Brummans & Vézy, 2022).

to compose–with organizational fields of relation by feeling–with the moments GIVING **RISE** TO THEM

7

Clifford Geertz (1973) is well-known for proposing *thick description* as an ethnographic technique in anthropology. As an extension of Geertz's original idea, *thick co composition* is a second technique for becoming with organizational becoming that complements the mapping or tracing technique described in commentary 6. Thick co-composition is inspired by Erin Manning's (2013) concept of *composing-with*, which she describes as follows: 'To compose-with is to place language within an ecology of practices. It is to think-with in the time of the utterance's becoming-expression. To compose-with is to collectively write time in the shaping' (p. 16). Following this line of thought, thick co-composition is a technique that enables you, *in the creative act of writing*, to sense the unfolding organizational field of relation you're investigating by *feeling-with* the micro-moments that give rise to it. For example, together with the tracing technique, this technique enables you to gain deeper, multidimensional, multisensorial, and multimodal insight into the dis/organizing effects of series of events that are brought into being by the moments giving rise to the foundation of the Buddhist monastery in the Indian Himalayas, or the moments giving rise to the boy's escape from a youth detention in France (see commentary 6; for more details on this second technique, see Brummans & Vézy, 2022). Both these techniques bring to light how important it is for process organization researchers to be reflexive of the ways fieldwork plays into the processes of becoming they're investigating. They acknowledge that you (the researcher) are an integral (*feeling* and *felt*) constituent of the relational field-in-formation, not a mere (participant) observer *of* it; someone who affects its enactment and is at the same time affected by it (see Ramos, 2020). These techniques therefore attune you—and potentially those with whom you're co-composing this relational field—to the complex ethical aspects of fieldwork, deskwork, and textwork (Yanow, 2000), well beyond traditional questions of consent, confidentiality, and so on.

to NOTICE *more*

in processes of organizational becoming

the less your mind is FULL

8

'Our "original mind" includes everything within itself', Zen master Shun-ryū Suzuki's (1970/2020) explains.

> It is always rich and sufficient within itself . . . This does not mean a closed mind, but actually an empty mind and a ready mind. If your mind is empty, it is always ready for anything; it is open to everything. In the beginner's mind there are many possibilities; in the expert's mind there are few. (p. 2)

The idea of *beginner's mind* suggests that 'people do not need to acquire more information, more logic, more ego, and more skills to make them wise', Eleanor Rosch (2008, 136) notes. 'What they need is to unlearn what they have accumulated that veils them from that wisdom. When they do this, it is believed, they find not only what they themselves really are already but what the world actually is, and, from that vantage point, they can live a good life.' There's no need to become a Buddhist practitioner to notice mindfully in process organization research. The trick is *not* to do what seems 'natural', which is clinging to forms of various kind (especially your-self, but also other-selves). Paradoxical as this may sound, practicing mind*fulness* entails cultivating mind*emptiness*: re-calling, re-attuning to the non-conceptual, non-dual ('original', 'natural') mind that's the ground of your existence (see Vyner, 2019), just like the empty ground of dependent origination that's the source of all forms of life (see commentaries 4 and 5). Cultivating beginner's mind enables you to engage in 'non-action or spontaneous action' (Rosch, 2008, 153) without getting entangled in and by a plethora of dualities that propel you out of the organizational becoming you're trying to understand. Beginner's mind allows you to become-with its unfolding by minding the ('empty') gaps between feelings, thoughts, sounds, words, actions, objects, and so on (see also Mingyur & Tworkov, 2019, 73). Noticing these gaps is crucial in process organization research, as Robert Cooper (2005) suggests, for it 'is the gap that makes possible the connection' (p. 1705). Less *is* indeed more.

References

Bigo, V. (2018). On Silence, Creativity and Ethics in Organization Studies. *Organization Studies*, *39*(1), 121–133.

Borges, J. L. (1998). The Ethnographer. In Borges, *Collected Fictions* (pp. 334–335; A. Hurley, Trans.). Penguin.

Brummans, B. H. J. M. (2012). The Road to Rizong: Buddhist Mindful Organizing amid Natural Disaster in the Indian Himalayas. *Qualitative Communication Research*, *1*(4), 433–460.

Brummans, B. H. J. M. (2014). Pathways to Mindful Qualitative Organizational Communication Research. *Management Communication Quarterly*, *28*(3), 441–447.

Brummans, B. H. J. M. (2017). Mindful Organizing. In C. R. Scott & L. K.Lewis (eds), *The International Encyclopedia of Organizational Communication* (pp. 1612–1620). Wiley.

Brummans, B. H. J. M., Hwang, J. M., & Cheong, P. H. (2013). Mindful Authoring through Invocation: Leaders' Constitution of a Spiritual Organization. *Management Communication Quarterly*, *27*(3), 346–372.

Brummans, B. H. J. M., Hwang, J. M., & Cheong, P. H. (2020). Recycling Stories: Mantras, Communication, and Organizational Materialization. *Organization Studies*, *41*(1), 103–126.

Brummans, B. H. J. M., & Vézy, C. (2022). Adventurous Ideas for Ethnographic Research on the Communicative Constitution of Organizations. In J. Basque, N. Bencherki, & T. Kuhn (eds), *The Routledge Handbook of the Communicative Constitution of Organization* (pp. 262–280). Routledge.

Chia, R. (1995). From Modern to Postmodern Organizational Analysis. *Organization Studies*, *16*(4), 579–604.

Chödrön, P. (2000). *When Things Fall Apart: Heart Advice for Difficult Times*. Shambhala.

Cobb, J. B. (2007). Person-in-Community: Whiteheadian Insights into Community and Institution. *Organization Studies*, *28*(4), 567–588.

Cooper, R. (2005). Peripheral Vision: Relationality. *Organization Studies*, *26*(11), 1689–1710.

Deligny, F. (2015). *The Arachnean and Other Texts* (D. S. Burk & C. Potter, Trans.). Univocal.

Endō, S. (2015). *Silence* (W. Johnston, Trans.). Picador Classic. (Original work published 1969.)

Faber, R. (2020). *Depths as Yet Unspoken: Whiteheadian Excursions in Mysticism, Multiplicity, and Divinity* (A. M. Davis, ed.). Pickwick.

Fan, V. (2022). *Cinema Illuminating Reality: Media Philosophy Through Buddhism.* University of Minnesota Press.

Geertz, C. (1973). *The Interpretation of Cultures: Selected Essays.* Basic Books.

Gethin, R. (1998). *The Foundations of Buddhism.* Oxford University Press.

Guenther, H. V. (1999). *The Life and Teaching of Naropa.* Shambhala. (Original work published 1963.)

Gyatso, T. (2015). *The Essence of the Heart Sutra: The Dalai Lama's Heart of Wisdom Teachings* (T. Jinpa, ed. & trans.). Wisdom. (Original work published 2002.)

Harris, A., & Holman Jones, S. (eds). (2021). *Affective Movements, Methods and Pedagogies.* Routledge.

Hussenot, A., & Missonier, S. (2016). Encompassing Stability and Novelty in Organization Studies: An Events-Based Approach. *Organization Studies, 37*(4), 523–546.

Khyentse, D. (2015). *Pith Instructions: Selected Teachings and Poems with Root Texts by Jamgön Mipham and Jigme Lingpa* (M. Ricard & V. Kurz, eds). Shambhala.

Lincoln, Y. S., & Guba, E. G. (1985). *Naturalistic Inquiry.* SAGE.

Manning, E. (2013). *Always More Than One: Individuation's Dance.* Duke University Press.

Massumi, B. (2011). *Semblance and Event: Activist Philosophy and the Occurrent Arts.* MIT Press.

Massumi, B. (2015). *Politics of Affect.* Polity.

Mingyur, Y. & Tworkov, H. (2019). *In Love with the World: A Monk's Journey through the Bardos of Living and Dying.* Spiegel & Grau.

Purser, R. E., & Milillo, J. (2015). Mindfulness Revisited: A Buddhist-Based Conceptualization. *Journal of Management Inquiry, 24*(1), 3–24.

Ramos, A. (2019). Affective (Im)mediations and the Communication Process. In C. Brienza, L. Robinson, B. Wellman, S. R. Cotton, & W. Chen (eds), *The M in CITAMS@30: Studies in Media and Communications Volume 18* (pp. 181–194). Emerald.

Ramos, A. (2020). Enter the Event: How Is Immanent Participation? *AM Journal of Art and Media Studies, 23*(October), 67–75.

Rosch, E. (2008). Beginner's Mind: Paths to the Wisdom that Is Not Learned. In M. Ferrari & G. Potworowski (eds), *Teaching for Wisdom: Cross-cultural Perspectives on Fostering Wisdom* (pp. 135–162). Springer.

Suzuki, S. (2020). *Zen Mind, Beginner's Mind: Informal Talks on Zen Meditation and Practice.* Shambhala. (Original work published 1970.)

Truffaut, F. (Director) (1959). *Les Quatre Cents Coups* [Motion picture]. Les Films du Carrosse.

Varela, F. J. (1987). Laying Down a Path in Walking. In W. I. Thompson (ed.), *GAIA, a Way of Knowing: Political Implications of the New Biology* (pp. 48–64). Lindisfarne Press.

Varela, F. J., Thompson, E., & Rosch, E. (1991). *The Embodied Mind: Cognitive Science and Human Experience*. MIT Press.

Vásquez, C., & Kuhn, T. (eds). (2019). *Dis/organization as Communication: Exploring the Disordering, Disruptive and Chaotic Properties of Communication*. Routledge.

Verma, R. (Producer & Director) (2013). *Journey of the Heart: A Film on Heart Sutra* [Documentary]. Telecommand Software India Limited.

Vyner, H. M. (2019). *The Healthy Mind: Mindfulness, True Self, and the Stream of Consciousness*. Routledge.

Wallace, B. A. (2011). *Stilling the Mind: Shamatha Teachings from Düdjom Lingpa's Vajra Essence* (B. Hodel, Ed.). Wisdom.

Weick, K. E. (1979). *The Social Psychology of Organizing* (2nd ed.). McGraw-Hill.

Weick, K. E. (1996). Drop Your Tools: An Allegory for Organizational Studies. *Administrative Science Quarterly, 41*(2), 301–313.

Weick, K. E., & Putnam, T. (2006). Organizing for Mindfulness: Eastern Wisdom and Western Knowledge. *Journal of Management Inquiry, 15*(3), 275–287.

Whitehead, A. N. (1978). *Process and Reality* (D. R. Griffin & D. W. Shelburne, eds). The Free Press.

Yanow, D. (2000). *Conducting Interpretive Policy Analysis*. Thousand Oaks, CA, SAGE.

10
Correspondences *with* a Business Meeting in a Time of Covid

Katie Beavan

> What I've been advocating for in my own discipline is an [approach] that is willing to join *with* other lives, to think and learn from them, rather than treating them as objects for ethnographic analysis. . . I would love to see a form of study that joins with and thinks with writing (or art or music, etc.) that shows how – by joining and thinking with it – we can open up differently to the world and perceive things to which we paid no attention before.
>
> **–Tim Ingold, 'Ecocriticism and "Thinking with Writing"'**
> **(Spencer and Ingold, 2020, 210, used by permission)**

Noticing Differently—Alluring and Perplexing

This edited book, of which this chapter is a part, is concerned with noticing differently in process organization studies (OS). Noticing differently in inquiring is alluring. It troubles knowledge making in our field, long overdue from my practitioner perspective. From the business schools around the globe, books and journal articles pour forth, though much of this research is unfortunately inaccessible and/or impenetrable to those working in organizations. For me, noticing differently is part of a broader quest to present accessible knowledge in ways that can help build flourishing organizations. I'm convinced this adventure does not have to involve simplification or popularization. It's reasonable to assume (organization) practitioners are as intelligent as (OS) scholars, capable of handling complex ideas and keen to make the effort (Ingold, 2021). We're usually invested in developing ourselves as leaders, our teams, and our organizations and looking for help.

Katie Beavan, *Correspondences with a Business Meeting in a Time of Covid*. In: *Doing Process Research in Organizations, Noticing Differently*. Edited by Barbara Simpson and Line Revsbæk, Oxford University Press.
© Oxford University Press (2022). DOI: 10.1093/oso/9780192849632.003.0010

Stories

Stories move us humans and writing helps me shape my thoughts. My research practice is to use writing as a method of inquiry (Richardson and St Pierre, 2005) and specifically écriture féminine (Cixous, 1976) for its potential to be *the very possibility of change* (879, original emphasis). Nothing is still or fixed in Cixous, everything, including her words, the unconscious, are in flux and speeding. It's a way of writing I've used elsewhere (Beavan, 2019, 2021a, 2021b) to capture the 'raw stuff of everyday [organizational] life', its 'psychic reality', both 'fictive and hyperreal' (Royle, 2020, 5–7, 13), its movement and our fluid subjectivity. It's writing that is freewheeling, freeflowing,

> a researcher
>
> being-in-the-process-of-writing
>
> writing fugue style, writing on the lam
> (Cixous, 2005: 26, 45)
>
> which can be perplexing
> though not unscholarly, says John Dewey
>
> rather, the privilege of science, of rationality, is rejected,
> 'reverie and desire. . .imagination is to be noted as much as refined
> observation' (Dewey, [1925]2008, 369).
>
> Though whether such writing is more accessible to practitioners dogs
> me.

Exploring a Blooming, Buzzing Confusion

Our Worlds Are Social

The daily worlds of living organizations bloom and buzz. Embodied, rich with affective intensities, dynamic and unfolding, relational; all our actions are interactions flowing in and out of our smart phones, laptops, telephones and filling our meeting rooms, hot desks, offices, cafeterias, and bathrooms. In Dewey's prescient conceptualization we exist in a social world which is constantly trans-acting[1] (Dewey and Bentley, [1949]2008). We humans share our world with a variety of more-than-human beings (from smart devices to toilets, office furniture, and coffee cups). We are porous entities, not self-contained; forming and reforming fluid stories of connectivity and ongoing differentiation (Ingold, 2021). How to go about noticing and representing what's going on in this dynamic, affective 'blooming, buzzing confusion' (James, [1890]1981, 462) perplexes me. I feel continuously confused. As a researcher, I'm in the ever-unfolding lifeworld I aim to study. Am I observer, observing, or observed? Is observing possible if I'm in the flow of continuous action? Truth is, I'm clinging to a moribund way of viewing selfhood. I believe it is 'absurd to look at the mind simply from the standpoint of the individual human organism. . . it is essentially a social phenomenon. . . arising and developing within the social process' (Mead, 1934, in Simpson, 2017, 62), but a part of me, infused with twenty-first-century ideas of free agency, refuses to embrace the idea of social selves. Restricted by false beliefs about my agency it's hard to open up to the myriad of trans-actions happening outside my conscious, rational awareness and the idea that it is impossible to have anything more than a partial and preliminary grasp of the living world (Dewey, [1925] 2008). The anonymous pre-personal lives of our bodies are somewhat invisible and we tune out shaping influences (Shotter, 1995). There is no *real* which can be known. What can be known? On, a bad day, this can feel so vexing that I feel tempted to give up with empirical inquiry altogether. If I can't see, can't represent, or interpret the world with, and for, my colleagues then what can I do as a researcher? My human I/eyes are implicated and humbled. Failure to represent is inevitable. How, to give voice to a multiplicity of beings interacting? How to avoid colonizing ventriloquism? How to grasp moving complexity? How, how, how? I'm lost in a labyrinth.

The Labyrinth

A labyrinth, unlike a maze, has only one way in and out. A labyrinth is a complex irregular network of passages and secret chambers, and it is

---

[1] Dewey and Bentley deliberately insert a hyphen between trans and acting stating '[w]e shall permit ourselves as a temporary inconvenience the irregular use of hyphenization . . . as a means of emphasizing the issues involved in their various applications . . .It has the particular value that it enables us to stress the inner confusions in the names as currently used' ([1949] 2008, 101).

difficult to find one's way. In anatomy the labyrinth is a delicate structure in the inner ear which contains the organs of hearing and balance.
The anatomical labyrinth consists of bony cavities (the bony labyrinth)
filled with fluid and lined with sensitive membranes (the membranous
labyrinth) gifting us hearing and balance. Spiritually, the labyrinth for
millennia has represented pilgrimage and wholeness. Journeys taken, like
those by Orpheus and Eurydice, to our own deep centre and back out into
the world. Figuratively, the labyrinth represents a complex or confusing
situation; an intricate system; a situation or condition from which it is difficult to extricate oneself; an entanglement (Oxford English Dictionary,
2021).

'To practise theory as a mode of habitation is to mix and mingle, in
one's thinking with the textures of the world. This means. . .not taking lit-
eral truths metaphorically, but *taking metaphorical truths* literally' (Ingold,
2021, 14–15).

> The labyrinth opens to the world in the way a maze does not.
>
> The maze puts all the emphasis on the traveller's intentions. He has an aim in
> mind, a projected destination or horizon of expectations, a perspective to obtain
> and is determined to reach it. . .
>
> In walking the labyrinth. . .[t]he path leads, and the walker is under an imper-
> ative to go where it takes him. But the path is not always easy to follow. . .. Once
> on the trail, he and his walking become one and the same. . .a mind immanent
> in the movement.
>
> (Ingold, 2015, 131–133).

Dewey's Denotat*ing* Method as a Way through the Labyrinth

Dewey's Concept of Experience

The path leads. Start, says Dewey ([1925] 2008) refreshingly, not with abstract theory, but with everyday (organization) experience. By experience
Dewey means the transactions, the goings on, between living organisms
(including humans and more-than-humans) and their environment. The
'value of the notion of experience for philosophical reflection is that it de-
notes both the field, the sun and the clouds and rain, seeds and harvest, and
the man who labors, who plans, invents, suffers and enjoys' ([1925] 2008,

384). It's active, engaged, experimental. Dewey has a very expansive idea of experience; it includes something 'as wide and deep as the earth' (370) and includes the sub- and unconscious where 'twilight, the vague, dark and mysterious flourish' (369). 'Devotion, piety, beauty and mystery [are as] real as anything else ([1925] 2008, 377). Applied to OS Dewey's notion of experience opens a vast universe for inquiry. However, it is not a world of subjects and objects. Dewey is asking us to think in terms of *functions* and *processes* (Alexander, 2019) and *fluidity*. It is an approach that remains revolutionary within social science inquiry (Clandinin and Rosiek, 2006) including OS.

Undergoing Experience

In undergoing experience, the organism is changed from within it. Every experience also takes up something from those which have come before and modifies in some way the quality of those which come after. 'Something of their meaning and value is retained as an integral part of self' (Dewey, [1934] 2005, 108). This brings us to Dewey's important principle of habit, 'through habits formed in intercourse with the world, we also in-habit the world. It becomes a home and the home is part of every new experience' (Dewey, [1934] 2005, 108). By undergoing, *in*-habiting, experience, we are changed recursively and continuously generated; experience is continuous. In this sense we both *act* and *undergo* experience in the environment. It involves both passivity, a surrender, and an active going out of energy, which we must summon and pitch at a 'responsive key' (Dewey, [1934] 2005, 59). The active part happens within the undergoing or, as Ingold frames it, as '[d]oing undergoing' (2016, 15). We *in*-habit experience, we dwell in it, undergoing trumps our agency and this is humbling. In the surrender part of this experien*cing*, it is no longer possible to say I do this, or I do that. The I isn't upfront, our agency and differentiation lags. Though, the active, responsive part is fecund with future potentiality. Mead, I murmur, presciently made the distinction between a passive, objective, ostensive 'me' and an active, performative 'I'. My 'me' in undergoing is humbled and my 'I' spontaneously and generatively responds to the present moment, (Mead, 1934, in Simpson, 2017).

'Active undergoing continually digests the ends of doing, and extrudes them into pure beginning' (Ingold, 2018, 22) or becomings. Communication is also integral to experience, and for Dewey in this highly responsive, emergent, and mutually constituting environment, communication is *not* about the transference of information. Dewey's struck by the affinity between the words 'communication', 'community', and 'common' (Dewey, [1916] 2008, 7) and for him communication is a mutual coordination of action which is *anticipatory*, an imaginative stretch, a casting of experience forward, in the hope of finding a common path, a way of living together, communing. The common path emerges out of the creative process of communication. Imagine person A asking person B to bring him a flower which A is pointing to and looking at. B, following A's gaze, responds to A's movements and sounds from the standpoint of A, as A is experiencing it. A in making the request conceives the flower not just as he experiences it, but as something that B can grasp and handle. Thus, '[s]omething is literally made in common' (Dewey, [1925] 2008, 141). Experience is thus simultaneously a process of differentiation and sharedness, and communication and experience are mutually dependent. 'For it is in joining with others that each of us comes into our own as a person with a singular and recognizable voice' (Ingold, 2016, 15). All this is to say Dewey's concept of experience, of living in culture, is broad and complex and revolutionary. How do we research it?

Dewey's Denotative Empirical Method

Help arrives. 'Dewey's Denotative-Empirical Method: A Thread through the Labyrinth [of Experience]' writes Thomas Alexander in 2004, summarizing how Dewey presents his denotative-empirical method as *philosophical* method ([1925] 2008). Dewey's intent is to avoid intellectualism and abstract philosophical theory. Provocatively, he's already rejected philosophy's Ruling Law that Reality equals what can be Known ([1905] 2008). His quest is to find a method which 'discloses' experience without transforming it into a 'theoretical object' (Alexander, 2004, 249). Dewey intends his method as a corrective. His first-class test for philosophy is does it refer 'back to ordinary life-experiences and their predicaments, render them more luminous to us, and make our dealings with them more fruitful' ([1925] 2008, 18). Dewey's quest is a difficult enterprise and one in which he assays and assays again, sometimes oscillating in his position. I'm following Alexander's (2004, 2019) and Ingold's (2016) interpretations. Dewey is searching for a method to approach, attune to, explore, and correspond *with* the mutually constitutive processes and functions of a dynamic, transacting world with practical ends in mind. He is decades ahead of Deleuze and Guattari, of Barad and Braidotti, but he is seeking and trying to describe a method that breaks with epistemology as realist and mimetic and is mutually generative. He is presciently into the territory of non-representation (Lorimer, 2005, Stewart, 2007; Thrift, 2008; Vannini, 2015), of research as a communing endeavour and as a practice of future making.

Dewey is perhaps clearest on what denotative-empirical method is not. We can't start with secondary cognitive experience. We can't equate the Real with the Known. The having and undergoing of an experience is 'indescribable'. We mustn't cut off an individual event from its context or environment (Alexander, 2004). What it is—is a bit muddier. Of course, such a method cannot lay down a blueprint; it's an emergent and situated approach. In the labyrinth there is no point-to-point, one follows the trail, undergoing. Dewey, in a course syllabus, *Types of Philosophic Thought*, describes denotation as a search and the creative side of science (Dewey, [1921-22] 2008, 389). He wants us to start with raw, non-reflective experience. He is asking us to pay careful and patient attention to the world. It is not about any specific scientific pointing out but an *art* of remembering the world. In remembering we need to be both open to evolutionary histories and to future potentialities that are contained in the present. We are to begin and end with an awareness of the world which *transcends* thought, approaching with open curiosity (Alexander, 2004). Overall, Dewey's approach is a 'doctrine of humility' and direction, and he asks us to 'open the eyes and ears of the mind' (372), to be sensitive, sensory, aware, and receptive. It's what today we would call a contemplative practice, a pathway to becoming more 'fully *aware* of the world *beyond* our ideas of it' (Dewey, 1929 in Alexander, 2004, 252) by staying present to it. He is putting reflection back in the lifeworld itself. Denotative method he tells us 'is the only method which can do justice to this inclusive integrity of experience' (Dewey, 1929 in Alexander, 2004, 252).

Art as Experience

I follow Alexander in that aesthetics is a 'significant, though neglected aspect of Deweyan philosophy' (2004, 248), and that *Art as Experience* (1934] 2005) is a golden key to understanding Dewey's denotative method. He originally delivered it as a series of lectures to a wide audience (Haskins, 2019). Art as experience, not as something we regard but something we do. Art as everyday embodied aesthetics, something we hunger for, an adjustment between intelligence and the environment. Inquiry as collaborative, a correspondence, an artistic ideal of qualitative unity and intensity, as a mode of travel across a landscape (Haskins, 2019; Ingold, 2021). '[A]rt as enactment is also a "doing" in response to an "undergoing"... Art provides the forms of (or for) our affective and cognitive experience of suffering' (Kelly, 2012 in Haskins, 2019, 448). Dewey, I believe, is asking us, in our inquiring of the social world, to correspond *with* it; thinking and feeling, and trying to represent it, like *artists*. He is calling us to make art.

The Middle Voice

Written language inhibits us. Dewey sowed confusion with his choice of the word experience, which he came to regret, and desired to replace with culture. If we *in*-habit experience, undergoing it in the social world, in unfolding trans-actions, where our 'me' is humbled, then we need a mode of expression that can capture this; a 'me' that lies between active and passive verbs. Ingold, recently coming to Dewey's work and taking much from it (more on this soon), offers us an 'overture to social life' (2016, 9) and following the Greeks, advocates adoption of the middle voice where the subject is both the cause and the focus, the agent and experiencer, of an action. It's a fascinating grammatical move, as in Greek middle voice many verbs have a reflexive quality about them. Some verbs that mean *come and go* in Greek occur only in the middle voice. A subject is participating in, and thus within, the action of coming or going (Major and Laughy, 2021), in the midstream.

Writing *In*-habiting Experience

How to be in the writing of *in*-habiting experience? What might *in*-habiting mean for writ*ing* as a method of inquiry? Do I relinquish my observing writing self? Can I slip inside the verb, losing myselves? I think so. Cixous does this, her *The Book of Promethea* (1991) is an exemplar. I'm taken with Ingold's move, following Dewey, to 'replace our nouns for naming things with verbs' (2021, 7). Ingold is speaking of us noticing the stone in its stoning, the mountain in its rising and falling, the human in his/her/their humaning, to which I add the Zoom meeting in its zooming. In this manner, '[t]here is no beyond-of- reflexivity in this mode of research – the self cannot stand apart from itself and reflect on its self from the god-like, transcendental position of a self beyond itself. Rather, the self-records a becoming self in motion' (Fotaki and Harding, 2018: 187) *with others* using poetic language the 'material, affective, emotional, embodied, conscious and unconscious, tacit and known' (Fotaki and Harding, 2018, 187). Can the middle voice be writing that touches us, can it be used to tell stories? I search for examples. I find a short essay by Stewart (2019) 'Granite' from a series by the Society for Cultural Anthropology called 'Correspondence'. How, I wonder could this middle voice be used in OS? The series' introduction leads me back to Ingold and his argument for a relational and generative orientation that seeks a 'correspondence' with the world, 'in the sense not of coming up with some exact match or simulacrum for what we find in the things and happenings going on around us, but of *answering* to them with interventions, questions and responses of our own' (Ingold, 2015, vii and original emphasis). There is uncanny resonance here with Dewey's denotative method. Has Ingold been reading Dewey? Yes! Ingold was invited to give the 2016 Dewey Lectures and this provided an incentive for him to do a deeper dive into Dewey's oeuvre. He moves, directly and humbly following in Dewey's footsteps to offer us a 'theory of correspondence'. What he says he proposes is not new, '[i]t was already adumbrated a century ago in the writings of the pragmatist and theorist of education John Dewey' (Ingold, 2016, 14). For Dewey and for Ingold, the life process is social and it is about forging connection and community as the outcome of communication (Dewey, [1916] 2008; Ingold, 2016). The hopeful discovery of a 'common understanding. . . which secures similar emotional and intellectual dispositions Dewey, [1916] 2008: 7'. Though, in my view, Ingold is leveraging his own fifty years of anthropological study, he is giving us further articulation and direction which he then implements in his accessible, freed from the chains of writing academically, recent book *Correspondences* (Ingold, 2021).

To Be *In-Corresponding*, Creating Correspondences

A Phenomenological Approach of Humility and of Direction

Ingold (2016, 2021) is suggesting as researchers that our phenomenological attention is directed towards a place from which we see something happening, goings on that spill out into surroundings including ourselves. Following Dewey, what Ingold is showing us in *Correspondences* is the application of an empirical, *phenomenological approach of humility and of direction*. He crafts twenty-seven essays or correspondences throwing 'off the shackles of academic convention' (p. 11), inspired by art and as art, 'proceeding in gradual steps from world to words' (p. 15). His intent is to 'stay close to the grain of things' showing us that 'the practice of thinking we often call "theory" doesn't have to lift off into a stratospheric realm of hyper-abstraction. . . .. Quite to the contrary, theoretical work can be as much grounded in the materials and forces of this world as the conduct of any other craft' (p. 14). We can he suggests practise theory by mixing and mingling in one's thinking with doing in the living world and that will be my intent in this chapter. 'The theorist can be a poet' and he urges me to take '*metaphorical truths literally*' (p. 15, original emphases). If, he suggests, we employ a metaphor of digging with a spade, then we should pick up a physical spade and dig the earth. Then we can bring the lessons learned from physical digging to our thinking. My intent here too is to experiment with applying Ingold's theory and practice of correspondences in my OS research and it is to these trails I now wander. Companion texts, a 2016 academic journal article explicating his theory and his 2021 book of short essays where he accessibly shows me how to *correspond* with the moving world, crafting words with affection, longing, and care.

Ingold's Theory of Correspondence

Ingold (2016) *corresponds with* Dewey's principle of continuity of experience, answering to him, and offering to me a theory of correspondence that helps me along my path. Co, or rather to co, is the lynchpin, that to communicate is to *common* with others, a finding of common ground, a participatory process of listening and responding. He suggests three principles of corresponding. (1) Habit, the Deweyan idea that in every experience we are doing undergoing. As we've seen it's both passive and active, we're in the verb. (2) Agencing, (not agency), there are 'no I's or you's to place before any action' (p. 17). We are forged with others in the undergoing of social life, forming and transforming in a 'meshwork of knotted and entangled lines' (p. 18). Our agencing is ever emergent. (3) Attention, in the contemplative sense, as a stance of resonance where we wait patiently for emergence, using our sensory awareness to open to the other, to be *with* them, to attune to them. '''[W]ith*-ness'' saves the other from objectification by bringing it alongside as an accomplice. Othering becomes togethering, interaction into correspondence' (p. 20). To these three principles Ingold adds two other practices; caring and longing. Caring is ethical. 'To care for others, we must allow them into our presence so that we, in turn, can be present to them. . .we must let them be, so they can speak to us' (p. 20). This has deep implications for my research. To let the other become, so they can speak to me. Longing, for Ingold, brings together the 'activities of remembering and imagining. Both are a way of presencing: remembering presences the past; imagining the future' (p. 21). In footnote 10 (p. 25) Ingold acknowledges both similarity to, and difference from, Barad's theory of agential intra-action (2007). They share the idea that agency is not something we have but arises from within an enactment and for Ingold the purpose of Barad's intra-action is similar to his for correspondence. The difference he states lies in the direction of travel. Intra-action reverses the between of interaction. For Barad we are *in* intra-activity, it's onto-epistemological. With correspondence, it's a ninety-degree turn from interaction; we're in the relational and processual midstream. 'Always in the middle: one can only get to it by the middle. A becoming is neither one nor two, nor the relation of the two, it is the in-between' (Deleuze and Guattari, 2004, in Ingold, 2016, 18). To correspond we join *with* the swimmer in the relational and processual currents of our shared material lifeworld. Crucially this is not intersubjective. Correspondence is not interaction traded back and forth between us as independent entities. Rather to *be in-corresponding* is an intertwining of our movements. We're in the flow together simultaneously and continuously both coming together and differentiating from each other. We are in the flow and our individuality emerges from of our connectedness. And from this position of *with*ness, he wants us, with a practice of care, great patience and attention to the present moment, to write stories (Ingold, 2007). He wants us, like Dewey, to stay, *in* the experience close to the 'grain of things' (Ingold, 2021, 8).

In *Correspondences* Ingold introduces the written word, returning to the intimacy, spontaneity of thought and observation, longing, and care, we used when we wrote letters by hand. 'Corresponding with people and things – as we used to do in letter-writing - opens paths for lives to carry on, each in its own way but nevertheless with regard for others' (p. 3). Such writing is attentive and deliberate and we feel the care taken over each word and sentence and this facilitates from us a deeper, more sensitive response. In his essay 'Words to meet the world' he suggests that 'perhaps, we need a new understanding of language, one that brings it back to life as a practice of "languaging"...endlessly creating itself in the inventive telling of its speakers – words can be as lively and mobile as the practices to which they correspond... Let's not be afraid then, to meet the world with words...[offering] inscriptions as things of beauty in themselves' (202–203). Perhaps after Hélène Cixous we need to learn to DRAW—'Dreamer, Realist, Analyst, Writing. With the caveat that they are not really separable but rather at every instant interwoven and interweaving' (Royle, 2020, 3).

Researching as *Corresponding*

Ingold invites me to do my research*ing* by *co*rresponding with things in real time. A going along relation. A *between* relation, a dwelling in the '*in-betweeness*' (2021, 9). Ingold corresponds with trees, snow, stones showing me how to align my whole body with the subject of study empathically, with responsibility, with care, joining *with* things. Though I'm assaying to join with a business meeting conducted via Zoom. To be *in–corresponding* with the meeting using a careful, attentive, soft rigour to stay close to the grain of things (2021, 14). Will I be able to discern heterogenous flows between the human and the non-human, empty out my conscious ego and allow in a communal subjectivity? Attentionality is a difficult principle. I spent a spring semester during the pandemic struggling to develop my contemplative poetic gaze as part of my MFA course at Naropa University. One of the artists we studied was Marina Abramović, whose ability to be present and to attune to affective intensities of her audience and environment is legendary.

The Artist Is Present

In 'The Artist is Present' which Abramović performed in the Museum of Modern Art (MOMA) in Manhattan in 2010, she sat over the course of three months, on a chair silently, for over 716 hours locking eyes with over 1,500 people, staying *with* the moment, (Abramović, 2012; Biesenbach, 2010). It was an extra-ordinary artistic and endurance feat. Abramović was able to produce and focus her own energy field and was also able to absorb, contain and change the affective intensities of the public audience in MOMA. 'I saw Abramović's face change into many different shapes, varying sometimes from babies to wolves to abstract constellations of lines and light. And sometimes, she completely disappeared. If there was a body, it was a body of light and darkness, quicksilver, humming' (van den Hengel, 2012, 14–15). At the time of the MOMA exhibit Abramović had been practicing performance art for more than four decades. I'm a beginner lacking unique talent or honed mastery, but 'The Artist is Present' teaches me about how I may be able to attune through my body *with* others, togethering, and in a way that can bring into visibility conscious and unconscious happenings answering them with responses of our own (Ingold, 2021).

Art is a method of corresponding *with* the social world including the more-than-human (Cixous, 2005; Dewey, [1934]2005; Ingold, 2021), to noticing organizational life differently and creating correspondences.

Correspondence as Participating Agents

Corresponding has no doer nor deed. 'Every correspondence is a process: it carries on. . . is *open*-ended: it aims for no fixed destination or final conclusion. . .correspondences are *dialogical* (Ingold, 2021, 11, his emphasis). To be in verb, *with*, the 'it' of my/our story is to be attentional. To care I must be present, so it can speak to me, I have to let 'it' be (Ingold, 2021, 20). This provokes interesting questions. What is my responsibility to my/our story? How can I let 'it' be so it can speak to me? How are we becoming together? Can we view stories as future possibilities of semiotic relations, influencing the present? (Rosiek and Snyder, 2018). In their essay 'The Story Is a Living Being: Companionship With Stories in Anishinaabeg Studies' Garroutte and Westcott (2013) observe that in Anishinaabeg philosophy stories are seen as living beings that exist outside time and space *whether or not* people tell their stories and they ask narrative researchers to consider how they can be good companions to their stories. Cathy Coutler (2020) in her 'Diffractive Story' takes up this point in exploring the 'possibilities of magical realism as a posthumanist narrative research project'.

Magical Realism as a Way to Be *In*-Corresponding

Magical realism treats the ordinary as miraculous and supernatural or magical as ordinary, 'a trickle of blood can cross a village along streets and through houses—avoiding rugs—to arrive at the feet of a loved one' (Coulter, 2020, 1216). Opposites fuse together, borders dissolve, mix, change, time is non-linear, indeed the narrative can seem outside of time (Coulter, 2020, 1216). '[U]rged on by an intuition that a deeper truth lurks. . .[M]etaphorical truths [are taken] literally' (Ingold, 2021, 15). Many of Ingold's essay titles in *Correspondences* have a magical realist air to them: 'In the shadow of tree being'; 'The foamy saliva of a horse'; 'A stone's life' for example. With Dewey's denotative method and Ingold's corresponding I'm seeking to be in the midstream, to be with attentively, *in*-habiting a place of agencing not agency, where I's and you's and they's are dissolved, where I'm in the verb corresponding; zooming with Zoom; whatsapping with WhatsApp. To be *in*experiencing, wishing a little magic. In the Imaginarium of OS, what might we create, patiently, joining *with*, in the midstream? Flickers from the feathery increments of iridescent half-lives, catching ideas on the fly?

A Tale from a Time of Covid

> But what I want to call imagination always evades capture, always escapes the grid of conceptualization. It is because of imagination that thinking goes beyond the limits of the already thought. And it is what enables life to go on. . .Art rekindles wonder and astonishment. . .rekindl[ing] the senses so that we can learn to attend directly, even lovingly, to the world around us, and to respond in kind—with precision, sensitivity, and wisdom.
>
> **–Tim Ingold, 'Ecocriticism and "Thinking with Writing"'**
> **(Spencer and Ingold, 2020, 211, used by permission)**

> Contexts are unfolding that even a movie couldn't represent. We live amidst and, however unconsciously, partake in constellations of the real that cultural standards, narrative givens, etc. can't make sense of, or even perceive. Simply to realize that they are here, emitting flickers from the feathery increments of their iridescent half-lives, requires the kinds of time that we are rarely, if ever, permitted to have.
>
> **Lyn Hejinian, *Positions of the Sun***
> **(2018, 53, used by permission)**

Click on Google calendar. Tap on meeting invite. Click on Open zoom.us. Tap on launch meeting. A practiced quickstep launching me into this Zoom meeting. Passing through the cloud joining you in your space, 'Hi Zoom'. Immediately unhinging, greeting myself up way too close and personal, a mirrored crow gazing back at me, a hidden cat on my knees purring loud, yellow kitchen dresser as a frame. Good morning again Zoom. Suspended in a curious, momentary stillness. Blue Admit button blinks. Clicking again I let J in, or you let him in, or we both do. Meetings with Zoom, crash-in begin, startling. Intercourse without preliminaries. No shaking hands, pecks on cheek, laughter, coffee, tea, or water poured. Missing touching, small talk, social pleasantries. Hanging there in social-less moments waiting for your audio and video to couple.

Click, tap, click, cha cha. One, two, three, cha cha; one two three cha cha.Strains of quick-step click-tapping echoing through attics, bedrooms, kitchens, dining rooms, garden sheds, closets, laundry rooms. Unmasked, up close, humans sitting, squatting, standing, walking around, on the treadmill, their Peloton, in every nook and cranny of this world where a half-stable internet signal is accessible and people can afford and own phones, tablets, laptops. Meeting, educating, cocktailing, birthday celebrating, dying, getting buried. Communing Human Life in its full panoply enacted through and with you. Everyday naked life seeping out from your interstices. We dress from the waist up for Zoom. Anything goes (on) below camera.

Odd the lack of smell. Polite, socially conditioned not to smell each other, unlike dogs. Yet we do sniff and inhale. Our noses and brains can distinguish roughly a trillion scents. English language lacks words to express our olfactory sensations. Constraining at work to coffee breath, someone's fart, garlic from last night's Indian curry seeping out through pores. Sniffing out unconsciously each other's sweat scent, registering, and distinguishing between, heat, fear, shame, pain. Our incredible dog-human sniffing faculties disabled on Zoom.

Yet, curiously, affect is transmitting through the cloud as every therapist has pandemic learned. Sight and sounds accentuated, up-close, and personal in unusual intimate laptop proximity. Humans taking cues from skin pallor, eye blinks, our slightest hesitations. And our intimate locations, bedrooms and bathrooms; intimate companions, pets and partners, children.

A whirlpool of corresponding.

With you Zoom we are a becoming magnificent, a shimmering In-gold-ian flickering meshwork. Your accelerating pandemic induced puberty. Wondrous promiscuous couplings. Pre Covid pandemic, you had 10 million partners, by April 2020, 300 million. Zoom, downloaded 34.4 million times in January 2021 alone. Baby Zoom tendrils spreading like silver lace vine interlacing our shared earth.

More intricate than a millennium of spider's webs shimmering in fall dew, glinting in slanting sunlight.

Morphing to Mobs of Connectivity, spinning, and turning across continents, oceans, and time zones. Knotting, untying, retying, new knots, old, becoming knots. The stronger the knot the more vivid the plot says Hejinian.

A frictionless environment declares your founder Eric Yuan. Zoom Dreamtopias for our workplaces, our families. Happiness is your value system. Zoom, sponsors of happiness for clients, for employees. We're warmly invited to join your annual Zoomtopia event. I'm signing up. Why not? Easy to be cynical but your Dad Eric was unhappy at Cisco, unhappy developing the WebEx platform. A melancholic first-year student at Shandong University in 1987, taking ten-hour train rides to visit his girlfriend Sherry, developing prototype and fantasy inspired videotelephony on the long train ride, imagining other ways to *visit* his beloved. Searching for magic. A love-sick mathematical dreaming.

Eric marrying his sweetheart at twenty-two. Moving to America after nine attempts to get a visa. My cat shifts, jumps down. Eric and Sherry have a family—three human children. Though, Zoom, aren't you his fourth beloved child? 'I did not see a single happy WebEx customer', your Dad recalls, 'I had an *obligation* to fix that problem.' Leaving Cisco, embarking on the unforseeable life of a tech entrepreneur. Telling Sherry 'if I don't try, I am going to regret it later'. A team of forty engineers, birthing you. Eric, Zoom and Zoomers, spreading happiness. They designed you better than any competition, though privacy issues an ink blot on this fairy tale. Pirate intruders requiring blocking. Still, a Silicon Valley pot-of-gold-at-the-end-of-the-rainbow fairy tale; Eric's current net worth $15 billion (Forbes, 2021). Hoping Eric pays his taxes, as all obligated billionaires should do. Eric dreaming-on imagining a world where there's no distance barriers, no language barriers, no cultural barriers to communicate.

Celebrating father-in-law's ninety-eighth birthday on Zoom. Thirty minutes of frustration, until a grandson marvellously connecting Poppa, Nana and the I-pad to his Zoom birthday party. Happiness palpable, wafting as a baby great-grandson waves his breadstick in the air.

How many million kids, high schoolers, undergraduates, pandemic-educated? Vital virtual doctors' visits made? Therapy sessions given and received. Easy to mock, critique as outrageous late capitalism, from an ivory tower pedestal. I shameful confess to intriguing to visit the Imaginarium at Zoomtopia in September 2021. I'm anticipating *Smellosophy: What the Nose tells the Mind* (Barwich, 2020).

Happiness. Though as human beings we also seem to thrive on provocation, separation, reparation. Happiness judged by our habitual behaviour is variably desired. Frictionless—not so when Wi-Fi signals oscillate. Unstable connection you declare as if we humans have dominion over cable companies, routers, internet traffic volumes. My friend-colleague P gets frustrated in her soothing lilac home office, switching home networks, huffily blaming her husband and you. A contagious condition. Our home signal withered, spookily declining from 250Mbps—megabytes per second—(extra fee paid Comcast for speed privileges) to 20. Zooming our bodies freeze, vital business calls rudely severed. Comcast dispatch their high-tech A team. Men climb ladders into high wires and poke about in our dusty basement. Modems and routers are replaced. Beards are stroked. Hands waved. A conundrum temporarily unsolvable. Oh, Google-signal booster boxes have blown out. A mystery? A virus? Signal boxes replaced. Cheque written. Happiness retrieved. Retrieving into our ordinary daily zooming lives.

Though our pandemic lives are far from ordinary. Fears lurk in the toilet, the casserole dish, toothpaste. Months pass by but fright has settled in. The three of us on this Zoom call are over sixty, rudely feeling unwanted, unexpected undertows of mortality. J, suffering from Long Covid. Your exhaustion coming and going. You're a hiker with a daily Iron Man practice, two-hour Stairmaster stints in the local gym. You, dear J, have small blood Covid clots on your lungs, a deep vein thrombosis (dvt) on your leg. The Royal Free Hospital's thrombosis clinic thrumming with Covid induced dvts. You too P, also have a dvt in your leg from too much sitting around all day Zooming. Both of you on blood thinners; I quiver and stretch.

Human fear fusses. Epidemic traumas carried in our DNA. The 1918 Spanish influenza. An uncle lost. The 1950s polio epidemic. Cousin Penny catching polio in its season—late summer—even when the town's public swimming pool was shuttered. Photographs of children imprisoned in iron lungs I spied as a child in our family's Encyclopaedia Britannica.

> I scream
> The body electric,
> This yellow, metal, pulsing cylinder
> Whooshing all day, all night
> In its repetitive dumb mechanical rhythm.
> Rudely, it inserts itself in the map of my body,
> Which my midnight mind,
> Dream-drenched cartographer of terra incognita,
> Draws upon the dark parchment of sleep.
> > **Mark O'Brien, 'Man with an Iron Lung' ([1988] 1997, copyright
> > 1999, Lemonade Factory—a small press. Used by permission.)**

Jubilation for sugar cubes administered at school with its red blob polio vaccine, relieving parents. Too late for too many.

Ordinary yesterday, thirty years ago yesterday, three of us, on today's Zoom, meeting face-to-face for the first time in Citibank's offices on The Strand. Three young leadership and organizational development professionals. J with your Scottish red hair and impressive Chatham House and Cranfield Business School credentials. P with your newly minted MBA, black bobbed hair, and cheery red beret. Me, Celtic, Cotswold, Cambridge, a closet bluestocking.

Next week five years or so later, P and I pregnant, walking around Maida Vale with your parents and husband as your labour begins. What was I doing in London anyway, seven and a half months pregnant myself? Oh, receiving the Opportunity Now award on your behalf for the diversity work we'd done together. J cradling my new-born in Connecticut after 9/11; a visit to design a leadership development programme attenuated in the face of disaster. Memories circling in and out of our meeting knotting us, commoning us, forming us, reforming us. Lasting knots. Humaning, our lines interlacing. A continuous participation in each other's lifelines, travelling the same path, growing older together (Ingold, 2016).

Today the three of us, this today, Zooming, sense-feeling anew the silky mercury undertow of our mortality. We're working on a design for a senior leadership program for the top 100 in P's company, to connect them across the firm. It isn't just that the pandemic has disjointed them. Financial services firms are fiefdoms, rugged individualism pervades, patrolled borders. The idea of a one-firm-firm, ha—J and I were seeking that philosopher's stone challenge long-ago yesterday before the century turned. Today, this day, this spring day in 2021 on a Friday, we're discussing the unexpected and unexplained death of a younger member of P's company's executive committee. Shock a thorn piercing hardened executive flesh, reverberating through and around the leadership community, blanketing the firm, swirling through you Zoom into P's home office where she is sitting today in gloomy London late afternoon light, spilling onto J's Murcian terrace where he sits bathed in sun, and gusting into my Connecticut kitchen where I glance out at a late spring snowstorm icing the blue hyacinths. Perforating our meeting, rupturing us.

We falter. A collective shiver. The Ferryman, passing by us, waves.

How do you contain Zoom the oceans of affect passing through you? Did Eric have an (un)conscious plan; creating you as a Brobdingnagian Therapist?

Spectres are arriving looming over our shoulders. My brother, a fatal accident at thirty-two just before I met the two of you. My Dad, then yours P. Our babies. Workplace deaths. A heart attack in a crowded open space office. An analyst pitching to his death down the sky-high glass atrium. Our meeting's becoming a phantoms' picnic.

Sight senses firing. Stirring, glimpsing your tear, urgent desiring to reach through my laptop screen and sit beside you P, touch your hand, remembering our dads. I lean in towards your face, your fortitude. Seeing and hearing, that's all we have with you Zoom. No smell, no taste, no touch.

Our meetings going forward will carry a brume from today. '[E]very experience enacted and undergone modifies the one who acts and undergoes, while this modification affects, whether we wish it or not, the quality of subsequent experiences. For it is a somewhat different person who enters into them' (Dewey, [1938]2008, 15).

Perhaps we are all reaching for the clues to our continued existence? Fears transmitted and admitted, we resume our meeting task. P takes a photo of some Power-Point slides and WhatsApps them to us. We mull on the overall leadership development plan for these leaders within which this part nests. Seek inspiration. Though the gloomy shade lingers, and we perceive its veil across P's workplace. Top leadership reluctance to discuss *the death* enclosing like a larger Russian doll nesting existential smaller and smaller or perhaps larger and larger worry-dolls, Covid, quarterly results, board pressure. P recounts euphemistic, unsoothing, repeating refrains, 'he would have wanted us to carry on'. Mourning minimalized. Minimalization of mourning a silent, seeping poison through the firm.

We parry back and forth following each other's verbal volleys through you. Brainstorming, rhythming, zooming. Our minds and bodies attuning to our task. Laughing, we are Scalextric cars zooming around a well-worn, homemade track. A terminus. Our emergent antidote to the presenting issue a discrete in-treatment. Create commoning between these leaders through successful cooperation in action. Veiling Dewey's philosophy, these are not the specific words I use with P and J. In any case, there is no need. We three have all long-learned this principle in our action, decades behind us developing senior leaders. We are masters as well as ongoing students of our craft. Settling into a design of peer groups of eight leaders, enabling intimacy, disclosure, normalizing, offering safety, coaches as containers. A variant of a design J and I have used before. Offering spaces in which the leaders can cast their lives' experience in ways to join each other midstream: commoning, and individuating; knotting, untwining, reknotting; mourning and healing. A potentia; though whether your colleagues will buy-it, contract with J and me, is divination.

P's husband pops his head in and says hi and J and I wave. 6pm on Friday and time for the two of them to unwind with a glass of wine. J, without his family in Spain and Long Covid tired, will sit awhile on his terrace, take photos of the sun setting over the mountains, a video of two birds in twilight flight to share with our students at Navarra University and WhatsApp before bedtime to me.

I click on the red button 'End Meeting for All',

another leaving, though connectivity lingers between our meshwork positions,

flickers, anticipating,

References

Abramović M. (2012) The Artist is Present. *Imdb.com*, Available from: https://www.imdb.com/title/tt2073029/ (accessed 8 January 2020).

Alexander, T. M. (2004) Dewey's Denotative-Empirical Method: A Thread through the Labyrinth. *The Journal of Speculative Philosophy, New Series*18(3): 248–256.

Alexander, T. M. (2019) Dewey's Naturalist Metaphysics. In: FesmireS (ed.), *The Oxford Handbook of Dewey*. New York, NY: Oxford University Press, 25–52.

Barad, K. (2007) *Meeting the Universe Halfway: Quantum Physics and the Entanglement of Matter and Meaning*, Durham, NC: Duke University Press.

Barwich, A-S. (2020) *Smellosophy: What the Nose Tells the Mind*, Cambridge, MA: Harvard University Press.

Beavan, K. (2019) (Re)writing Woman: Unshaming Shame with Cixous. *Management Learning* 50(1): 50–73.

Beavan, K. (2021a). EXPRESS: Becoming Visible: Uncovering Hidden Entanglements of Power, Performativity and Becoming Subjectivities in a Global Bank. *Organization Studies*. February 2021. https://doi:10.1177/0170840621997609

Beavan, K. (2021b). (Un)felt Ferments: Limning Liminal Professional Subjectivities with Pragmatist–Posthuman Feminism and Intimate Scholarship. *Management Learning*. https://doi.org/10.1177/13505076211027566

Biesenbach, K. (2010) *Marina Abramovic*. New York: Museum of Modern Art.

Cixous, H. (1976) The 'Laugh of the Medusa', trans. Keith Cohen and Paula Cohen. *Signs* 1(4): 875–893.

Cixous, H. (1991) *The Book of Promethea*, trans. Betsy Wing, Lincoln, NE: University of Nabraska.

Cixous, H. (2005) *Stigmata: Escaping Texts*, Abingdon and New York, NY: Routledge.

Clandinin, D. J. and Rosiek, J. L. (2006) Mapping a Landscape of Narrative Inquiry: Borderland Spaces and Tensions. In: Clandinin, D. J. (ed.), *Handbook of Narrative Inquiry: Mapping a Methodology*. Thousand Oaks: SAGE, 35–76.

Coulter, C. (2020) A Diffractive Story. *Qualitative Inquiry* 26(10): 1213–1221.

Dewey, J. ([1905] 2008) The Postulate of Immediate Empiricism. In: Boydston, J. A. (ed.), *Middle Works 3*, Carbondale and Edwardsville, IL: Southern Illinois University Press, 158–167.

Dewey, J. ([1916] 2008) Democracy and Education. In: Boydston, J. A. (ed.), *Middle Works 9*. Carbondale and Edwardsville, IL: Southern Illinois University Press, 1–370.

Dewey, J. ([1921–1922] 2008) Syllabus: Types of Philosophical Thought. In: BoydstonJA (ed.), *Middle Works 13*. Carbondale & Edwardsville, IL: Southern Illinois Press, 349–396.

Dewey, J. ([1925(rev. 1929)] 2008) Experience and Nature. In: Boydston, J. A. (ed.), *Later Works 1*. Carbondale & Edwardsville, IL: Southern Illinois University Press, 1–396.

Dewey, J. ([1934] 2005) Art as Experience. In: Boydston, J. A. (ed.), *Later Works 10*. Carbondale & Edwardsville, IL: Southern Illinois Press, 1–329.

Dewey, J. ([1938] 2008) Experience and Education. In: Boydston, J. A. (ed.), *Later Works 13*. Carbondale and Edwardsville, IL: Southern Illinois University Press, 1–369.

Dewey, J. and Bentley, A. F. ([1949] 2008) Knowing and the Known. In: Boydston, J. A. (ed.), *Later Works 16*. Carbondale & Edwardsville, IL: Southern Illinois University Press, 1–279.

Forbes (2021) Eric Yuan & Family. *Forbes Billionaire List*, Available from: https://www.forbes.com/profile/eric-yuan/?sh=17eb4bf061bf (accessed 9 June 2021).

Fotaki, M. and Harding, N. (2018) *Gender and the Organization: Women at Work in the 21st Century*, Abingdon: Routledge.

Garroutte, E. and Westcott, K. (2013) The Story Is a Living Being: Companionship with Stories in Anishinabeeg Studies. In: Doerfler, J., Sinclair, N. J., and Stark, H. K. (eds), *Centering Anishinaabeg Studies: Understanding the World through Stories*. East Lansing: Michigan State Press, 61–80.

Haskins, C. (2019) Dewey's Art as Experience in the Landscape of Twenty-First Century Aesthetics. In: Fesmire, S. (ed.), *The Oxford Handbook of Dewey*. New York: Oxford University Press, 455–470.

Hejinian, L. (2018) *Positions of the Sun*, Brooklyn, NY: Belladonna Collective.

Ingold, T. (2007) Materials against Materiality. *Archaeological Dialogues* 14(1): 1–16.

Ingold, T. (2015) *The Life of Lines*, Abingdon and New York, NY: Routledge.

Ingold, T. (2016) On Human Correspondence. *Journal of the Royal Anthropological Institute* 23(1): 9–27.

Ingold, T. (2018) *Anthropology and/as Education*, London and NY: Routledge.

Ingold, T. (2021) *Correspondences*, Medford, MA: Polity Press.

James, W. ([1890] 1981) *The Principles of Psychology*, Cambridge, MA: Harvard University Press.

Lorimer, H. (2005) Cultural Geography: The Busyness of Being 'More-than-Representational'. *Progress in Human Geography* 29(1): 83–94.

Major, W and Laughy, M. (2021) The Middle Voice: Part I. *Ancient-greek.pressbooks.com*, Available from: https://ancientgreek.pressbooks.com/chapter/21/ (accessed 1 June 2021).

O'Brien, M. ([1988] 1997) The Man in the Iron Lung by Mark O'Brien | Poetry Foundation. *Poetry Foundation*, Available from: https://www.poetryfoundation.org/poems/56110/the-man-in-the-iron-lung (accessed 9 June 2021).

Richardson, L. and St Pierre, E. (2005) Writing: A Method of Inquiry. In: Denzin, N. K. and Lincoln, Y. S. (eds), *The Sage Handbook of Qualitative Research*. Thousand Oaks, CA: Sage, 959–978.

Rosiek, J. L. and Snyder, J. (2018) Narrative Inquiry and New Materialism: Stories as (Not Necessarily Benign) Agents. *Qualitative Inquiry* 26(10): 1151–1162.

Royle, N. (2020) *Hélène Cixous: Dreamer, Realist, Analyst, Writing*, Manchester: Manchester University Press.

Shotter, J. (1995) *Talk of Saying, Showing, Gesturing, and Feeling in Wittgenstein and Vygotsky*. Available at: https://www.massey.ac.nz/~alock/virtual/wittvyg.htm (accessed 1 June 2021).

Simpson, B. (2017) Pragmatism: A Philosophy of Practice. In: Cassell, C., Cunliffe, A. L. and Grandy, G. (eds) *The Sage Handbook of Qualitative Business and Management Research Methods*. London: Sage, 54–68.

Spencer, A. and Ingold, T. (2020) Ecocriticism and "Thinking with Writing": An Interview with Tim Ingold. *Ecozon@: European Journal of Literature, Culture and Environment*, 11(2), 208–215.

Stewart, K. (2007) *Ordinary Affects*, Durham, NC: Duke University Press.

Stewart, K. (2019) Granite (from the series Correspondence). *Society for Cultural Anthropology*, Available from: https://culanth.org/fieldsights/granite (accessed 30 May 2021).

Thrift, N. (2008) *Non-representational Theory: Space, Politics, Affect*, London and New York: Routledge.

van den Hengel, L. (2012) Zoegraphy: Per/forming Posthuman Lives. *Biography* 35(1): 1–20.

Vannini, P. (2015) Non-representational Methodologies: Re-envisioning Research. Abingdon and New York: Routledge.

11

Opening Conversation on Doing Process Research

Alecia Y. Jackson, Lisa A. Mazzei, Line Revsbæk and Barbara Simpson

LINE: The purpose of this conversation is to explore aspects of the *doing* of process research, whether it's in education (which is Lisa and Alecia's field of expertise) or in organization studies (the primary readership targeted by this book). All of the chapters in the volume have been selected as exemplars of process ontological research, showing how this brings about noticing organizational phenomena differently—in the doing. Many of the chapters draw explicitly, and some more implicitly, on process philosophy, exploring how it informs the practice of empirical work that can investigate and bring about organizational phenomena differently. So let us talk about the doing of process research. In relation to this, you—Lisa and Alecia—have introduced a *thinking with* way of doing process research. In a recent article you said that you 'think *with* whatever you are reading at the moment' (Jackson & Mazzei, 2017, 725). How do you do this? How is the doing situated? Is that a good place to start?

LISA: You mentioned this in your invitation to us: what is the beginning? I think that it is not a question of beginning. It's a question of, perhaps, a starting point. The significance of starting with what you're reading and immersed in at the moment—in the middle of what you find yourself thinking about—is that it allows emergence and newness whether it's a new question, or a *different* question, a different beginning—not in the sense of an origin, but in the sense of a starting place.

ALECIA: In response to 'how it's done', I recently talked with doctoral students about this in a class I'm teaching right now. So many of them want to do inquiry differently, and it's natural that they ask a lot of 'how to' questions and what this doing differently involves. We read my *Thinking without Method* article (Jackson, 2017) that came out a few years ago, and in that piece, I grappled with where to start if inquiry is positioned as an emergent yet fragmented strategy, one that is not pre-given. If we're going to do something differently, then maybe the question to pose is what do we *not* do? What should we give up, and what should we let

Alecia Y. Jackson et al., *Opening Conversation on Doing Process Research*. In: *Doing Process Research in Organizations, Noticing Differently*. Edited by Barbara Simpson and Line Revsbæk, Oxford University Press.
© Oxford University Press (2022). DOI: 10.1093/oso/9780192849632.003.0011

go? Doings may actually be as much about *undoings*. Again, in my article *Thinking without Method*, drawing upon Deleuze's new image of thought, I wrote that we have to do what Deleuze calls 'forgetting everything'—and I plugged that concept into the context of qualitative inquiry. How do we 'forget everything' about qualitative method—how do we do away with method—so that we can proceed differently? Because in this process methodology, there is no 'how-to' method: it's a commitment to reading, and reading in particular ways to allow encounters that engender new thought and doings. It's not reading for meaning—but reading to see what comes through, what sparks (to put it in Deleuzian language).

Bettie St Pierre[1] (who was my doctoral advisor and remains my mentor) always told me, just do the next thing—even when you really don't know what that next thing is. Doing process research involves uncertainty and unpredictability. Zourabichvili wrote that 'every beginning is also a return. But the latter always implies a divergence, a difference, never a return to the same. There is no arrival. There's only ever a return' (2012, 206). In our *Thinking with Theory* book (Jackson & Mazzei, 2012) we emphasize this idea of returns and repetitions: the way that we return to theory or we return to whatever it is we're thinking with. It is not a beginning, as Zourabichvili says; it's always a return, but it never goes back to the same thought to reproduce what is already known. These returns—as process—keep us open to what's to come, the new, the unthought. So, this doing and undoing and redoing and returning and staying in the middle is the work of process methodology.

But in my teaching, I have to be aware of what students assume by *process*, when they have heard 'the research process' over and over again—as opposed to process research. Part of an undoing, then, is what is signified by the word 'process'. This is also a matter of language and signification, paying attention or noticing what they think something means when I might be referring to something very different, based on the paradigm I'm in. For those of us who are working on process methodology, we have to ground that in our ontology: what it is to be in a process, or become-with a process. Obviously, it's not a linear step by step plan that's laid out. To return to your question, that's part of the challenge of how to position or situate a *thinking with* process that is both contingent and emergent, creative and experimental.

BARBARA: Yes, this is a challenge that I have encountered with my students as well. What I talk to them about is the capacity, or the ability to dwell in uncertainty. That is so hard for them to contemplate because much of what we learn, many

---

[1] Elizabeth Adams St Pierre.

of the theories that we teach, these are intended to give us some sense of certainty. And yet what ontologically-oriented process inquiry invites us to do is to actually acknowledge and embrace and celebrate the doubt, the uncertainty that permeates our lives. That's a hard thing to teach—

LISA: —it's a hard thing to live!

BARBARA: It is a hard thing to live. But that is precisely what living is about, always contingent, always emergent, and always precarious. The shifting sands of process, in the ontological sense, oblige us to move with our fields of inquiry rather than trying to fix them into stable states.

LISA: I want to go back to the question of reading, again. Reading intensively, and we're talking about students. One of the things that I say to my students is there's not a correct theorist or concept. Alecia and I wrote about this in our book (*Thinking with Theory*, Jackson & Mazzei, 2012). I say to students, yes, you have to read intensively! You have to be immersed in a particular set of questions or assumptions. But just because that's where you start, it doesn't mean it's going to do the work that you need to do. So, I often say to students: you start with a particular concept, let's say you start with deconstruction, and this is what you're thinking with. But if deconstruction is not doing the work that you need it to do, then you need to be open to another concept. A concept that actually helps produce questions that you're wrestling with, starting in the middle. That is how Alecia and I talk about our plugging in process, the way in which questions emerge as we bring different theorists and their concepts together with what we are trying to think about. Staying with something and seeing what it does. This happened to me when I was at Manchester Metropolitan University in the mid 2000s, when I first started trying to think with Deleuze. I was presenting some ideas in our weekly methodological meetings and Maggie Maclure always, always, always would say to me, what is Deleuze doing for you that Derrida doesn't? And if you can't tell me that, then you need to put that aside and go someplace else in terms of a different emergence or different encounter, which is part of that process.

BARBARA: Can I ask you that question then, what does Deleuze do for you that Derrida doesn't?

LISA: I've written about this in making sense of it for myself (Mazzei, 2011). I started with Derrida in my work in terms of trying to account for silences that were present in my conversations with white teachers talking about race, or rather, *not* talking about race. I found the concept of the absent presence (Derrida, 1976) to be a way to explain that silences weren't empty. In fact, there are two scholars from Denmark (Bang & Winther-Lindqvist, 2017) who published a book titled *Nothingness* and the idea that nothingness implies an emptiness or void, but they approach it as fullness, the presence of absence. Derrida helped me account for the silence.

But then I kept running into the problem of why did the silences persist, and what were they doing? And so then Deleuze helped me theorize the persistence, the productive nature of the silences, and why they continued. It was as if, although I can look back and say this now, it was as if Derrida took me to a certain place, helped me theorize certain things but I was in a 'stuck place', as termed by Patti Lather (2007): a place to dwell in for its fruitful potential, instead of something to avoid or flee from. I can't say that I thought at the time, 'Oh, well, Deleuze is going to help me out of this'—but it was because of the reading and the studying I was doing at *that* time, that it opened up a different way of thinking.

LINE: As you speak, I begin to think about what it is that we need the concepts to do? What I find myself doing—after reading, and reading harder, as St Pierre (2011) encourages us to—is noticing *when* in an interactional flow what is going on comes to a halt for me. When it tends towards a potentiality of paradigm negotiation, like a gesture to possibly respond to. A cross-road of worldings with a sense that my response will either take us down a habitual lane (which I, from the reading, am now myself alienated from), or make everything in the next different, unforeseen, potentially inspiring, new but also possibly unrecognizable or even upsetting. Productive alienation is how I have come to think of this potentiality to the occurrences where theory, in Spivak's words, 'comes in as a reflex' (Spivak, 2014, 77), not in the form of an answer, but in a sense of alienation inviting improvisation (or a new worlding). For me, this could be in interaction with students, or with research partners in action research collaborations, when the encounter produces occurrences—or emergent events, as I understand them with Mead (1932[2002])—that then make noise in my writing afterwards, in my writings of the empirical. So, for me, that's where the reading becomes troubling, in the field, constitutive of an experience that settles into a different noticing.

LISA: I like this idea of making noise, the readings making noise. I have Whitehead on the brain right now. He writes about this concept of ingression (Mazzei, 2021, Whitehead, 1978), of things that break in and are all part of becoming. And in terms of thinking about your project and some of my own thinking: how do we articulate that which is happening that is not just initiated by us, and by us I mean humans? These ingressions are happening all the time, whether we respond to them or not. This idea of, as you said, the readings making noise—it's the something else. Returning to the idea of doing, that Alecia was talking about: Something else is doing the doing, and how do we attend to that in thinking about process methodology? What are those things; what are those doings? And I don't know that we always necessarily *can* name them or *need to* name them. For example, Alecia and I wrote an article years ago to deconstruct autoethnography (Jackson & Mazzei, 2008). One of the critiques we made was that, at least in the manuscripts that we deconstructed, the author allowed for his or her own becoming, but froze the research participants in a static position. In preparing for our conversation today I was thinking a lot about that in the sense of how life continues to unfold and the way in which traditional practices often do not allow for becoming and emergence.

LINE: So would this be about how *agencement* is playing out with forces beyond subjects and intersubjectivity? In many of the volume chapters there is this concern with environmental forces (e.g. Silvia Gherardi and Michela Cozza in Chapter 2, Timon Beyes in Chapter 7, Ariana Amacker and Anna Rylander Eklund in Chapter 3) as co-emergents and continuously generative in the process of noticing differently. Barbara, do you have any thoughts about that?

BARBARA: What strikes me about the chapters in this book is that I think the authors are certainly well-read, and they work from specific domains of writing. That resonates with what you're talking about, Lisa. But they're also working very strongly in an empirical sense. So, a lot of what they're talking about comes from the noticings that they experience empirically. They want to reject representationalism, and they want to reject intellectualism. And the step that they take is into the aesthetic, the more-than-representational (Lorimer, 2005). So what we find are authors talking about colour (Timon Beyes, Chapter 7) and rhythm (Charlotte Wegener, Chapter 4) and social poetics (Steve Linstead, Chapter 6) and performance art (Katie Beavan, Chapter 10). That seems to me to be a little different, perhaps, from working from a strong theoretical foundation, although they do all have that as well. What's your thinking about that?

LISA: Alecia and I have written and talked about, and we've talked about this with Elizabeth St Pierre, that there's still a centring of the human and humanist subject. Even in talking about aesthetic or colour or art: a centring of 'this is how *I* experience it'. And so going back to Line's comment about making noise, it's easy to conceive decentring, theoretically. It's much more difficult to enact it, methodologically. How does one *not* start from the position of the 'I'? And how does one talk about these beings? Whitehead refers to entities rather than beings or subjects, and he also asserts that thought is not necessarily a conscious awareness. I don't know if I'm answering your question, Barbara, but one of the things that struck me as I was reading your introductory chapter and thinking and trying to situate it in the context of my own work and conversations that Alecia and I have had, is the idea of noticing. Noticing that you refer to is a different positioning, but it's still based on this empirical project of the 'I' who notices. Thinking with Whitehead, what happens if we shift from noticing to being? Then it is not starting with an 'I' who notices, but it's starting with a different way of thinking about *being in the world*, with the world. These words I'm using now are borrowed from Karen

Barad (2007), from Erin Manning (2013), and others. For me, part of this process is an interrogation of what do we mean by beginning? What do we mean by noticing, and how do we think about existence in a way that informs our doing of inquiry?

ALECIA: Your questions, Lisa, lead to one of mine: Is it possible to do inquiry without perception? So even when we attempt to be anti-representational, even if we're claiming that we are worlding, how much are we still relying on perception? Earlier I referred to undoings, and now our conversation is making me wonder about the role of 'cutting' in this process methodology: I think that if we focus on doings and undoings, then it's also important to focus on cutting, especially in the way that Karen Barad (2007) writes about agential cuts in her book *Meeting the Universe Halfway*. Cutting is always involved in a making. As we stay in a process, becoming-with, we not only create and stay entangled, but we also discard and do away with. I don't know if I have a response to your question that set this off, Barbara, about aesthetics. But imagination, creation, aesthetic methods, and unleashing worldings that we encounter in philosophy are things that we don't do all that well in qualitative research or social science or educational research: interpretive and critical forms of inquiry are so bound to representation that any attempt to be experimental oftentimes results in keeping the world very static, as Lisa mentioned. Reflecting and representing, rather than creating. So I think that that's a vexing problem, this idea of how do we get outside the trap of representation when we are still perceiving and noticing and using all of those ways of doing research that are deeply embedded in our disciplines. Lisa and I, too, have been reading Manning and the way that you, Line and Barbara, write about attunement and sensing is very much in line with what Lisa brought up earlier about Whitehead. And that's hard to capture in writing. It's difficult to describe or explain what we think we are doing when we're sensing what is on the horizon, the not-yet. That's all just part of the challenge and the paradox of these doings. So, how do we pay attention to the cuttings as much as the doings and the noticings? One provocation in your introductory chapter for this book is how do we recondition the ways in which we notice what is happening; how do we recondition the ways of noticing what has previously gone unnoticed? How do we attune to that? I would question further, how do we even sense the process itself? How do we know we are 'in' a process, if we want to avoid setting out on a path, intentionally? So, those are just some of the questions that I'm thinking about right now.

Lisa and I have both used the concept of encounter in our conversation here. In *Difference and Repetition,* Deleuze (1994) writes about 'the encounter' as being the thing that, by chance, forces us into thought. Like you were saying about the noise that comes up—not knowing what to do, not knowing how to write, not knowing how to think about something, because it's so outside of how we notice, or what we notice, that the encounter forces us into thinking otherwise. So that might be something to consider as part of this overarching question of what it is to do process research, to respond to those encounters as they occur. Deleuze (2007) explains that a spider spins its web with no concern for the outcome; it is only interested in the doing, learning as it goes, and responding to what happens. So *how* one writes about process—*as* the happenings happen—without concern for beginnings and endings is probably a Deleuzian strategy, in a sense. A strategy that, retroactively, reveals itself at the end.

LISA: Alecia and I have talked about this. I suppose we were doing process methodology a long time ago in the way that we have discussed today, but we didn't think about that or call it that at the time. An example of what revealed itself at the end happened in my initial dissertation study in which I was working with white teachers in a large urban school system in the US and thinking with Derrida to deconstruct race. The teachers in my study were in the majority of the teaching force as white teachers, but in the minority in terms of the demographics of the student population. I had lots of good field data, if you will: interviews, focus groups, observations, you name it. When I started to really focus on analysis, which is often how students are taught—you do your analysis at the end of your field work, at the end of this process, rather than as part of what was going on—I got to a place where I had all this information, but not anything that was a response to 'how do white teachers talk about race, especially their own race as whites?' Returning to how aesthetics function, I ended up using aesthetics in order to get me out of my rigid way of writing and thinking, reading poetry and fiction to do this. As part of my 'unlearning', I happened to attend a poetry festival and was in a session in which poets discussed the intentionality of silence in poetry, which shocked me into a different way of thinking. I had been so obsessed with what was right in front of me, the presence of words spoken, instead of a consideration of the gaps or Derrida's absent presence (1976) to rethink the way in which silence was functioning as voice. The teachers were using silence to talk about race rather than articulating it in a conventional sense. And again, when Alecia is asserting that this is all retroactive, I can go back and talk about this now, but it was the aesthetic, it was the poetry, it was the poets talking about the way in which silence functions and how they purposefully use silence in poetry that was a way to bring the theoretical concept to bear. I remember too, that at that time, Laurel Richardson, a sociologist, was looking at using poetry as a form to present ethnography (1993), although I'm not interested in a poetic representation. I am interested in how poetry helps me think differently about the language and the pauses and the gaps and so forth. So, it was a way of thinking differently *through* the aesthetic form, but not *using* the aesthetic form as a way of trying to represent something.

LINE: Several of the chapters mention and exemplify how formats grow from the rhythms of the context in which what is going on is going on. For instance, Steve Linstead (Chapter 6) refers to his and Garance Maréchal's (2010) exploration of Jacques Jouet's metropoems as a particular way of writing, sitting on a metro train, conditioned by the rhythm of the train, by its periods of motion and stops at stations, conditioning the form of expression in the poem, and leaving the reader with a sense of the constituting rhythm. As I was reading the metropoem presented in Chapter 6, it tuned me towards the emergence of format in context or, we might say, the emergence of methodology in context.

BARBARA: This example of the metropoem is interesting because it describes a specific poetic form. It is built around rules that you need to follow in order to create the poetry. This brings to my mind the idea of improvisation, like jazz for instance, where you have a form. It's a very specific form, but the point about the performance is to push the boundaries, to explore the boundaries, to exceed the boundaries, to go to new places because of the form. So it's not about getting rid of the form, it is actually working through the form to create something new. I think that's what poets are doing as well with their sonnets and haiku, forms that shape but never fully determine what they write. And it's the same in research. Research has a well-rehearsed form that we work with as we push it into different shapes and do different things with it.

LINE: In the back of my mind this question about how one can be noticing anything if one is trying to escape the 'I' as a site for knowing, still sits with me as a deconstruction. What is left on the other side of that? How are we then to talk about the doings? I think you're right in pointing out an assumption about perception in the idea of noticing, although the idea of noticing differently for me refers to those occurrences in which paradigm becomes an issue, where a possibility of understanding differently and assisting what takes place into its otherness by the responses we make to the potential of difference arising in a situation, is at its most intense. In his chapter, Boris Brummans (Chapter 9) suggests Buddhist-inspired ways of being mindful, one of which is 'to drop your-self as principal tool' of research, hinting at a similar concern for letting go of the 'I', un-selfing in order to sense differently. Sideeq Mohammed (Chapter 8) argues for the proliferation of an ethnographer's multiple conceptual personae, each 'with its own way of noticing', enabling the ethnographer to engage and bring out multiple realities of a site.

BARBARA: I agree. The conventional Humanist conception of the 'I' as individual, in-dependent, and hermetic is problematic for process researchers. The idea of subjectivity needs to be refurbished if it is to be of any use for inquiring into worldings that are perpetually on-the-move. To the extent that the 'I' continues to be defined dualistically in opposition to the 'other', as some 'thing' that can be either centred or decentred by researchers, it remains inadequate as an apparatus for processual inquiry. This is where I find Rosi Braidotti's (2019) thinking about posthuman subjectivities helpful. She argues for subjectivities that are not merely human, that are necessarily plural, and that are continuously evolving in their encounters where, as Erin Manning (2013) reminds us, we are 'always more than one'. Several of the chapters included in this book deliberately seek to open up this more complex understanding of subjectivities and the researchers' 'I's that are thoroughly entangled in the *agencements* of their inquiries. For instance, Katie Beavan (Chapter 10), Sideeq Mohammed (Chapter 8), and Anne Augustine (Chapter 5) challenge us to think about the multiplicities of researcher subjectivities in their respective engagements with a Zoom meeting, a shopping centre, and a medical general practice, while Charlotte Wegener (Chapter 4) explores the rhythms of her own multiple selves that are at play as she writes. They are each, in different ways, probing questions about what research is and how we can engage with research as posthuman subjectivities.

ALECIA: I would say the question is bound to the workings of power in process methodology. All of these new approaches that we are currently engaging—such as posthumanism, feminist new materialism, all the postfoundational philosophies—are any of these approaches or strategies ways that we are trying not to escape power, but instead to account for power relations? What are the workings of power in process philosophy and process methodology? Drawing upon Barad's ethics and agential cuttings, and being accountable to those cuts and the moves that we make in our doings, is a way to consider power in an ethical way. The 'I' will always be there, so perhaps it's accounting for it in a way that is an enactment of power, in relation to process. And to notice that the 'I' is not acting or enacting alone—but bound to relations of power, to a collective, to an assemblage. I don't know the way out of it, but if we pose the question of power and ethics, we might do more than problematize or decentre the 'I' and instead account for it differently—the 'I' as produced and producing, constituted and constituting. Entangled and enmeshed rather than distant, observing, and static. This is all the language of becoming, isn't it?

BARBARA: I've grappled with power a lot as well because it is a difficult concept from a process point of view (Simpson, Harding, Fleming, Sergi, & Hussenot, 2021). Traditionally when we think about power, it's a very dualistic notion: some have got it, and others haven't. In this sense power is something that divides, whereas process unifies. I think Foucault was definitely heading towards a processual understanding of power. But I still struggle with the whole notion of power in a process context. I can understand forces, movements, energies, and so on. But I'm stuck on how to deal with power because it does feel to me as if it simply doesn't belong in process thinking—it's a paradigmatic misfit—so I resist using that word. It comes as no surprise then, that when you read people like Whitehead, for instance, he doesn't really deal with power. And Deleuze prefers the notion of desire rather than power, doesn't he?

ALECIA: Barbara, I like the way you bring us back to forces and movement. To go back to your earlier point about aesthetics, even when we're using aesthetics or adopting the approaches of the genre as Lisa described, or pushing the edges of boundaries, it seems that there are power relations and forces working. In his book on Foucault, Deleuze (1988) writes about force having the power to affect and be affected, basically claiming that power, as exercised, shows up as affect. He is tying Foucault's concepts of power as productive (rather than a possession) to his own concepts of thought and the outside. And whatever is 'outside' of our thought—what opens to the not-yet—is a force that is of resistance. So, while Deleuze doesn't specifically use the word 'power', he is writing about non-dualized forms of relations that are imbued with forces, affects, and desire. And for Deleuze, desire is not dualized as have/have not, but desire as a creative and productive force. I can sense how Deleuze might refer to desire, force, strategies, and affect in a similar way as Foucault's exercise of power and forces that resist.

BARBARA: Power is not the only concept that is challenged by process thinking. Many of the familiar concepts that we encounter in our research domains require reformulation before they can be usefully engaged in processual inquiries. For me, critical thinking still tends to be dualistic in its way of engaging with the world, whereas process is trying very hard not to be dualistic, to actually move with the flow. For this reason, I very much appreciate Deleuze's approach to desire, for instance. I think it's a helpful response to more dualistic notions of power.

LISA: Coming back to an earlier question of yours, Barbara, what is research or why do we do it? I'm situated in a college that has very strong post-positivist traditions, it's all about scaling up and replicability and research that supports these aims. I say to the students that I get from other programmes: If your goal is to answer a question that you already think you know the answer to, then why do research? To me, that's not research.

In *Thinking with Whitehead,* Isabelle Stengers (2011) wrote that if we're only interested in asking questions in order to find answers, then what we're doing is staying in the same feedback loop. What she suggests is that Whitehead was interested in problem posing. So, it's not that we aren't interested in things or questions; it's not that we aren't concerned with how to think differently. But if we only are asking questions in order to find an answer, then we're going to come back to the same place because we're asking a question that we know to ask and that we can answer (rather than posing problems which then open us up to other ways of thinking or to other questions). And so, I try to get the students that I work with in teaching, and this is an introductory methodology course, to engage with how to think about what it is that we're doing from the start and not just situating ourselves as researchers interested in answering questions. That idea of problem posing that Stengers talks about is helpful for me in my own work and my teaching.

BARBARA: It's nice. I think there are still fundamental problems in reaching across to a post-positivist audience: Why would you want to notice differently? Why would it be of interest to think differently? How do you respond to that sort of question?

LISA: It's getting us out of the fix that we're in. The same methods and the same questions aren't helping us. And so, how do we ask a different set of questions? I guess that's my issue with post-positivism. This is the question I wrote down from reading your introduction and the chapters: What newness or difference is made possible? That's a very abstract question, I guess, for someone who is interested in answering something very specific. Let me also add that the students I work with are much more receptive to being pushed in this direction. The difficulty I have is often with the faculty who are supervising them. The students get introduced to new theories and concepts that challenge post-positivism, and they are so excited that they start seeing possibilities. And then often, you know, they're working with faculty in another department, and their ideas and creative thinking get shut down. As an outside person, I try to encourage them to do this work, to get their degree, and then to be able to shift the field otherwise. Let me share an example from a former student whose work centres on individuals with disabilities and complex communication needs. She was in a class where we were studying posthumanist theory, and we were reading Karen Barad. We also watched a segment of the film *Examined Life* in which Judith Butler takes a 'walk' with Sunaura Taylor who is in a wheelchair. Prompted by our reading and encounter with this 'walk', this student wrote a final paper in which she focused on the way in which individuals encountering one of her clients, intra-acted (Barad, 2007) with the wheelchair instead of the person. It opened up a different way of thinking about the services or the education we offer to students in a situation when people respond to the machinery or the apparatus, not the person. Or thinking about the way in which the machinery is an extension of the person— as in Donna Haraway's Cyborg. It's the way in which all of this is part of who the person is, not apart from the individual. It's Erin Manning's (2013) idea of bodying and extension and so I think there is possibility of rethinking relationality. But it's hard work. Her committee would not allow her to think with this theory for her dissertation, although she has presented at conferences and authored papers for publication.

BARBARA: I have to say that one of my great pleasures is teaching MBA students. Our MBAs are post-experience, so they've been out there, they've been working and they've come back to university with practical puzzles they'd like to address. They're actually looking for new ways of thinking. They love this stuff; it's blindingly obvious to them that this is the way they need to think about working in their businesses, and developing their practice in ontologically processual ways. But I also teach undergrads and PhDs and, as you observe Lisa, it's disappointing that they often get channelled into there being only one way to do research. I think it's incredibly destructive for our world actually that people are not gaining a bigger and better picture about what research is and how it might contribute to making better worlds.

ALECIA: I'll tell a quick story to respond to your question about why people should care about process methodology or thinking with theory and the ways in which our book is trying to do something different. I was talking with someone at a social gathering, someone not affiliated with the university. It happened to be a semester when I was teaching a class in feminist theories. This person commented about how great it must be to teach a class like that, to read and discuss feminist theory together. And I thought about that comment for a moment and I said, you know, this is the fourth or fifth time I've taught it over the course of ten years and we're still talking about the same issues over and over and over. Nothing is really different. It can be a little depressing! And so when I think about research, process methodology, thinking with theory or any of these new approaches and strategies and techniques that are trying to push out the old, I hope that this work is engendering new conversations to challenge the status quo. So that over the course of ten years, those who teach qualitative methodology are in a discipline that is constantly transforming and responding to the world. I challenge students frequently by asking them: Can we use research to create a different world and imagine different possibilities for all lives to flourish? I mostly teach school principals, and they are inundated with testing data and discipline policy and having to manage all the things that are not the good parts of school. They're so focused on those managerial things, and they want to do research that studies the 'impact' of those practices. And then we go back to what Lisa brought up earlier as 'you already know the answer to this question'—why do you need to do a study that may cause harm and stress, only to reproduce what we already know, or fortify common sense? A theme throughout chapters three and four of *Difference and Repetition* is Deleuze's (1994) famous proclamation: reject the problem *and* the solution. Both Deleuze and Foucault claim that every solution produces another problem. And that's the deconstructive task, right? So in my classes with doctoral students we talk a lot about, for example, why do you want to research how to keep kids' test anxiety low? That's not your problem! Your problem is that you're testing them. I imagine a world in which our research is not about solving problems or even asking better questions, but just throwing out the problems and the questions and instead seeking: what is it to use research or inquiry to create a new world? That's what we talk about in class all the time, especially around problems in education that need to be addressed. And it's privileged white hetero-cis men, as school principals, who are working to try to solve the problems and they are not able to notice the things that have gone unnoticed, to use your language from the introduction. To your question of what it is to do research: I do believe that process methodology and thinking with theory can help us begin elsewhere, start elsewhere with a framing that's not deficit-oriented or damage-based, but looking at the institution and the structure as the problem—rather than the individual. Don't focus on youth as being the problem, or having a problem. Focus on this high-stakes testing culture as productive power, as the creator *of* these problems.

BARBARA: Indeed, I passionately believe that we should all be activists working towards new worldings. Academic activism is what we are invited to do by the posthuman. It opens us to thinking about an appreciative and positive world, and how we might make it.

ALECIA: I think it's not teaching people how to do research. I think it's teaching people how to think, and how to trouble the 'topics' that we think should even be researched.

BARBARA: I agree—

LINE: Alecia, you mentioned that your reading into the chapters of this volume which are aimed for organization studies was a different reading experience. Is there anything more to be said about that?

ALECIA: When I was reading the chapter about the shopping centre in particular (Chapter 8), it was very affective. I felt immersed not in the representation itself, but to what is going on in that place, what was happening. Admittedly, I felt a little out of place! I tried to use my imagination to think about the last shopping centre I was in, which I can't even really remember. My reading experience was a sensation of feeling out of place and attuning to what's happening here, and why is this important? When I read about schools or higher education, I kind of know what's the important thing that's going on and why I need to pay attention to it. So, I entered into newness with these chapters. The conceptual persona piece by Sideeq felt like a warm invitation into *What Is Philosophy?* (Deleuze & Guattari, 1994) and the concepts. So, I just had different experiences of being a reader of those pieces, which produced an unexpected affective response. And maybe as far as a non-ending here to this conversation, what emerges for me is Deleuze's phrasing of 'a people to come' (1994, 218). Maybe that is the purpose of our writing, and our inquiry, in using a process approach. We're writing not *about* the places and the people in the environments and the atmospheres that we've experienced, but *toward* that which we actively seek or long to think with: the people to come, the world to come, the environment to come. As a reader of the chapters in this book, I sensed the not-yet: like something was coming. I didn't really know what it was; I wasn't trying to figure things out. Not reading to understand, but reading with an anticipation of having/needing/wanting to re-read: a second or even third reading. The anticipation emerged *with* reading, engendered by a reading *without* an intention of understanding. Maybe I would even call it a reading to come. It was that *with-ness* that I sensed, because in the chapters, I could not recognize what I already 'know'—or even myself! I always talk to students in my courses about 'don't read to understand; read to see what emerges and what sensations are felt'. And be open to reading as playful and blissful (Barthes, 1975), rather than as consumption or for mastery. So, being unfamiliar and somewhat out of field was affectively productive in that I didn't read for meaning but for play, for process itself.

LISA: Reading to sense. Not reading to know.

BARBARA: The chapters we've included in this book don't really conform to the disciplines that they might be rooted in either. So, the hope is that even people within the business and organization disciplines will have the same reading experience that you had: 'this is something different. This is taking me out of my familiar comfort zone that prevents me from seeing all these other things'. Hopefully these pieces invite us to drop our blinkers, at least temporarily.

LINE: The phrase of 'a people to come' and writing for the people to come made me think about Ariana Amacker and Anna Rylander Eklund's contribution (Chapter 3) about *Learning to see the Forest for the Trees* in which they set out to connect and become-with, in different ways, with the forest as a living organism. I now imagine their text as developing an attitude for a people to come, moving towards this new people. . . . And on that note?

LISA: I think that is a lovely place to pause

BARBARA: Yes

LINE: Let's do so . . .

References

Bang, Jytte & Winther-Lindqvist, Ditte (eds) (2017). *Nothingness*. London and New York: Routledge.

Barad, Karen (2007). *Meeting the Universe Halfway: Quantum Physics and the Entanglement of Matter and Meaning*. Durham, NC and London, UK: Duke University Press.

Barthes, Roland (1975). *The Pleasure of the Text*. New York, NY: Hill and Wang.

Braidotti, Rosi (2019). *Posthuman Knowledge*. Cambridge, UK: John Wiley & Sons.

Deleuze, Gilles (1988). *Foucault*. Minneapolis, MN: University of Minnesota Press.

Deleuze, Gilles (1994). *Difference and Repetition*. New York: Columbia University Press.

Deleuze, Gilles (2007). *Two Regimes of Madness: Texts and Interviews 1975–1995*. Cambridge, MA: Semiotext(e).

Deleuze, Gilles & Guattari, Felix (1994). *What Is Philosophy?* New York: Columbia University Press.

Derrida, Jacques (1976). *Of Grammatology*. Baltimore, MD: The Johns Hopkins University Press.

Jackson, Alecia Y. (2017). Thinking without Method. *Qualitative inquiry, 23*, 666–674.

Jackson, Alecia Y. & Mazzei, Lisa A. (2008). Experience and 'I' in Autoethnography: A Deconstruction. *International Review of Qualitative Research, 1*, 299–318.

Jackson, Alecia Y. & Mazzei, Lisa A. (2017). Thinking with Theory: A New Analytic for Qualitative Inquiry. In Denzin & Lincoln (eds), *The SAGE Handbook of Qualitative Research* (5th ed.), 717–737. Thousand Oaks, CA: SAGE.

Jackson, Alecia Y. & Mazzei, Lisa, A. (2012). *Thinking with Theory in Qualitative Research: Viewing Data across Multiple Perspectives*. London and New York: Routledge.

Lather, Patti (2007). *Getting Lost: Feminist Efforts toward a Double(d) Science*. Albany, NY: State University of New York Press.

Lorimer, Hayden (2005). Cultural Geography: The Busyness of Being 'More-than-Representational'. *Progress in Human Geography, 29*, 83–94.

Manning, Erin (2013). *Always More than One – Individuation's Dance*. Durham, NC and London, UK: Duke University Press.

Maréchal, Garance & Linstead, Stephen (2010). Metropoems: Poetic Method and Ethnographic Experience. *Qualitative Inquiry, 16*, 66–77.

Mazzei, Lisa A. (2011). Desiring Silence: Gender, Race, and Pedagogy in Education. *British Educational Research Journal, 37*, 657–669.

Mazzei, Lisa A. (2021). Postqualitative Inquiry: Or the Necessity of Theory. *Qualitative Inquiry, 27*, 198–200.

Mead, George Herbert (1932[2002]). *The Philosophy of the Present*. Amherst, NY: Prometheus Books.

Richardson, Laurel (1993). Poetics, Dramatics, and Transgressive Validity: The Case of the Skipped Line. *The Sociological Quarterly, 34*, 695–710.

Simpson, Barbara, Harding, Nancy, Fleming, Peter, Sergi, Viviane & Hussenot, Anthony (2021). The Integrative Potential of Process in a Changing World: Introduction to a Special Issue on Power, Performativity and Process. *Organization Studies*, 42(12), 1775–1794.

Spivak, Gayatri Chakravorty (2014). *Readings*. Calcutta, IN and York, PA: Seagull Books.

St Pierre, Elisabeth Adams (2011). Post Qualitative Research: The Critique and the Coming After. In Denzin& Lincoln (eds), The *SAGE Handbook of Qualitative Research* (4th ed.), 611–625. Thousand Oaks, CA: SAGE

Stengers, Isabelle (2011). *Thinking with Whitehead: A Free and Wild Creation of Concepts*. Cambridge, MA: Harvard University Press.

Whitehead, Alfred N. (1978). *Process and Reality: An Essay in Cosmology* (Griffin & Sherburne eds. Corrected edition). New York: The Free Press.

Zourabichvili, François (2012). *Deleuze: A Philosophy of the Event*. Edinburgh, UK: Edinburgh University Press.

Author Names Index

Subject Index